D0776816

ALIENATED AFFECTIONS

BEING GAY IN AMERICA

ALIENATED AFFECTIONS

BEING GAY IN AMERICA

by

SEYMOUR
KLEINBERG

ST. MARTIN'S PRESS
NEW YORK

Parts of this book, in somewhat different versions, have appeared in the following periodicals:

"Finer Clay" in *Shenandoah*
"Passing or Memories of Heterosexuality," "Friendship: Gay Men and Straight Women," "Where Have All the Sissies Gone?," "Prisoners: The Three R's," and "Those Dying Generations" in *Christopher Street* magazine

COPYRIGHT © 1980 BY SEYMOUR KLEINBERG
FOR INFORMATION, WRITE: ST. MARTIN'S PRESS,
175 FIFTH AVENUE, NEW YORK, N.Y. 10010
MANUFACTURED IN THE UNITED STATES OF AMERICA

Library of Congress Cataloging in Publication Data

Kleinberg, Seymour, 1933-
    Alienated affections.

    1. Homosexuality, Male—United States. I. Title.
HQ76.2.U5K54   306.7′6   80-21648
ISBN 0-312-01857-6

DESIGN BY MANUELA PAUL
10 9 8 7 6 5 4 3 2 1
FIRST EDITION

To Sonia

CONTENTS

Introduction.

CHAPTER ONE.

Names Can Never Harm Me: Jew, Commie, Fag   1

CHAPTER TWO.

Finer Clay: The World Eroticised   38

CHAPTER THREE.

Passing or Memories of Heterosexuality:
Gay Men as Straight Men   70

CHAPTER FOUR.

Friendship: Gay Men and Straight Women   93

CHAPTER FIVE.

The Flesh as Fantasy: Gay Men as Women   118

CHAPTER SIX.

Where Have All the Sissies Gone?
The New Masculinity of Gay Men   143

CHAPTER SEVEN.

Sexual Pioneers or Uncle Tom's Bondage: S-M, F-F, ETC.   157

CHAPTER EIGHT.

Prisoners: The Three R's—Reading, Rape, and Riot   197

CHAPTER NINE.

Those Dying Generations: Harry and His Friends   213

CHAPTER TEN.

Beyond Gay or Gloomy:
The Ordinary Miseries of Everyday Life   243

ALIENATED AFFECTIONS

BEING GAY IN AMERICA

INTRODUCTION

In 1979 the news broke that Anthony Blunt, the curator of the Queen of England's private art collection and a noted art historian, was the "fourth man," a Soviet agent like Guy Burgess, Donald Maclean, and Kim Philby. He had confessed to the authorities more than fifteen years ago, confessed that he had been recruited and done recruiting, had access to enough information in his high circles to warn the others they were about to be arrested (they escaped to Moscow), yet he was never prosecuted. Apparently, this tardy business only came to light because the imminent publication of Andrew Boyle's book, *The Fourth Man,* had forced Prime Minister Margaret Thatcher's hand.

The circle of upper-class Cambridge men to which Blunt belonged was also known as the "Homintern," for the men were as open among their peers about their homosexuality as they were furtive about their politics. The British press thought the political-sexual connection overdone, perhaps a coincidence. Philby was a "ladies' man," and Maclean was a father. After all, John Maynard Keynes, a known homosexual, was a Cambridge peer of the others; could his economic theories be attributed to sexual orientation? One London wit then concluded that perhaps "sodomy is the cause of inflation?"

The British press closed ranks, relying on the nation's purported tolerance for sexual deviance among its upper class. Members of the press did not, however, dismiss the connection between class and radicalism; that was fascinating for them. Those born to English privilege are almost born to caste; how interesting that they chose to betray the very system that had given them so much.

For Americans, the connection of class, politics, and sexual deviance is not coincidental, at least not for this American. Class in America is less rigid than its British counterpart; we have racial and ethnic minorities instead. To be a first-generation Jew in America or a black of any generation is to enter the world almost as if caste-born. And radicalism in America is one of our most orthodox traditions; the nation began in revolution and has barely stopped protesting since. And deviance in America, that too has its orthodoxies and its caste coloring. This book is about how class and sex and politics have been the loom on which one life and one sensibility have been woven, and I hope the fabric is recognizable to others as part of a common cloth. I changed the class I was born into, changed my politics (more than once), and changed my sexual orientation. Perhaps such a statement could only be made by an American.

It wasn't that I couldn't make up my mind; I made it up all the time. A friend once said of me, "Seymour's always certain; he's not always right, but he's always certain." I liked it when I heard it. There was plenty of time to be "right," whatever that was, but I was "too hot for certainties in this our life" to rest content with doubts. But I was not prepared for the "dusty answers" which George Meredith promised in his poem were the fate for those in such heat.

American experience seemed to justify changeability. As I saw the country—growing up in the Depression, the war years of the forties, and the fifties—it seemed as protean as my convictions. A child of European peasants who were entirely apolitical and religiously indifferent, unlettered and conventional, I chose to enter the academy to study Shakespeare and found politics almost as early as I discovered I was homosexual. While I did not dare confront the family with sexual deviance, I compensated by irritating them all with my political "notions." The Jewish radical pursuing high culture is no stranger in modern society, but homosexual as well, he is not so familiar a figure. Being alienated from mainstream America on three counts is more than multiplying estrangement by another third. It is to be an outsider in these ways, particularly the latter, that concerns this book.

To change class or change politics in America may simply be the nature of things; to become homosexual is not—at least so far it has not proven so. While I sometimes felt foolish or ill at ease with my political naiveté or my pretensions to culture, I often felt profound unease in homosexual life until it became politicized and offered possibilities I hadn't imagined before.

Homosexuality is now a proper subject of sociologists, and gay life has had its share of confessional testimony; this work is neither confessional nor social science, though it is highly personal and relies on psychoanalytic thought. It is an approach chosen from dissatisfaction with "objectivity" about an issue where controversy and speculation are always present and confusing. I am not dismissing Kinsey or Masters and Johnson, from whom I have learned, if nothing else, to think for myself about the questions they ask and the answers that seem inadequate. The sociology of sexuality is a relatively new subject, and someday no doubt the answers, or the questions, will strike home. As for the confessional, it can be wonderful, as J. R. Ackerly or Quentin Crisp's biographies were, but it is also limited, if infinitely more entertaining. Part of this work, especially the beginning, is frankly confessional, but I think it appropriate for that place, as I introduce myself to you. The rest of it concerns other aspects of the homosexual condition, but I have tried to connect speculation and generality with my own experience, to use myself as evidence, as well as the observation and testimony of others. I hope it is not naive to think common experience is enough for me to speak for others, as I hope that it can also speak to others.

Seymour Kleinberg
New York City, 1980

CHAPTER ONE

Names Can Never Harm Me:
Jew, Commie, Fag

1

I first became certain that I saw things differently in 1952 in my junior year at the City College of New York. I was president of the English Society and responsible for bringing Langston Hughes to campus; I was also poetry editor of the school magazine *Sound and Fury* and had published two of my own poems, which were much talked about, even by professors. These successes were a trifle duplicitous. Two months before he came to campus, I had never heard of Langston Hughes. I was auditing a course in Negro history at the Jefferson School for Social Research, paid for by the woman who had indoctrinated me into the Labor Youth League, the Communist Party's official youth organization, and it was from my instructor that I learned a Negro poet was living right there in New York. As for publishing my own poems, well, I had become the poetry editor for that very reason: even then I knew one didn't leave matters of publication to mere chance. However much reputation these achievements brought me, nothing was publicly odd as yet, for at City College one was admired as much for his boldness as for the issues he brazened out. I was nineteen, and it was my wheeler-dealer semester. I was also eager and ambitious; I simply didn't know how I wanted to earn a living. Until I found out, school and the city provided plenty of diversion—educational if not vocational training.

In my first months at college, I had discovered the civil rights movement and that I could write poetry. But my academic interests remained moribund. Everything meaningful happened *outside* the classroom. In the required speech course, for example, we studied the formalities of debating, which though not difficult, I found dull and absurd. City College students were already ferociously argumentative; what we needed to learn were enough good manners to listen to each other respectfully for more than ten seconds at a time. The instructor drilled us in *form;* we got the forms right and sat distracted through each other's speeches about euthanasia and capital punishment, the electoral college, and statehood for Alaska. When my turn arrived the solid subjects had been exhausted; I could think of nothing appropriate to talk about.

As it happened, my mother had just been forced to duplicate a payment to Con Edison under threat of shut-off. So I argued that Consolidated Edison should be nationalized. At the end of my speech, Belle, a classmate in her late twenties, applauded; later she asked me to have lunch with her in the cafeteria. I was flattered; the adult students, mostly veterans and women returning to college after some years of working, usually kept to themselves. We chattered about how rotten Con Ed was; then Belle invited me to her home to meet others who gathered there each week to discuss social questions, but on a "broader" scale.

Belle and her husband lived on the Upper West Side, in a large apartment filled with books, a casual assortment of furniture, and an even more eclectic assortment of friends, mostly young adults who worked full time. Of the few students present, I was the only white male. I had never been in a Manhattan apartment below Washington Heights, nor in one where the living room furniture was not a "suite"; I certainly had never been anywhere socially with blacks. Belle and her friends were discussing a pamphlet called *Dialectical and Historical Materialism.* I was smart enough to know that I was having coffee and cheesecake with Communists, but I didn't understand a word they were saying. At the end of that exciting and bewildering evening, I agreed to return the following week.

I had had few political feelings in high school (I was a Democrat; they were for the Jews). Mostly, I was indifferent. My father had always spoken of his birthplace in Polish Russia with nostalgia, so I was less rabid about the Cold War than others my age. I was more frightened of Nazis than Reds; I had not advanced beyond the idea that the Soviets had been our ally a few years before. Besides, I knew there were injustices in America; the people I met at Belle's were the first to speak of them seriously, and they did not patronize me when I asked questions.

At Belle's request, since I was headed uptown, I escorted Cora, a black student, to her apartment in Harlem. The trip was uneventful; I agreed to pick Cora up the following Friday on my way to Belle's. Riding the subway home that midnight, I felt exhilarated: everything I'd done that evening could destroy my family's harmony and complacency; everything I had learned contradicted my parents' assurances about *schwartzes* and Commies. I remembered with some chagrin their anxiety about my going to City College: they had predicted I would become a Communist.

I had entered college to prepare for medical school though I had never seriously wanted to be a doctor. In fact, I had no professional ambitions except *not* to be a small shopkeeper like my father. College life began classically: I was delighted to be rid of the misery of high school but afraid of the choices ahead, which I could not even identify. After a semester loaded with science courses, I ended up on probation, with a D in chemistry and C's in everything else except history and English, where I distinguished myself slightly. My advisor told me to forget medical school; the quota for Jews was small and As in science were expected. He suggested that I take a psychological test to find out what actually interested me.

I *knew* what interested me: opera, dance, movies, theater, novels—and sex. Though I had not yet discovered my first gay bar, no less the gay world, my sexual hunting was already obsessive. I had first discovered sexual play with my cousin when he and I had been dumped together in the same crib whenever our families visited.

One day when I was eleven, I had a cold and ran out of Kleenex on the way home from a movie. So I went into the subway men's room when I got off the train and stood near a booth snatching toilet paper. I paid no attention to the man at the urinal who suddenly groped me while I blew my nose. I couldn't believe it: he looked just like anyone else. I pushed his hand away and fled the restroom. Halfway down the steps I stopped cold, immobilized in sexual heat, did an about-face, paid another fare, and returned to the restroom. He was still there. I repeated my gestures and he repeated his, more tentatively this time. I did not resist.

It was all over in a minute. I had never been done before, had not really believed people *did* that, despite having heard "cocksucker" yelled in the streets since I was a toddler. I was stunned by the memory of pleasure, which left an after-burn of shame in my groin. Less than thirty minutes later, I was downing cocoa and cookies in my mother's kitchen, trying to pay attention to her questions about the movie. Seeing that I was moody, she soon gave up talk to go on with her cooking.

That scene became typical. Fresh from the subway johns, I would nibble and sip and remember until it was time to collect my books for Hebrew school. While the other boys recited from the sacred *Torah,* I mused on my profane moments, vivid as the mixed smells of ammonia, perspiration, and semen. Part of me hoped it was just a phase, that I would settle down and begin to enjoy girls. I was intensely romantic and sexist at the time: I knew absolutely that sexually permissive girls were no good, and that good girls weren't sexual. Meanwhile, I avoided the temptations and confusions of girls by getting blown by some man, any man: after that first refusal, I never said no again.

In the next six years, I systematically discovered the tea rooms of Manhattan, places in Central Park, and an eerie Turkish bath in the basement of the Penn Post Hotel (now a parking lot near the main post office) where I paid a dollar to "use the showers." At first, my contempt for my partners was twofold: they were content with an unreciprocated sexual activity (I could not understand what their excitement was), and they were doing it to *me,* a minor if no longer a child. They were inappropriate enough in their sexual tastes to be criminal. I was haunted with a sense of my own power to betray them, for which I have never quite forgiven them. Ever since, I have been skeptical about pederasts' claims of nurturing tender affection among boy lovers. It is not so much that I was seduced by pederasts, though that is an accurate enough statement. I never felt endangered by them, threatened, or abused. On the contrary, the danger was to be discovered with them, and I felt it was I who used them: their needs had brought them to their knees. At a time when I chaffed at the restrictions of every authority elsewhere in my life, I felt a thrilling power that I could betray these grown-ups, so sick, so indiscreet.

What I saw at the Penn Post was lust in action: silent, genital, brief, and somewhat grim. It was also public and furtive; there were no rooms or corners, no place for privacy and therefore no place for foreplay. I did not see two men kiss for years; the first time it happened, in the midst of an orgy, I was embarrassed at such a display of intimacy. By then, the Penn Post was attracting younger men with its growing reputation as the raunchiest baths in town.

With boys who knew nothing of my life as trade, my sexual experiences were fiercely democratic: one did nothing that the other did not solemnly promise to imitate. Sex with my cousin had been intense but also playful; there were lots of giggles. With men, it was tense and serious; there was no talk, let alone laughter. I assumed homosexuality was entirely an issue of lust. I made efforts to ask questions when I could, but the men who did me were either uninterested in talk or unable to tell me anything that added to what I already saw. I could have done without such high seriousness, without the nasty thoughts of betrayal that did little for my pudgy self- esteem. Most of all, I could have done without the corrosive fantasies.

For my experiences at the Penn Post led me to feel that I was no longer a tourist, that I belonged among these men. My guilt still inhibited what I allowed to happen, yet my fantasies made it clear what I wanted; not to be standing up against the wall being done, but to be kneeling myself in that mysterious lust I felt in the men who did me. I could no longer pretend that I was just getting my rocks off. This growing desire to touch them, to engage them, to *go to bed with them* frightened me. These men were sick; slowly, I was becoming leprous. I already knew I was bad, but I could live with badness; it was probably caused by my defective nature, some freakish criminal streak. That wasn't the same as being sick. Could I live with sickness, with helplessness and unknown debilitations?

No doubt I was well on my way to a very neurotic adolescence anyway, but for years I believed that my problem was homosexuality rather than the kind of homosexual I was becoming. Before I found myself on my knees, humiliated and beneath contempt, I would try to change. I wasn't like my cousin, with whom sexual play had stopped abruptly as "kid stuff" when he was sixteen and I a year younger. I explained to the school guidance counselor that I had "problems" I thought needed professional attention, but no money to pay for treatment. She gave me a list of agencies, alphabetically arranged, that saw patients at reduced fees, sometimes free. I made an appointment at the Alfred Adler Consultation Center.

My first interview was with an elderly woman who spoke with a heavy Germanic accent. She asked me why I had come; I was embarrassed. I had not expected to be interviewed by a woman. How could I bring up the topic of homosexuality? I had never discussed any sexual issue in front of a female, not even my sister or mother. I muttered that I had "feelings" about men. She asked for details. I was speechless.

"Do you perform fellatio with them?" she asked, trying to be helpful.

Although I had been blown hundreds of times in the last six years, I had never heard the word before. I asked her what it meant.

"Suck," she clarified with a touch of impatience. "Do you suck them?"

It was one of the low moments of my life. I had not expected the question, certainly not after fifteen minutes and from a stranger, moreover one who resembled my grandmother. I told her that I didn't, and further-more that I didn't think she was a lady. Free or not, Alfred Adler and I were not getting along.

She asked me what career I was planning; I said I thought I might teach English. She insisted I was being self-destructive in choosing a pro-fession that constantly tempted me with adolescent boys. I explained that since I was barely seventeen myself and I hated straight adolescent boys, who I thought were barbarians, it didn't strike me as a serious problem. But she knew better: after all, I wouldn't be seventeen for long, and I might come to like barbarians; besides, it wasn't right for homosexuals to teach. Some part of me agreed with her, but I kept these moral reservations from the other homosexual English majors preparing to teach high school, as I also concealed from them my studies at the Jefferson School and my asso-ciation with the Labor Youth League.

When I reluctantly kept my appointment the following week, I was surprised to be greeted by another therapist, also a woman. After a while, I confessed that I did not see how I could talk about what was bothering me with any woman, no matter how motherly, patient, or professional she might be. She asked me to try again, to think over this embarrassment—and to consider telling my parents about the center so that it could determine my fee.

I had no intention of telling my parents. My mother would only deny that I needed therapy, and my father would ask why I wanted it. I believed that I had a social disease from which society had inadequately protected me; I wasn't responsible and I wasn't going to pay good money to be cured. And how could I tell them it wasn't some vague desire for men that I found undiscussable, but actual orgies?

My third appointment was with yet another therapist, this time a man; he gently assured me that *he* was my therapist, that the matter of the fee would be postponed until I could discuss it at home, and that no one would pressure me about it. Over the next two years, my vivid transference filled me with romantic longings for him; I was eager to try out some of my sexual fantasies as well. But I did not discuss these with him, afraid to embarrass him, nor did I mention my homosexuality except to inform him that I "had" it. He waited, I waited. He assured me that one day I would trust him enough to talk freely. I was beginning to agree with him when he completed his internship with the center. I was transferred to another therapist, the leader of the group I had recently entered.

Group therapy began uncomfortably and became an ordeal. But it gave me something to talk about in my private sessions, where I was now more guarded about everything else. After five months, I began to know the men and women, all in their early twenties, well enough to talk about my family, my fears, my future—anything but my sexual past and present. One evening a new couple, fiancées, entered the group. The rest of us tried to go about our usual business, each member speaking briefly about his or her problem of the week, which took up nearly the entire hour. Then the therapist, puffing on his pipe, asked the new couple what they thought of the group.

The young woman demurred, but her fiancé said, "It's too soon to tell much, except that I can't stand fags," pointing at me. He added, after a few moments of silence, that he thought some of the problems discussed were trivial.

Everyone waited to see what I would do; I waited to see what my therapist would do. Despite my panic, I would not deny it now that it was said aloud. But would anyone else in the group deny it? I had never mentioned my homosexuality. This secrecy had led me constantly to falsify experiences by changing pronouns or trying to avoid them completely. Finally one woman, the most aggressive member of the group, said that she thought our new member was a pretty crude number. The therapist ended the session, promising we would continue to explore these feelings the next week.

I was in the street in seconds; no friendly cup of coffee tonight. One of the men caught up with me at the corner, touching me tentatively while I waited for the light to change. He was the handsome man in the group, whom, of course, I'd had a crush on for months.

"You can stop running now," he said.

"You think so?" I asked rhetorically. But I joined him and some of the others for coffee, where I was assured that the new member was a real brute and that the group would never be the same. I didn't stay long enough to find out. I left within the month, never having confronted the brute. I was sure there was little real sympathy in the group for me, even if there was none for him. I had expected it all along: heterosexuals, no matter how friendly, were at best indifferent if not secretly contemptuous of homosexuals' problems. I was no longer foolish enough to expect protection from my heterosexual peers or therapist. Besides, it had been said: I was a fag. What the hell did I need therapy for?

2

Three years later I was still passing as a good son, a believing Jew, and a dutiful student loyal to my parents' aspirations for me: that I work, marry, and have their grandchildren. In fact, I considered myself an atheist and a revolutionary, a committed worker for Negro civil rights, a secret aesthete, and a sexual pervert. There was no part of my life where I did not lie about some other part of it. Among Marxists, I was embarrassed at not being a member of the proletariat (my parents owned a small grocery store); moreover, their intensity about social issues made my love of literature seem politically trivial. Among homosexuals I concealed my politics, since this was the height of the McCarthy hearings and guilt by association was hardly an idle phrase. And at school with other students of literature, I wondered why I felt differently from the way they did about the writers we read.

My two favorite courses were Shakespeare and Modern American Literature, which in those days began with Henry James and ended with

Hemingway. Both courses were taught by sweet, erudite professors, one trained at Harvard, the other at Princeton. I flourished in Shakespeare until we read *Twelfth Night,* which I expected to be treated like that other grim comedy, *The Merchant of Venice.* But my professor thought it wonderfully funny and exquisitely sad. Now, there was nothing funny about the humiliation of Malvolio, the only worker in the play. Furthermore, Sir Toby was not a charming advocate of the carefree life of pleasure; he was a drunkard like my Irish neighbors who fought bitterly every Saturday night, a plain case of the ne'er-do-well. Who could care about these people, this Orsino and Olivia who were self-indulgent, spoiled aristocrats exploiting workers? How could Shakespeare have made Malvolio the biggest fool and knave in the play?

I gingerly asked my gentle professor why Malvolio's humiliation was any more deserved than Shylock's. He cast me a disappointed glance, baleful but patient, and explicated the letter scene exposing Malvolio's ambition, sensuality, and vulgarity. Now I knew that vulgarity was bad; I had an uncle who farted loudly in public and mortified my mother. However, ambition and sensuality I had always thought of as proper.

Besides, *why* was he vulgar? Shouldn't "Count" Malvolio wear branched velvet gowns and play with jewels? Some instinct, which later got me through graduate school, told me to shut up. After class, I asked Alan, my best friend, if he understood vulgarity, and while he swore he did, his explanation was muddled. It wasn't helpful for the English Society President-Poetry Editor to be unacquainted with mysteries as central as good and bad taste. I suspected this gap in my knowledge had much to do with being Jewish, but I was uncertain; it might have something to do with being poor. I was hopeful since I planned to acquire money but could do nothing about being Jewish. I told myself that Malvolio was vulgar and *he* wasn't Jewish.

For more precise definitions, I consulted the professor. He was shy and puzzled. What could be clearer? He had even read from the text of the play. I said maybe it was the same issue that ruined *The Merchant of Venice,* poor Shakespeare's unconscious prejudices, the benightedness of his times, but I was assured the analogy was entirely mistaken. By 1952, everyone knew that Jews were victims of hideous anti-Semitism, but class climbers without sensibility were as guilty of unforgivable ambitiousness now as then. The professor offered to resume this discussion if I still had any questions after I reread the play, which I actually determined to do, and in the quietude of the library rather than on the subway or at home where the sound of the television filled every room. I knew trouble was brewing for me along these shadowy lines of taste and class, subjects I felt deeply about but had yet to find the words for.

As long as I used my involvement with literature for such good works as bringing Langston Hughes to campus, the Labor Youth League approved my somewhat inexplicable passion for literature. But sometimes my aestheticism was immune to political influence. I had been warned, for example, that T. S. Eliot was anti-Semitic, reactionary, and decadent; like my friend Shifra, also a promising radical and future English teacher, I was ready to dismiss *The Waste Land* as elitist and, I hoped, even trivial. I had read only the first fifteen lines when I found to my mortification that I was in love with the poem. I understood little of it but felt it was magical and I knew it was important. Slyly I asked Shifra what she thought. Perhaps Eliot's political rottenness was exaggerated? Maybe it was a generational issue: older Communists were sometimes so narrow. No, it was me. Shifra had no such lapse; she pounced on the opening line. "Ridiculous. How can you *breed* lilacs out of a *dead* land," she flung at me. Upper-class nonsense. I began to avoid Shifra.

I might have to adore that rat Eliot secretly, but surely Shakespeare was safe, the plays often performed in socialist countries. I could forgive him *The Merchant of Venice;* what could he know of Jews in England where there were none? Anyway, Shylock's hatred of Christians never bothered me; I'd grown up with that all my life. It was his avarice, which I was also too familiar with, his "O my daughter, O my ducats." All that was missing were a few farts. It would be cold comfort to discover that in Shakespeare both Jews and workers were vulgar.

On a Saturday morning I returned to the school library to read *Twelfth Night* in a hardbound edition with scholarly notes. As I read slowly and carefully, something unexpected happened. Malvolio's vulgarity vanished beside my new discovery: the play was queer; it was a gay play! Why else didn't it seem to matter to the hero that Caesario was girlish, or was it that Viola was boyish? And Olivia! All she seemed to care about was the lush loveliness of the pageboy; his sexual ambiguity was the very thing that was turning her on. The ending was outrageous; Orsino was marrying Viola while she was still dressed in her boy's drag! The notes explained all about the disguise convention and Shakespeare's boy actors, but drag was drag; I was not to be put off with academic euphemism. If it was just convention, how come Antonio was hysterical when he thought Sebastian abandoned him? Why had he risked his life for Viola's twin brother saying, "I do adore thee so that danger shall seem sport." Why was Antonio acting like a jealous lover?

A voice whispered that I was seeing faggots everywhere. I knew that syndrome: out one year and suddenly the whole world was gay, any man in loafers was suspect. But I was really stuck. I couldn't possibly ask Shifra what she thought, or my professor, for it was beyond my courage to raise the subject, tantamount to public confession, nor, incidentally, did I find the courage for another twenty years.

I decided to drop the matter; it was more than I wanted to cope with. The increasing seductiveness of literature was a source of ambivalence I did not understand, and my growing aspirations about serious literary study I regarded with suspicion. What was I doing? The world was hard enough to understand; why was I trying to explain a society and an art I knew little about and would probably always feel alien exploring?

What I did want was a serious involvement with the adult world, and politics and sexual adventures provided enough scope for my immediate ambitions. I wanted to change the world so I could claim my place in it, and I wanted fervently to believe such changes would enable me to sleep with men without remorse. I was still grossly unfamiliar with the society I wanted to change, particularly when I was confronted with it in literature. I did not understand Protestant culture and was fearful of it. Its political, economic, and moral defects had been amply argued; I knew the catechism of its faults by heart, but I had not made much acquaintance with its virtues.

Neither my family nor the university helped me reconcile my idealism, my sexuality, and my love of books. Both emphasized vocation, security, and status. Both taught that capitalism was benign, that for verbal white males it delivered on its promises. But though I was verbal, I was also Jewish, not quite white by Protestant standards, and homosexual, which in the gray fifties meant not really male. While my classmates, their eyes on

Harvard, were attracted to the social sciences, mostly psychology, my experience in therapy had made it clear that for a homosexual such a choice was self-defeating. But the students in literature classes were far more diverse in their expectations; being gay seemed no particular handicap. In fact, most of my gay undergraduate friends were in the humanities or the arts

Exciting intellectual experiences were not limited to English classes, but personal ones were. I had drifted into studying literature when I began to write poetry. In my sophomore year, to fill a gap in my program, I followed an acquaintance, a boy I was attracted to but knew only slightly, into a course called Technique of Verse. It was taught by a genteel man near retirement who loved poetry, treated his students like ladies and gentlemen, and showed extraordinary patience with their first poetic efforts. On the first day of class he handed out copies of the opening twelve or so lines of *Paradise Lost* and asked us to write our own ten or twenty lines of blank verse. Despite a year's survey of English literature, I had never heard of blank verse and barely remembered who wrote *Paradise Lost.* My teachers had always wanted "interesting discussion": What did you think of Chaucer? Did you like Shelley? Such questions easily took a week of babbling to exhaust. The "facts" were in the texts, always available; there was no hurry to learn them. By the end of my term of writing ballads and sonnets, imitating Milton and Shelley, I had learned more about reading and responding to literature than I thought possible. No course in literary study that I took during the next ten years made a comparable impact on me.

Encouraged to write, I took a course in short-story writing with Theodore Goodman, a teacher legendary for his discipline, his misogyny, and his passion for his students. Assignments were never late; women were not allowed to enroll in his courses, and when one accidentally or defiantly did, she was summarily told she was unwelcome. But we each had biweekly conferences of intense probing criticism from the master. His aim was clear: we were to learn to write so that *The Saturday Evening Post* would publish our work. Art would come later; now we were to learn commerce.

In my first conference, Goodman was brutally frank about the dullness of my fiction. Write only of your experience, he had exorted us, but he also banned sexual topics. At our age, he said, we knew nothing about sex that could interest anyone besides other adolescents. I felt this did not apply to me since most of the men I slept with were adult: they would be interested in what I wrote. But I was far too timid to argue the point. Since I was also too cautious to write about my political world, I was left with the family, which I didn't want to write about. Everyone else was writing about chicken soup, and I had nothing to add.

I finally broke through with a story about a boy and his dying father which carried conviction. At my conference, Goodman told me there was "something there"; then he looked at me closely and asked whether he could give me some personal advice he thought important to my writing. The advice was to keep my writing "clean"; it should be the "clean room" in my house. He had guessed that I was gay; I was not a hard case to read. I waited for more, for some details: why was this good advice? Instead, he stared at me fixedly and waited for me to leave. After that, I handed in my stories, dry little imitations, and cut the conferences; Goodman ignored me from then on. But I was learning fast, mostly to shut up in classes where my mannerisms might betray me and to gather what prestige I could from the literary magazine and the English club. There was little else engaging on campus—no political activity; the licit organizations were the Young Republicans or Americans for Democratic Action, neither very active, and there certainly wasn't any homosexual activity.

When I left campus, I left the university world behind. I walked directly into Harlem and politics, which that year was preoccupied with the Willie McGee case and with preparations for the school desegregation case soon to come before the Supreme Court. Occasionally I would meet a black comrade at Lucky's, a local bar, that catered to a mixed crowd of blacks and whites, straights and gays, but I was usually nervous in such situations. Concealing my homosexuality from my political friends was more important than hiding it at school.

On weekends, after clerking at National Shoes, I prepared for my long nights on the town. I would stand with friends at the Metropolitan Opera House or sneak into the second balcony of the City Center Theater to see Balanchine's ballets. If I could afford it, I bought the cheapest ticket to a play. Then, the proper part of the evening over, the improper part began.

First we toured the bird circuit, favoring The Blue Parrot in the East

Fifties under the shadow of the Third Avenue El, where we rarely scored since we looked like jail bait beside the men in Brooks Brothers' suits. But it was safe; no one we knew was likely to be in that neighborhood, which was as far from our homes, school, and work as social geography allowed. The Blue Parrot, narrow-aisled and crowded with handsome men listening to Judy Garland or Peggy Lee, was a far cry from the tea rooms, the locker rooms of Riis Park, and the quickies off Central Park West.

At nineteen, I had seen a remarkable variety of sexual activity among other men, but I had never been kissed. All that was soon to change: Larry, a giddy hairdresser who looked lovely and feminine in drag, invited me to my first gay party. I had never seen drag queens before, never danced with men nor seen how gay men with money lived. I met a young painter and promptly fell in love. The affair was brief; the novelty of my naiveté soon wore thin for him. Thus was I embarked in the gay world. At least now I knew the names of my sexual partners.

At home I was a horror. I was there as little as possible, and then there were arguments. What had happened to their good son, their nice boy? my bewildered parents complained. Where was I til all hours? They suspected me of randy nights in Harlem with black Communist women; I would surely end up marrying one of them. I stoutly and sincerely denied it, but the truth would hardly have made them any happier. No matter which priority was at the top, my life with my family was at the bottom. Home was both tense and boring. I was obsessed with being thin, so I even rejected my mother's cooking, nearly the last straw. Recently I had been in gay men's apartments where the furniture came from Sloane's, the food was served with wine, and people ate with cloth napkins on their laps. I had been in other places where there were no luxuries at all except the excitement of political argument and the new pleasure of communal work. And at school, I was deeply involved with writing poetry and reading literature. I was becoming a snob from many points of view; anything my family offered was subject to criticism from one alien standard or another.

As my activities as a student grew more demanding and my sexual life more time-consuming, I began to neglect my political commitments. I would have to make a decision about how I was to earn a living; distributing leaflets was not a profession.

By my senior year, the tensions of my fragmented life began to show;

to my consternation, I was acquiring a reputation for eccentricity. Shifra and the radicals approved of Hemingway because he had fought on the right side in the Spanish War; I thought him a prig but was too embarrassed to point out his homophobia. Even my gay friends thought I was being oversensitive; after all, those swishy numbers with their telltale bracelets running around with Brett in *The Sun Also Rises* were only symbols of *her* sexual corruption. Like when reputable writers used black as a symbol of evil: hadn't I read *Benito Cereno?* Well, I'd whimper, doesn't all that butchness depress you? What about *that,* I said, pointing accusingly at someone's massive identification bracelet modeled on Marine Corps issue?

In Marxist study groups young radicals who used "fag" as a synonym for bourgeois decadence assured me that in socialist countries there was no perverse sexuality. In group therapy, I was accused of sexual hypocrisy, while at the Labor Youth League I was told that literature was corrupting not only my political but also my common sense.

Like other gay friends, I resolved on graduate school, on teaching, on the good *safe* life. If that required me to marry and keep my homosexual affairs secret, if that demanded that I learn the caprices of Protestant taste, if that implied, finally, that I should retreat from leftist politics where it was so dangerous to operate, then I would.

Like so many my age at the universities of New York City, I was a first-generation Jew whose culture was Yiddish. I was preparing for life, not a job. Unlike the psychology majors, the social workers, the pre-med students, or the future mathematicians or biologists, I *presumed* the eminence of literature. I was learning nothing less than the ways of the world. Despite lapses like Eliot and Hemingway, to me literature was what my professors claimed it to be: the finest minds at their finest moments. Taste, moral distinctions, ethical values, aesthetic sensitivity—these words were a maze through which somehow I would make my way. I resolved to become a gentleman: not only would I understand Henry James' novels, I would *live* in them.

I sensed something sexually peculiar about the men in this world. If there were a place for Ralph Touchett or Hyacinth Robinson, surely I could be accommodated. If they were normal, I might pass. That they were also tragic was an issue I was unready to face. I hesitated to say I thought Gilbert Osmond was queer because he hated women and he reminded me of men I'd met in gay bars, but I believed that the customary expectations about masculinity were less applicable in James. And there were other writers whose ideas of male normality were flexible. To find this kind of world, I thought, both Jewishness and radicalism would have to be "deferred." I was deviant; why compound my alienation with communism and Yiddishness? At least homosexuals weren't being sent to jail or concentration camps, I assured myself smugly.

It was clearly a poor time for leftists; no time had ever been a good one for Jews. Ironically, it didn't seem terrible to be homosexual. It was only abnormal. In 1952, "queer," not "gay," was the preferred term among ourselves. If one were discreet, later known as closeted, if one acquired manners and taste and discrimination by going to the opera and ballet and theater, if one saw foreign movies and read *Partisan Review* and modern poetry, one would uncover in himself that finer clay.

With the right values, the conventional life was still available. What was perforce denied by radicalism or ethnicity was still allowed to perversity. I had quickly noticed that my literature professors made less fuss about sexual propriety than others. If there was any place to store this baggage, it was academia. I would become an English professor and guarantee myself the elusive respectability that was finally more precious than either the memories of dead European Jewry or the promises of justice in socialism.

3

Graduate school was the promised land in 1953. My boldness, my poems, my advocacy of civil rights were bread upon the waters: I won a fellowship to the University of Connecticut to teach two sections of freshman English a semester for $1,560 a year, minus tuition. At Storrs, the master's program was new and there was as yet no doctoral program, just thirty-two students, thirty of whom had fellowships. At the first staff meeting, I sat next to a chic young woman with mannishly bobbed hair who was smoking a cigarette through a long amber holder. After the formalities, during which I nervously cited my alma mater as C.C.N.Y., she turned to me and asked in a Southern accent more delicious than any I'd heard off stage, "What's C.C.N.Y.?" I thought she was joking, but spelled it out, and since I'd never heard of her school, I asked her where Wellesley was. Her eyes narrowed; she exhaled deeply and said, "Honey, don't be a bitch."

There was only one other New Yorker, a Jewish woman from Barnard whose father played violin for the New York Philharmonic. The remaining twenty-seven fellows came from either Ivy League or prestigious state universities. I was unique. Within the first two weeks of classes, I knew I was being talked about. Who else casually mentioned seeing Martha Graham as Jocasta, sneaking into theaters to see ballets, or "visiting" Monet's Water Lilies at the Museum of Modern Art. I was New York Jew, and like Midas, I turned all I touched to a golden haze of approbation. Our teachers were again Ivy League, but much younger; for many, this was their first postdoctoral job. They invited us into their homes to meet Richard Eberhardt and Dylan Thomas, to share meatloaf suppers, or to babysit. The days glistened with dewy information: Armagnac, Monteverdi, Firbank, medieval literature—I'd never heard of any of it.

My two seminars were in Mythology and Literature and Henry James. The myth course was scholarly and dull. I decided to trace the legend of Clytemnestra, who I felt had been sadly misunderstood, and submitted it with my own lengthy poem on the subject. In the James seminar, I had already established my brilliance after an oral explication of "The Altar of the Dead," a preparation I had finished only hours before class after working on it all night. I didn't really understand the story, but I had a flashy, quick delivery. No one noticed much else. The teacher asked a few generous if sticky questions: Did I mean that it was X or that it was Y? Well, neither had occurred to me, but I guessed X. He sighed with relief, nodding sagely.

From then on, I pursued the most eccentric readings. James' concern with money was vulgar. Kate Croy was the real heroine of *The Wings of the Dove*. James did not understand the class struggle in *The Princess Casamassima*. *The Golden Bowl*, which I spelled "Bowel" most of the semester, was really an epic poem. Whatever feeling the reading inspired—a sentimental sympathy for a corrupt young woman, an impatience with James' difficulty, or anxiety about his hardness—immediately became the meaning of the work.

I adored the course, I loved the reading, and I believed all the outlandish things I said; I just exaggerated a bit to make *me* more interesting, which was as important as being right—in fact, much more important. The two words I used a lot in talking about James were "elitist" and "vulgarity." The word that never passed my lips was "homosexual." It had disappeared from my vocabulary. Nor had anyone else heard of it: not my friend from Wellesley and the eerie dancer from Bennington she shared a cottage with, not the young man from Duke with whom I was having an affair, not my advisor for whom I babysat and with whom I occasionally went to bed.

After the final examination in the James course, I went to my conference to find out my term grade. The professor had not given marks before, just extensive comments on papers. I knew he found my work interesting; he wrote more on my papers than on others though he was forever arguing with me.

He looked up when I entered and offered me coffee. He told me I had done an A exam, which especially pleased him since now he could pass me in the course. PASS ME? He told me I was going to get a B, his expression drenched in compassion; he did not have to give me a C. My mind went blank; I grew stony silent. Finally I thanked him and then lurched across campus wondering whether he was anti-Semitic. Perhaps he had found out about Duke and me? Was it because I'd said that James didn't understand the class struggle?

My B was a scandal. Most of my fellow students assumed I had fallen apart at the final examination, and I encouraged this less humiliating explanation. After a while, I reread my papers and his comments. At first I was sure it was all personal animosity. Here was the evidence: on my discussion of Kate Croy alone he had written two closely scrawled pages of criticism the point of which I'd not fully understood at the time. It was plain to me that what a professor said mattered far less than how much he said. One weighed excellence: interesting work got lots of commentary, dull work got little.

Slowly, what his commentary said seeped in: "unsupported," "contradictory," "arbitrary," "wrong word," "not true," "misunderstood," "misreading," "unclear" . . . I couldn't understand; it was my boldest work, my most *original*. My teachers at City College would have kissed me for such carefully typed papers. I bitterly remembered my comparative literature professor who had adored my Freudian-Marxist analysis of Strindberg's plays, all of them, in eight succinct pages. He had told me how much he'd admired my enthusiasm, the eagerness of us all; we children of immigrants were so vital. What was going wrong? Could one be too enthusiastic? It was absurd, like saying one was too good.

I was now studying metaphysical poetry and taking a course in modern drama with Richard Eberhardt, the year's visiting poet. He was delighted with my suggestion that I write a full-length play instead of a term paper. In the poetry course, I discovered the knack of explication. I was good at it; by the time I got my master's degree I could analyze the structure of a laundry list. And these Christians, Donne and Herbert and Crashaw, were interesting stuff. They made sense; if I could personalize the class struggle and sexualize my ambitions and doubts, why shouldn't they? That the material—passionate religious conflict, Anglo-Catholicism and spiritual doubt, all immersed in an extraordinary intricate poetic style— was emotionally foreign to me was unimportant. I did better with a cool head. The lesson of the James seminar was worth the humiliation: "vitality" was a risky business.

In the spring of my last semester at Storrs, a friend in the New York chapter of the N.A.A.C.P. wrote to tell me that a black college in St. Louis was trying to integrate its students and faculty to qualify for federal aid. They particularly needed English teachers. I applied and was offered a contract which I proudly showed my departmental chairman. He commended me for my convictions about civil rights: so few people were willing to *do* anything, but he also felt it was his responsibility to warn me. If I went into full-time teaching now, I was unlikely to return to graduate school, and if I taught at a black college and decided to go back, it might be difficult to get into a good graduate program.

I was frightened about living in the South, but it was white rednecks I was afraid of. In 1955, the black-Jewish alliance was still comfortable, and among the Jews of St. Louis I knew I'd find other socialists. And of course I'd find the homosexual underground. From what I knew about bars like Lucky's in Harlem, it might even be easier to be open with blacks, among whom homosexuality seemed a less explosive issue.

During the next two weeks some of my professors spoke to me about my decision; my favorite was a poor Southerner, who had struggled through Harvard on scholarships and sympathized with my shyness about decorum, my hesitancy about table etiquette, my confusion on matters of class distinction. He urged me to try doctoral work for just one year. If I really hated it, I could take the job I was now being offered, or one like it, since integration was only beginning in the colleges. He warned me that as a New York Jew, I didn't know American anti-Semitism. Smartly he underplayed the racial issue, but he understood my vulnerability about class and Jewishness.

When friends began the same pressure, I surrendered. So much attention! It would be ungrateful, even rude, to ignore their good intentions, their affection. Everyone urged me to apply to doctoral programs; what did I have to lose? I could always not go.

4

After a year in Ann Arbor, I was much cleverer about teaching, graduate work, and being different among Protestants. I was still ignorant, brash, awkward, and unsure of myself, but I knew how to bluff others into thinking I wasn't. There were so many Jews at the University of Michigan, that it hardly seemed worthwhile exploiting. Everyone was political, but the politics were national issues like getting rid of Eisenhower and ousting the Republican party. With the end of McCarthy's power, radicalism began to seem naive. Truly sophisticated intellectuals were interested in power and pragmatic change, not utopian dreams of social revolution. Most seductive of all, Ann Arbor was gay. Faculty and graduate students (never undergraduates) mixed freely at discreet dancing parties. I discovered the amenities of cooking little dinners, serving French wine, using tablecloths and china.

I had not altered entirely; I stretched my meager income from teaching by moonlighting as a janitor for free rent. I hated sweeping halls and lugging garbage pails around, but I made sure everyone knew I did such work. On the one hand it was amusing, young intellectual manual laborer; on the other it was discomforting: I could never have lived in the building I cleaned if my apartment wasn't rent-free. I actually saved money; money was always sneered at, yet it was present in almost everything I did or said.

I wanted it now: there were so many *things*. I had never noticed things before; anything could be a thing—an ashtray could be lovely, a water glass—it was astonishing. But even had I not discovered materialism so tardily, there was Europe. I had to go to Europe.

While I still believed that the study of literature would make me morally superior, it was more important that it make me respectable. Truth, knowledge, and beauty were fine, but a job in the academy, now America's most coveted occupation, was much closer to the state of grace I aimed for: a confirmation of the efficacy of capitalism and democracy. If *I* could become an English professor, then this was truly a society that rewarded merit and work, and being Jewish or homosexual was merely an inconvenience; being politically radical was totally beside the point.

In Ann Arbor in the mid-fifties, the poor were students, not the working class. Blacks worked at the university in menial jobs, but their salaries were not significantly lower than those of junior faculty. Even the bank tellers, shop clerks, and maintenance men for the telephone and utility companies were often graduate school dropouts. The center of life was the campus, and it provided my first full glimpse of how richly ivoried that cloistered tower could be.

I still felt fraudulent as a doctoral student; the real business of literature remained a private experience, and being able to teach while I was reading was a gift. In fact, without my own classes, I couldn't have endured the ones I had to take. Most of the English department faculty were decent men, but untalented teachers. Some were not even decent.

Professor Reinhardt of medieval literature was a legendary terror, but I was unimpressed by his nastiness; I intuited that he was really no more than an irritating eccentric. He, at least, loved the literature he taught, and much of his irrationality was the result of his students' apathy for his material. One survived his class by pretending to love whatever he taught. He despised modern scholarship and criticism; the Early English Text Society had done all the work he thought necessary. While my classmates labored on their papers, trying to guess what would please him, I dashed off sycophantic bits of praise, nicely phrased, empty-headed, and false-hearted.

Toward the end of the semester he announced to the class that at least one student had understood the material and knew how to write about it, then proceeded to read my twaddle aloud to twenty-five men and women appalled at his bad taste. I was sincerely embarrassed. My earlier warning that they were wasting valuable time taking the course seriously now made things worse. I might have been forgiven had I been as sentimental as my paper, but I was just a slick New Yorker, and my success was a mockery of their efforts.

The chairman, Warner Rice, was another matter—less susceptible to slickness. I first met him just before the semester began to request another freshman section; I could not live on the thousand dollars a year my fellowship paid. He was icier than anyone I'd ever spoken to; he seemed to weigh every word I uttered as evidence against me. I explained that I was self-supporting and needed another section, that I was used to the load that I had carried easily for two years at Connecticut, and besides, while one class might be reasonable for a new teaching fellow, I was experienced. His silence lasted as long as my argument had. Then he told me the rule was inflexible; freshmen classes were a practicum for graduate students and were never meant to be regarded as an income. Gentlemen and scholars needed such contact while immersed in serious study; if I could not afford to live on what I had, perhaps I should reconsider entering a doctoral program until such a time.

I left his office knowing I'd made a serious mistake; the best I could do now was to avoid the man. After four years I thought I had evaded him, but he had not forgotten me. When I finally chose a thesis subject in Renaissance poetry, he made himself the chairman of my committee (Michigan students had no say in such matters) and paid me back fully for my earlier presumption.

My queasiness as a scholar and a former radical was fleeting; my unease as a gentleman remained unmitigated. I needed to know more about gentility and was ambivalent about the desire. I learned about proper style through other homosexuals and I acted out my ambivalence about elegance and materialism in their society. Other students were as strapped for money as I was; the married ones lived barely above the poverty line. But they had fewer pretensions. They moonlighted to pay the babysitter; I did janitorial work to go to Italy. They scrimped so they could go to the movies; I needed extra cash for the gay bars of Detroit. They furnished their cramped flats with books and posters; I shopped the thrift stores for antiques.

The years in Ann Arbor teaching, reading, discovering good taste, and idling my time observing the workings of academic politics were crucial to the creation of a veneer for myself. I was living a life whose quality I had not even imagined before my early twenties. They were good years for the mind: the pleasures of new writers, new music, modern art, the seriousness of the world of ideas, all came in a rush; the intellectual and cultural excursions were exciting, and the information I acquired then has lasted. I can't complain about the education.

On the other hand, some experiences I would have been happier without, have also lasted. First, I did not know how to integrate my present life with my suddenly distant past, particularly my identity as a Jew and a radical. Not only did Ann Arbor offer little opportunity for continuity in those areas, but I was too self-conscious in my new costume of gentility to risk the wrong accessories. Left-wing politics now seemed a dabbling, something naive I had done between being apolitical and provincial before college and unpolitical and intellectual in graduate school. When the pressure of trying to conform to obscure standards of conduct and taste grew too strong, I would search for comfort among reminders of my New York Jewishness. After a year of grueling and meaningless cramming for doctoral exams, reading much material that gave me no pleasure and little knowledge, I rebelled by immersing myself in Jewishness. I took a year's course in Biblical Hebrew with the university's leading specialist in Near Eastern languages. I joined a small off-campus group devoted to mastering Yiddish. I attended synagogue on the high holy days.

Though I understood Christian culture better than I ever had before, I felt frightened by it. When I was younger, Western civilization had been *theirs,* the world of *goyim,* and I had not questioned my xenophobia. Besides, the years of my childhood and adolescence substantiated that the Christian world was a dangerous one for Jews. The Second World War had supplied me with abiding nightmares of being wrenched from my parents and shoved into a cattle car hurtling toward the crematoriums. Long before American newspapers publicized the concentration camps, the Sunday supplement of the Yiddish daily, *The Forward,* the only paper my father could read, featured pictures of Jews being rounded up, their yellow stars badges of doom. After the war, there had been a mysterious outburst of violent anti-Semitism in New York, predominantly in Washington Heights with its large population of Irish working-class youths. Jewish boys were beaten and slashed; synagogues were vandalized; "Hitler was right" appeared scrawled on subway advertisements.

I did not let my guard down until I began to feel successful at City College; not until then had I spoken socially to a gentile adult. My professors were my first experience of Christians I did not fear. By the time I went to Storrs, I was cocky enough to exploit being Jewish among intellectuals who were still horrified by the Holocaust.

While the feeling that I was unqualified for the place I was claiming in the dominant culture was disquieting, it was also sporadic. A vivid source of my growing cynicism was also the gay life of Ann Arbor. The life was varied, and all of it frustrating. The active tea room trade was dangerous and seductive. At least once a semester, someone was caught *in flagrante* and left campus suddenly. There were no prosecutions since the police were hired by the university, but there was repeated evidence of enticement. At least one professor resigned in midyear and a number of graduate students left town abruptly.

The two bars, The Flame and The Bucket of Blood, were both unsatisfying. The Flame, catering to whatever was seamy in town, was the one bar that tolerated prostitutes. Because it was mixed, the gay men were almost as closeted there as they were everywhere else in Ann Arbor, clustering toward the back in booths, surreptitiously cruising. The Bucket of Blood was the only black bar in town; the atmosphere was raucous and free-wheeling, but the gay liaisons were usually commercial. It was a long way from Lucky's in Harlem, but at least it was sexually charged.

Most sexual contacts were made on the streets after 11:30 when the last of the movie crowds had gone home and the town looked nearly deserted. Then one would stroll about waiting to be picked up by a traveling salesman or a fraternity boy in a sports car. Sex behind the wheel or snatched in an alley was adventurous and novel for some of the men I knew, but I was tired of it, having exhausted the thrill of hurried public encounters in New York.

The heart of the life was partying, and there were two unofficial grand hostesses, one a relatively well-off graduate student and the other a charismatic university professor. Both had places where discreet dancing parties could be held. Al, the graduate student, rented an entire house in the business section of town, a small frame, outwardly rundown and un-kempt, wedged between warehouses behind the main street of shops. In-side, it was faggot *à la mode:* painted, papered, carpeted, and ornamented with original prints and pottery by local artists. Isolated and posh, it was somewhat like a gay speakeasy. There was always plenty of beer and the newest records to dance to. The largest room was cleared, lit only by a few inadequate candles, and smoochy couples glided the evening away.

Tom, the professor, rented a duplex at the dead end of a remote street in a house whose owners were perpetually away. Here the parties were much more select. Anyone could crash Al's parties—the more the mer-rier—but no one came to Tom's unless invited. His apartment was elegant and his furnishings choice: a fine Oriental rug, a Steinway, a *real* Italian Renaissance painting, crystal glasses for the good white wine he served. The dancing did not begin until the crowd thinned in the very last hours of the night; until Tom deemed it proper to dim the lights and put Peggy Lee or Ella Fitzgerald on the phonograph, the guests chattered and camped.

At Al's one dressed collegiate—chinos and plaid shirt; at Tom's one wore a jacket and tie. Everyone had a ball at Al's and then bitched about him the next day, envious of his money and contemptuous of his egalitar-ianism. Tom's was less fun; the aura of the select few was priggish. For his evenings I splurged for a new tie and polished my shoes. The repartée was incessant and the bitchiness much nastier. The wit was high and the malice just as welcome. It was prime time to show off the newest everything. At Tom's I first learned of Elizabeth Schwartzcopf's leider singing, of Man-nerist painting, French recipes, and gay arrogance. We were all the finer clay; from that assumption came a barrage of funny, mean comments on the provincialism of Midwestern heterosexual Ann Arbor. It was also at Tom's that I first understood that no degree of elegance could make life in a university town really cosmopolitan. These men always looked eastward: to New York, London, Paris, Florence. But the New York they knew and adored was as foreign to me as the other cities they venerated.

None of this would have been a source for unhappiness had I been a sexual success. But I hadn't acquired the knack; my clothes were too cheap, my looks too unfashionable (I never managed to look boyish after adoles-cence), and my mouth too acidic. Dressed up, groomed with twice my usual care, I would still end up a wallflower, ignored by the pretty boys for whom I was neither sophisticated nor old enough and by the older men for whom I was not pretty enough. As I got more frustrated, anger made my tongue cleverer—at some point in the evening, usually too early, I would give up hopes of romance and turn into an outrageous camp, the terror if not the life of the party. At my meanest, I could be hilarious. Naturally, the host kept inviting me back; inevitably, I went home alone.

There I was in graduate school, at one of the important centers of American education, and my brains were good for a laugh. The vacuous or pretentious pretty fag was taken as seriously here as in the haughty bars of New York that catered to ribbon clerks. Oddly, I was both vehemently aggressive and timid at the same time. Despite more sexual experience than most of the men my age, I had few of the social graces required at gay soirées. I did not know how to talk to strangers; my experience told me that talk before sex was poor form. Ten minutes of stupidity were enough to turn me off the prettiest face; I couldn't understand how men who praised me for being so smart required so little intelligence in the boys they wanted for the night.

I sought commiseration with my closest friend, a Southern middle-class black some years older than myself. Wilfred understood my frustration and unease; his own had been of much longer duration, but he had mastered it. White academia had become an easy place for him. After a narrow education in a small black college in North Carolina where he also taught for a few years, he had resisted the lure to remain a local success, the best and richest black teacher in town. His family had had money from the earliest years of the century; he was, in fact, a slum lord, though the business was handled by lawyers and he himself had rarely seen the family property. He was pragmatic about money, race relations, and his homosexuality. He was closely tied to an extensive family who admired him unqualifiedly; he was the first of his generation to earn a doctorate and become a professor, though education was common for them all: his mother had graduated from Howard before World War I.

He had been raised to regard himself as privileged and to esteem himself. He was wary in his dealings with white authority but carried them off with rare self-assurance. The department had rewarded him with favors of grants and an instructorship with the implied promise of a tenured future. His extravagance about clothes and food made him the best-dressed host in Ann Arbor. With his Southern manners and his largesse, he was much sought after. He seemed to have done everything I wanted to, and I was frank about my envy. He was black, his education had been even more provincial than mine, his past was a living testimony of American politics. What had made the difference?

Partly, as we both acknowledged, he was the only black in the vast English department and one of the few at the university, which had more than its quota of Jews. But mostly, it was that he was middle class: his values and his money and his manners expedited it all, and he had the wit to exploit them. He was not ambivalent about his success nor did he feel disloyal to his past; on the contrary, this was what he had been groomed for.

Wilfred counseled patience and caution, two qualities I sorely lacked. He would have advised tact, but we both felt it to be beyond me. It was with Wilfred that I went to the Bucket of Blood and to Detroit for wild gay parties where I was often the only white present. I trusted Wilfred because he understood the ghetto past, and he found in me someone who did not regard his blackness as exotic.

My friendship with Wilfred taught me that in the lottery of success being a member of a minority and a homosexual mattered little compared to being *déclassé*. Jews who learned Protestant mores and already had middle-class manners did well in graduate school. Without these, even unusual intelligence was an unreliable asset. Eccentricity and aggressiveness were secret sins, discretion and amiability the public virtues. I did the best I could by retreating into an obscurity that might get me by, for I had little hope of learning charm and I could not depend on poise. I was rattled by situations where being witty, if not bitchy, was regarded as uppity, and where the small talk that was expected to pass for social intercourse often left me speechless. At the end of four years in Ann Arbor, I had observed enough and practiced sufficiently to pass as a gentleman when necessary: a very angry gentleman.

I was happy in my own classroom; I wanted to be a charismatic teacher. There at least intelligence, aggressiveness, and serious discourse were proper and rewarding. But I was not sure that I belonged in the university world, always uneasy with my colleagues and afraid of my superiors. However, I was also spoiled for the public schools: their long days and regimentation were unattractive after the academic freedom and the flexible days of college teaching. By Midwestern standards of the late fifties, I was quite advanced erotically compared to so many of the men my age who had come out recently, but the emotional territory of homosexual life was still uncharted. I had a history of fifteen years of sexual familiarity with men, but less than five months of romantic intimacy, the sum total of two short relationships in my late teens and early twenties.

I had lost my assurance as a New York Jew; I no longer found America ridiculous or its culture something to patronize. In my forays back to Yiddishness and my visits to New York, I increasingly felt like a tourist, but I was not at home anywhere else. My absorption in politics had been erased by my disillusionment with Russian anti-Semitism and the dogmatism and sexism of the American Left. I was still interested in civil rights, but so was the rest of the country. To my chagrin, I had become a liberal.

Between the past I felt cut off from and the future I could not envision was this: the arduous creation of myself that I had begun when I left New York, an awkward collage, uncertainly glued together, threatening to fall apart.

5

My father's death set me in new motion. I had only learned of his lung cancer on the day in September 1958 when I returned from my first trip to Europe. No one had written to me; I had not left any addresses for them to write to. My father was fifty-seven; I was twenty-five. He was soon hospitalized with a prognosis that indicated little about how long he would live (from a few weeks to several months), so he took matters into his own enfeebled hands and threw himself from his tenth-floor window in the middle of the night. After the funeral, I found that my view of his suicide was singular among the family.

No one seemed to know how to console anyone else; instead, there was an unbearable pretense, an incompetent denial disguised as optimism, that I could not bear. My mother was puzzled and somewhat ashamed. My sister, in her last month of pregnancy, refused to see the manner of his death as significant. The rest of my relatives would not mention it at all.

The word "suicide," like the word "cancer," was never heard: he had *passed away;* he had *had a growth.* When I found the euphemisms no longer bearable, my family thought me odd and difficult, nervous. I fled to graduate school, six hundred miles away.

My grief and shock inaugurated a depression that allowed for absolutely nothing else, certainly not the completion of my doctoral thesis. Not long into the semester, I developed what seemed a slight headache or eyestrain, a pressure on the left temple, faint, persistent, and maddening. Nothing but drunkenness gave me relief, until I finally admitted myself to the university hospital for a thorough check-up. The possibility of a brain tumor was dismissed after the first day's tests. I went from department to department, until only gynecology and psychiatry were left.

Describing my ordeal to a resident psychiatrist, Doctor Vanderveer, and my chagrin at all those useless tests, I supposed it might have something to do with my father's death, but I was dubious. I wanted to assure him that the physical symptom was really driving me crazy with its subtle omnipresence and told him that if he took his forefinger, as I was taking mine, and just ever so gently touched it to his head—and I saw what I was doing: the finger of guilt stopped pointing, the pressure was instantly gone, and I was in therapy again.

I was still a teaching fellow, so my fees were minimal, some three or four dollars as I recall, but I recall very little else about that year. Except that I did not mention my homosexuality—it was "tacit"; I spoke of what mattered: my guilt at not helping my family through the ordeal, my sense that I was forbidden to surpass my father, that the degree had been for him, so that he could frame it and hang it with my others for his customers to admire. My grief was not only that he was dead, but that he had died before I had gotten to know him. All my growing up, all this grooming had been for that, so that one day we would finally meet, with ease, as men.

Dr. Vanderveer did not press me; he was in no position to, since he had told me he was leaving at the end of the year. He recommended I continue with someone out of residence and gave me a list of names. This time I decided that alphabetical order was not the way to approach my choices. I asked my friend Frances, who was finishing her degree in clinical psychology, to check around, and she narrowed the list to three names. I chose the one that sounded most Jewish.

My initial interview with Dr. Miller was late on a June evening after the normal working day. I drove to his office in the heat, dressed in shorts, sneakers, and T-shirt. When I met Frances later to report on how it had gone, she indicated that my attire was somewhat peculiar for an intake interview. I didn't see why, and she clammed up.

Six months later, ensconsed in a big leather chair facing a blank wall, I became uncontrollably squirmy and campy. This went on for weeks. I had said I hadn't minded the set-up when Miller, who was in psychoanalytic training, suggested we try it, but that blank wall seemed to provoke my nelliest behavior. If I could only smoke, I'd calm down long enough to say something sensible. Finally, he inquired with just a touch of weariness, "Mr. Kleinberg, would you like me to fuck you?"

I stopped squirming instantly and said "Yes." I added that if he *did,* I would not pay for the session. For the first time I felt free to talk about my homosexuality, to relate it if necessary to why I could not write, to my father's death, to my father. Unlike my first male therapist, whom I had sensed was gay and for whom my longings had been unmentionable, Miller was a taut, balding, sexy East Coast Jew who I knew was married and "therefore" straight. With him, my sexual yen was diffused in restlessness that might never have ended had he not confronted it. For most of the three years of treatment with him, I was in a fog, either ineptly seductive and coy, or dogmatic and angry. I try to remember now what he was like and cannot. I never fully saw him—literally, it turns out. Once, I admitted I found him attractive, saying that I liked compact men, trying not to insult him by calling him short. He asked how tall I thought he was. I knew he was a few inches shorter than I, and I was ordinary, five feet nine inches, but not to hurt his feelings I threw in a couple of inches. He informed me he was six feet tall. I exploded at the incredible hysterical nature of this whole experience; he calmed me by saying how conventional it was for patients to distort a little.

"After seeing you let me in and out of this office for nearly a hundred fifty times?" If I would not believe my eyes, what else did I refuse credence to?

The baths had been the first trauma that sent me to the couch; my father's death the second. The first separation had been my sense that I was no longer normal, the second separation, death. In some way, still unclear, both separations were the same, and all the ones to follow, all the deaths, were bound together, borrowing from each other so that each new separation, each new death accrued power from the past. In therapy I tried to forestall, to bridge, to soften them: I marked time.

The hard work of confrontation, interpretation, and reconstruction was infuriating; each symptom lost was wrenched away and mourned as if new deprivations were inflicted on me. I insisted I *could not* write; Miller said I *wouldn't*. I explained how my conflicts, my anxieties, were too embroiling to write a dreary dissertation; he said I was refusing to. I said it was probably just as well; he said to go home and write it.

Three years earlier when I was passing in my final grades for my freshmen, the departmental secretary had casually asked about my plans for next year, the only person in any official capacity to do so. I told her I was going back to New York to look for work. My fellowship had run out and there was no hope of a scholarly grant or an instructorship. She had understood this correctly to be my resignation and mentioned that the community college in Flint, some sixty miles away, needed an instructor.

I continued my doctoral work in Flint for the next three years, and it was in that quintessential industrial town that I came closest to feeling American. The city was an enormous working- class community entirely dependent on General Motors, a true company town whose single newspaper was practically an in-house publication. Unlike those in Detroit, where the racial tension was volatile, the black workers of Flint were a docile minority recently arrived from the South in search of work and less likely to question the discrimination that laid them off annually for four months during the automobile industry's slow season.

The town had forgotten how it had played a central role in the establishment of the U.A.W., and that the bloody sit-in at the Flint Chevrolet plant had sparked the violence that was eventually to give the union its solidarity and victory. Between unemployment compensation and welfare and the invidious installment plan everyone lived on, Flint represented all I had been taught to condemn as unjust and futile in capitalism.

The rich did not even live in the town; the last of the large estates belonging to C. S. Mott had been given to the city for the community college, a drab collection of cinder-block buildings set on the hundreds of landscaped acres that had been Mott's home. The architectural exception was a handsome cultural center built and lushly endowed with G.M. stock.

The small middle-class community of teachers, shop keepers, and professionals lived in enclaves, some of which were fenced and gated. For $100 a month I rented a seven-room apartment and garage, actually one quarter of a small apartment house, not considered a bargain since it was at the edge of a black neighborhood, albeit the best one. I bought a car, a used convertible whose former owner threw in a pair of Siamese kittens from a recent litter because I didn't haggle over the price.

I had joined the synagogue to say prayers for my father on Yom Kippur and met some of the local Jews who were eager to introduce so apparently eligible a young man to their daughters. The town was apolitical; the union could not even get its members to vote as a bloc: Flint was a Republican district. But I taught half my classes in the evening to white- and blue- collar workers from the plants; the junior college was used by the local G.M. factories as a company training program where the promising and ambitious were sent to become literate enough to do managerial work. At last I was teaching the proletariat.

In the beginning of my third year, I was twenty- eight and in therapy, with only one chapter of my dissertation done. I was seriously thinking of making Flint home. I had been given tenure and was being considered for the chairmanship of the department. I was making $6,000 a year, and the salary increased regularly, determined by seniority not merit. I spent a lot of my time and money on antiques and clothes. My apartment was clever and spacious; by local standards, I was a chic host.

Dr. Miller was encouraging my somewhat chaste courtship of a nice Jewish divorcée some ten years my senior, a secretary at the cultural center. For the first time in my life I was dating, a couple among couples. I reserved my homosexuality for excursions to New York, Chicago, Detroit, and Ann Arbor, and to occasional pick-ups of local working-class men. The doors to a modest respectability, if not normality, were opening.

Then I panicked. The last of my friends were leaving Ann Arbor for important university jobs, and Jeanne was pressuring me to marry her. I arranged interviews at the Chicago meeting of the M.L.A., and by February, I had an offer from the Brooklyn Center of Long Island University, which did not require that I have the degree in hand but which would reward me for finishing my doctorate with an instant promotion to assistant professor. I ground out the thesis in five months, a mediocre, patchy job but conventional enough. The day after Labor Day, I took my thesis defense. The committee was contemptuous of the work, but relieved to get rid of me. Since I was so neurotic and so weak a scholar, and since I was going to so inconspicuous a school, in Brooklyn at that, what real difference would it make?

I told Miller that I was leaving Michigan partly to get away from him, from the nasty business of paying to discover how nasty I was. He assured me that all Freudian therapy made one feel temporarily worse in the interests of long-range improvements. I was dubious; who did I need to be so nice for? He quoted Freud, "The good is the enemy of the best." I quoted Freud back; when he first came to America he told his enthusiastic admirers, "I am bringing them the plague." Freud saw psychoanalytic theory as even more wounding to man's prestige, his "narcissism," than Darwin's theories of evolution, and more diminishing of man's importance than Newton's discoveries.

If I felt alienated from academic society, was that really a loss? If the gay culture of such a society was unsupportive, mimicking the pretensions of the university world while it overtly endorsed prettiness and bitchiness, then why was I so concerned with self-improvement? I was alienated in Michigan because it really *was* America, where I would always have to be secretive and hypocritical. If I found no part of myself in this country, no sense of community, how could I find congenial work or love among strangers?

I would go home to New York, to the city that looked eastward more than it did anywhere else. There among my own I would find whether I were good enough, whether my failures were my fault or my choice.

6

I returned to New York in the mid-sixties, to an urban school whose students were usually the first of their families to get higher education, and joined a department permissively run by an avowed Marxist (often off marching in war protests). My colleagues were mostly Jewish and, like everyone else I knew, drifting toward leftist politics as the Vietnam War escalated. There were a number of closeted gay men on the faculty and, as I was later to learn, almost as many lesbians. Being Jewish, concerned politically, and homosexual were hardly distinctions, let alone handicaps.

In the next decade, teaching became the center of my life. For the first time I had a chance to teach advanced and graduate courses to students who wanted to learn about literature as much as I had, and who were as ignorant as I had been about the traditions that produced it. I was determined they would not go to graduate school with the same combination of arrogance and naiveté that had marred my career. My courses were popular since the reading was "light": the bulk of the syllabus was poetry, which my students could prepare by reading the assignment on their way through the door. Half the class attended stoned or tripping; I was often complimented on the good "vibes" they got listening in a drugged haze to me read and analyze seventeenth- century love lyrics.

After the arrival and success of Black Studies, some of the Jewish students demanded that the school offer Jewish Studies (we would have offered Albanian Studies if anyone had demanded it). I grabbed the chance to teach fiction, even if it meant Isaac Bashevis Singer instead of Henry James. Singer was invited to give the inaugural address to those in the new program, and the fashion lasted for a few years. While it did, I again immersed myself in Yiddish culture, reading everything in translation (still a small body of work). I became increasingly involved with the fate of Israel, at one time contemplating emigration as the war in Vietnam worsened and the university began to crumble under the dual attacks of student radicalism and surly vandalism.

Faculty offices were bombed twice, causing fires and millions of dollars in damages, but there was no apparent reason for the violence except that Columbia was under attack and some of our students missed the excitement. If there was a more serious reason, it was simply to destroy the campus and the school, since no demands were ever submitted and no group ever claimed responsibility for the arson. The hostility toward the school, which was so much more easy-going than any institution I had attended, was sad and ironic. There was lots of rhetoric in the air about how academia had sold out, was whoring for government grants, and was hysterical and compliant in its pursuit of the big money. But the small campus where I taught survived on student tuition, and its students were there because they often had no educational alternative. Amid the most political generation ever to attend college, these students were conventional by comparison.

College administrations, mine included, were confused and inept in handling the restlessness rife among undergraduates. No longer was the university a haven from class inferiority or the guardian of manners and morals. Given how parricidal young radicals sounded, it was time to abandon *in loco parentis*. As the credibility of the institution diminished, drugs and ideas of sexual liberation came to dominate campus life; the notion of decorum looked more and more absurd. So what if one colleague was fucking a student in his office or if another was always so stoned that not a word he said was intelligible? When I mildly objected to them at the lunch table, I was told being judgmental was dreary. What was important was relevance.

Secretly, I raged at my luck: here I had turned myself every which way to become genteel and now I was being told it was dreary. Worse, radical students sneered when I became nostalgic about Cold War politics and the Labor Youth League; one would have thought I'd said the Hitler Youth, given the reaction of some of the advanced Maoists. I didn't understand the rising anti-Semitism among blacks nor the idea that Israel was imperialistic, but the blatant homophobia among radicals I knew all too well: revolution was still macho business.

Relevance: the faculty scurried to be relevant. We were already sleeping with, smoking with, and bowing to our students, bringing loaves of bread to ritually break with them the first day of classes, rarely giving rigorous assignments or grades below C, but the best students still drifted away, contemptuous of graduate school or the notion of teaching, especially in the high schools, which were by now only slightly less violent and unattractive than prisons. Some faculty found consolation in the diversions of the city, clocking into work as little as possible; with some pull, one could be on campus exclusively on Tuesday and Thursday mornings. Others maneuvered increasingly into teaching graduate courses which were a bit glum, but where one could still command and demand.

I was content to separate my work from my private life; New York offered all the opportunities for distraction and discretion I could ask, though I was unsure of what I had to be discreet about among male colleagues bedecked in beads and jeans, with their hair in pony tails. Officially, I was in the closet. Then the popular young instructor who'd been asked by some undergraduates to teach a noncredit seminar in gay literature was fired. This was not because of his avowed homosexuality, but because everyone without tenure was being fired to offset the rapidly declining enrollment in the English major. He asked me if I would give the course instead.

I had already become publicly involved with gay issues. I was spending a great deal of time and effort on the Gay Academic Union, whose first conference was the most personally exciting public event I had ever participated in. I had always intended to come out at work, I really had. But what was the rush? Now I was caught without a single rationalization. Not only was I a tenured full professor protected by union seniority as well as by A.A.U.P. standards of academic freedom, but also coming out was a growing issue of supreme importance among liberationists. Every closeted gay man and woman made the silence more difficult for others to break. Every homosexual and lesbian who passed as heterosexual diminished the support and weakened the sense of community needed by those who were out.

When I began to discover gay politics, I was somewhat patronizing. It seemed second-hand, borrowed from the New Left, paraphrased and rhetorical. But the rage and the pride soon struck me as much more than homosexual theatrics. The initial protests against oppressive police departments and unresponsive politicians gave way to policy and action. The physical excitement of actually doing anything publicly was replaced by the moral exhilaration of thinking about what we were doing, of taking ourselves seriously.

That new seriousness was partly expressed in the aesthetics of sexual life, the androgynous look that swept away all the old fashions and stances. We were consciously and defiantly rejecting the verities about masculinity and role, virility and dominance. It was unclear where all this was heading, but it didn't seem to matter. Wherever, it was bound to be better than where we'd been.

The night the Gay Academic Union's first conference ended, we celebrated with a dance. More than a hundred gay men and women met in a loft, and for many like myself, it was the first time we had congregated socially because it was good to do so: not sexually expedient, not mutually protective, not merely fun, though it was all those as well. We were self-consciously creating a psychological community where we felt entitled to exclude our old secrecies, wariness, and anger. I could see that we admired as well as desired each other. The pride felt good because it was earned; what we were working for was admirable and new, and it was changing our lives. We had found the beginnings of solidarity.

I agreed to give the course in gay literature. At the opening meeting, twenty-two students showed up: eighteen women, most of them third-world, and four men, one of whom announced that he was heterosexual but doing research. Then the door of our room opened and a sociology professor I knew slightly walked in followed by his entire class. He wondered whether I'd mind (just me) if they quietly observed us; it would be so informative. I was so stunned I didn't even get angry. I laughed and wryly said I'd mind. When asked whether I were sure, I became a little testy.

To teach Shakespeare's sonnets, Colette and Gertrude Stein, James' *The Bostonians,* and numbers of modern writers in a gay context was to rediscover the works. But to teach them to third-world women, many of them only recently discovering their own lesbianism and feminism, was to confront at first hand the relationship between men in authority and women for whom education is the answer to oppression. The course changed my professional life: if I could dramatically alter my idea of my own authority in a classroom because my students were lesbians and feminists, then I could revise that idea for all students. If Puerto Rican women could find Renaissance homoerotic poetry interesting, what was the issue about relevance? The key remained what it had always been: not to assume that literature was a mirror of *their* lives, but to show how it pertained to *mine.* I could no longer be merely intellectual or scholarly or pedagogical; I could be *all* of those if I were also personal. All literature could be revealed as meaningful and contemporary if I chose to reveal it through myself.

I began to return to my beginnings.

CHAPTER TWO

Finer Clay:

The World Eroticized

1

The legend: deviance is aristocratic; homosexual sensibility decadent in the original sense of the word, the descriptive rather than the judgmental. Whatever the sterner stuff is, we are not made of it. Rather, genetically and culturally, by nature and by the nurtured habit of secretiveness, we are barometers of nothing less than the progress of civilization. Beauty, knowingness, and above all, aesthetic discrimination of the finest sort are the province of our sensibility which yields that degree of taste beyond even the good: the new.

So we have lived out the legend as the advance guard of fashion in everything and as a jury whose verdicts of conviction for conventionality, ordinariness, and philistinism have themselves become a tradition. Gay sensibility, even if it is a phantom, has haunted the citadels where powerful decisions affecting art and commerce are made. Even if it does not exist, like the Protocols of the Elders of Zion, its mythic impact has been felt as surely as if it were substantial.

But wherever gay sensibility is felt, it makes itself evident by its concern with the feminine and with eroticizing experience. Gay sensibility is truly subversive because it insists on the primacy of sexuality beneath its adoration of the civilized. While ostensibly it is concerned with disseminating new ideas about culture, its real concern is the dissemination of sexual knowledge, with which it is obsessed.

The tradition has it that homosexual men understand women better than their husbands; within that scope, gay men have been free to worship and exploit, control and serve women in a way that the men who engage them sexually have not. This does not mean that the interest in women is always overt, though sometimes it is blatant, as in the industries relating to clothing, cosmetics, and all that has to do with the appearance of women's bodies and society's idea of femininity. But often it is covert, and beauty and love, the world of romantic feeling, becomes the subject rather than the object of this sensibility.

The transformation of eros into romance is dramatized in the fantasies of gay men, fantasies psychological or cultural and sometimes both, which range in expression from the literal (clothing and costume) to the imaginative if not esoteric responses to art. I am not saying that gay men are more attracted to creative work or are more talented in the work they do. I do think that in their work and in their investment in themselves as creators, gay men act out their experience as homosexuals, experience that has been oppressive and enraging. What homosexual men have subscribed to is the idea that their vision is different because they are gay. Part of this must be true despite the lack of agreement about the importance of that vision or the nuances of its nature.

In addition to its roots in sexual feeling and ideas of gender, this is a response that is duplicitous, part of it made to the world, and part to homosexual subculture.

In our times, two dominant areas of this expression in art and commerce have been in ballet and movies. Gay men were the first reliable audience for the dance, amateur rather than professional connoisseurs, and gay men defined the glamour of women in films that created the fashions which heterosexuals of both genders were to accept as erotic.

Gay sensibility sexualizes the world, and because homosexuals are like other men, the objectification of women is the most imaginative arena in which they exercise this sensibility and legitimize it by actually influencing women's lives and, therefore, the lives of the men who love them. Perhaps this is the grand illusion: that homosexuals conspiratorially define the styles of upper-class taste which bourgeois society eventually mimics. It is a formidable legend which some of us have devoted our intelligence and talent to fulfilling, and it is the same legend that heterosexuals have claimed is the real source of their resentment of homosexual men.

The real rather than the legendary scenario for power is more complicated. Its beginnings are simple enough; it starts as ordinary ambition
fueled with that aggression Freud tells us is part of human nature. But gay
men discover that as homosexuals they forfeit access to power, first in their
estrangement from marriage and paternity, which offer most men sufficient territory to satisfy their need to dominate, and then in work where
their sexual reputations imperil their prestige. These frustrations transform
conventional competitiveness into a headier investment; success in the
world has to compensate for the limitations of the personal life and for the
anxiety of exposure that is unique to homosexuals.

Perceiving themselves as politically weak and socially insecure in the
larger world, homosexuals are most ardently determined to secure status,
especially since they have the skills to advance, skills systematically denied
women and minorities. Homosexual men acquire their acumen, learning in
the world as other men do, because they can conceal what they are as long
as they need or want to.

But they also perceive that their vision as gay men cannot be duplicated. Everything that would isolate them and keep them out also forces
them to exploit that position. Undistracted by conventional relationships,
often economically advantaged, clever with that special quickness attributed to gay men, they make their ambitions their virtues.

In culture, that ambition for power becomes an adoration of elitism, of
all that is literally aristocratic: ideas of rare breeding, inherent excellence of
line, and refinement of mind. But the motive for these cultivations is privilege, notably a freedom from bourgeois narrowness and a largeness of
choice that are the rewards of money and status. Thus, homosexuals seem
to identify with and support what is deeply conservative in civilization
while their own status is actually illegal and peripheral. They differ from
others who are eager to succeed in that they are burdened and distinguished by their awareness. No matter how secure they become, the rewards of their success, money and property, cannot mean for them what it
does for others: the creation of a patrimony for their children.

For gay men—more than for lesbian women, who increasingly can
choose maternity without the penalties of the past—there is in the exclusion
from paternity an utter isolation. Their ambitions, no matter how amply
fulfilled, can never be a patrimony for their children. They are lost to

patriarchy and are potentially its inherent enemies. The youth that follows age for parents and is for them a bittersweet reminder of their own mistakes and a true promise of their biological immortality is for gay men only the mirror of their own fading desirability. The next generation is merely an opportunity for aging men to cultivate their final romantic follies in a confusion of paternal sensuality.

It is because success—any success—is finally barren that gay men have been charged with decadence. And because gay men do not have that investment in the future, nothing inhibits their self-serving in the quest for power. Money is not enough, though of course it is the first necessity. Money alone cannot exempt one from scorn, though it is probably the only compensation for it. It is acceptance that is needed and deference that is wanted. And only among the rich and the sophisticated can either acceptance or deference be secured. Ironically, it is in that very class that the idea of patrimony, the legacy for the future, functions most enormously.

Gay men have found patronage among the rich for many reasons. First, upper-class notions of sexual morality are congenial, much less constricted by religious ideas of morality, and upper-class sexual mores are themselves traditionally permissive for men. Second, connoisseurship is a major preoccupation of the rich, though their occupations are devoted to the real sources of power, the acquisition of land and industry. Those are the provinces gay men have not found suitable: land is meaningless without the next generation to inherit it, and industry demands that gay men remain masked and function as best they can as heterosexual. It is then in the preoccupations of the rich with culture that gay men find their best opportunities for success.

There is another reason why gay men are accepted in upper-class society more easily than elsewhere, and it is more subtle than the need to delegate taste to the arbitration of others who will devote themselves to it exclusively. It is that the homosexual is seen as a symbol of the authenticity and viability of elitism. The very aspiration to be accepted and given deference confirms for the rich their power in an immediate way. It is one thing to know that the rich rule; it is another to act out that drama among men who neither question it nor wish to change it.

What follows are a number of priorities that middle-class and proletarian society abhor, chiefly the conversion of moral issues into aesthetic ones, the insistence that beauty yields its own pleasure and needs no social use to justify itself. For example, in the fiction of Wilde, James, and Proust set in London, Rome, and Paris—the durable symbols of sophistication in Western civilization—this theme is fully explored. Moral vision and innocence come to the city to be tragically seduced there. Born in another country, youthful optimism is corrupted by society, for whom civilized and sophisticated are identical in meaning. What is valued in intelligence is wit; in behavior, fastidiousness; and in feeling, refinement. Invariably, the plot centers on social behavior, which always alludes to sexuality. The fusion of the moral and the aesthetic, the social and the sexual provide the peculiar flavor of this fiction, which concerns a decadent world that cherishes a nostalgia for simplicity, but which protects itself from sentimentality by regarding its own longing with irony.

In matters of irony, the ironic vision and the witty expression of it, gay men excel; it is second nature. All that happens in experience to define them as gay also educates them in irony. In popular culture, the style of that irony is camp; in high culture, the style is less outrageous.

The idea of the decadent is not tangential to the world that gay sensibility hopes to shape. I use the word to suggest what a term like *fin de siècle* tries to convey: the end of the line, the sense that beginnings have finally ripened into what they were destined for, and that what had begun now begins to finish. The awareness of this imminence before the end, that the old is transforming itself, is the foundation for innovation. This taste for the new is a forbidden sensation because it heralds the end of the old ways, and because it is disloyal, it is also that much more enticing and irresistible. It is perfectly appropriate that advance-guard ideas are met with hostility by society at large, for they rarely are progressive or conservative; they neither come out of the past with a seeming inevitability nor do they show much concern to preserve the hallowed. Instead, they are original and ironic. New ideas and the fashions in which they are embodied are defiant in their indifference and satiric by their very existence. Gay men become a third column of subversives undermining the traditions they have come to serve, and it is not a trivial revenge.

Most of the world can't be bothered; it has all it can do just to survive. But those who are part of the world which has nothing to do but ask what they are surviving for relish the complexity of such a duplicitous vision. It is at once clever and innovative and fresh, contemptuous of whatever is not, and yet touched delicately with a longing for its own childhood, that sadness so Jamesian, so Proustian, the powerful nostalgia that makes the taste of a madelaine recall a lifetime.

For the homosexual, the nostalgia is more poignant because the innocence he recalls ends not merely with adult experience, but with the discovery of his perversity. If among the refined mere adulthood is disillusioning, what is it for the ultrarefined homosexual who discovered maturity and perversity simultaneously? Debarred by sin and burdened initially with primitive shame, one easily begins to question traditional morality which blindly condemns one and to substitute for that loss values taken from art and culture. There, good and bad refer to achievement. And in these achievements are models for success. Excluded from heterosexual institutions by patriarchal men, the fathers they are not, excluded by their own obsessive romanticization of sexuality, gay men turn to women in culture to exercise their appetite for power.

2

Gay sensibility is devoted to glamour, to the enhancement of experience with erotic aura, and this is stylized through incessant innovation. The constant change of fashions provides not only innovation, but also enormous commercial reward. Thus, the evidence that gay men have really achieved power is provided by both influence on others and by money. In general, the fashions gay men create are always reemphasizing aspects of sexual identity, playing with notions of gender, of what is feminine and therefore what is masculine.

The clearest example of this progress is the history of clothing. The rise of the couturier and the development of a massive industry to clothe the most widely affluent civilization in world history are two events that gave gay men an unprecedented opportunity to manipulate fashion and women for power and money. Such manipulation may be unconsciously sexist, but it is highly conscious about romantic glamour.

For example, in periods when women find a delightful freedom from the literal restraints of clothing meant to laden them in layers and pounds—

periods such as the twenties, the war years of the forties, the late sixties, and early seventies—one might think that a permanent liberation from the burden of clothing had arrived. But it is both puzzling and dismaying to see how precarious those claims to liberated dress in fact are. Recent history serves as a good illustration. By 1970, women looked radically different from any way they ever had before. Their appearance bespoke freedom: not only sexual freedom, but actual freedom to move vigorously. Their skirts were so short and their shoes so functional that they could move with comfort; they actually walked more briskly. The style had simplified everything, and in addition, it was healthier. Feet were accommodated for mobility rather than immobility; gone were the high heels that had been invented to shape the calf into something prettier than it usually is. The dress became a tunic, loose enough so that women could forego brassieres and girdles. Without the constant pressuring reminder of restraint, they seemed quicker, livelier. Those women who found the exposure of leg inhibiting took to pants. Here were choices and all of them said that women were actively engaged in the world. It was a style whose sexual appeal lay in its energy.

For some women, the legacy is permanent, and rather than give up this freedom of movement, they prefer to look out of fashion. But they are a small minority who probably always dressed to please themselves, with comfort their primary demand from dress. Most people are compulsively conformist in matters of dress, men in their way more rigid than women.

Now as a new decade begins, women look retrograde. It is not even a new style, as if designers were saying that in fact they could not improve on the liberated look they had made compulsory. Instead, the new fashions all recapture past modes: the thirties look, the forties look. People appear to be in costume, as if ignoring their own psychology or the sociology of the times.

Why haven't women objected to, and more, rejected, such callousness to their needs done in the name of chic? Why haven't spokeswomen taken the issue seriously, instead of preferring to think that the frivolities of fashion are unimportant to the feminist struggle? I remember when Paris designers decreed that hems would drop; longer skirts meant higher heels. Initially women resisted. Partly it was economic: one could shorten a long skirt if the fashion changed, but what could one do with a short one?

Rather than appear unfashionable, millions of Americans abandoned skirts altogether and took to pants where the issue was irrelevant. But soon what had looked utilitarian began to seem butch or drab; the incessant propagandizing for sexually alluring clothes undermined the resistance. In a time of stress about roles and about sexuality in general, when women are under more pressure than ever before to act consciously about their lives, the novelty of change may seem a harmless indulgence, as if what we look like has little to do with what we are. Women have fallen into a collusive effort with a part of society indifferent to their political status when they agree to resume seductiveness as a mode of dress. At this time in our history, when millions of women are agonizing over their relationships to men, to marriage, to family, the latest fashion defines sexiness in the tritest manner—all artifice—and a look of sexual availability, sometimes whorish, usually aggressive, is the remnant of a real bolt for sexual freedom.

Kennedy Fraser in her column on fashion in *The New Yorker* (June 19, 1978) writes incisively about how the Paris clothes of the season symbolize contemporary sexual politics, especially men's anxiety about "the aggressive new woman." The image of this new woman is designed to express autonomy but in fact really suggests a woman who "does not need the love or companionship of men. She seems determined, rather, to provoke fear." Her sexiness "shrieks" a message of one-night stands, and clothes are a costume "to caricature sexuality." Frazer claims that this idea of women has special appeal to homosexual men because it poses no threat, but she does not explore the notion. It is implied that there is a disservice done to the needs of women, that gay designers are exaggerating the confusion of women because they are comfortable with it, because it confirms that their own promiscuity is now much more commonly shared, and that sexual decorum for both women and gay men is out of style. Mostly, I agree: gay men are quick to note how they personally can profit when heterosexuals flaunt convention, and they are equally quick to articulate sexual suggestion in clothing. That the new models are easily more ugly than playful, more hostile than assertive, seems somewhat irrelevant. In a world as giddy as high fashion, who expects moral or political stances, especially if they are unprofitable?

Men and clothes are telling a similar story, though it looks more novel than it is. Every century except the twentieth allowed men to be dandies, even fops, allowed them to adorn and amuse themselves with clothing. If we are embarking again on a time when it is permissible for men to spend as much time and money on their clothes as women have, it is not the kind of equality one had in mind in supporting the E.R.A. Clothes are often the only expressive way people have of presenting themselves to the world, and there are few who are indifferent to them. Many may be depressed by their choices and resigned to appear in unflattering attire, but it is not a comfortable solution.

Because the world of fashion, in contrast to the clothing industry, has been regarded as frivolous, gay men have had an easier time establishing themselves in it. But in a society as affluent as ours—one in which even the cheapest clothing is expected to imitate the look of expensive items—fashion determines the profits of that large industry, and where the profits are determined, the power lies. In the past gay men have been allowed unhindered to be decorators and hairdressers, cosmeticians and clothes designers—occupations that provided services only slightly more prestigious than the manual catering of servants, but much more lucrative. Gay men took the path of least resistance; here at least was work that did not demand that one pass as heterosexual. But they were also quick to recognize that the servant can rise to master if he is witty enough to amuse his fretful client.

While it may seem unfair to blame women and gay men for the recalcitrance of fashionable clothing, one is at a loss to look elsewhere for the responsibility. I do not think that an individual mode is, in itself, expressive of any sensibility; certainly, what women or men wear is not the result of anything particularly gay except perhaps for the fetishism of leather. But the insistence on stylishness as style, the investment of class meanings in style, the suggestion of the haut-monde or the demi-monde (increasingly today the same thing)—all these are related to sensibility, to the view of the world that is filtered through intelligence and personality. Homosexuals carry it off with wit and irony because their own experience as objects in society has enabled them to understand how best to manipulate objectification. It may seem cheap to be an object, but it need not be profitless. Besides, some men adore it. Commercializing their sexiness makes it seem that they are controlling what happens. As a comparison, when feminist women accepted prostitutes as examples of liberated women, they were saying something similar. Since all women are forced to trade on their sexuality, prostitutes at least do it without the burden of sentiment, and they control the profits of the experience. I think this was a naive view of exploitation, but the conventional views are more misleading.

Fashion is a much more complicated world than I have tried to explore, but it provides a ready example of the thesis about sexual politics, about glamour and exploitation, about irony and ideas of gender in an occupation self-conscious about its role in culture. There is, however, an area of popular culture where these ideas were expressed powerfully and unself-consciously: the Hollywood movie.

3

The Hollywood movie was both a product, in part, of the sensibility of gay men and a major source of society's education in notions of femininity and masculinity; it also provided an analogy between eroticism and glamour for the entire nation, one that gay men accepted with enthusiasm. There were a number of movie genres, but the one I am concerned with is the women-centered dramas about love and family that dominated production in the thirties and forties, the period when Hollywood exerted its deepest and most damaging influence on popular culture. The impact of the fantasy of these films was unprecedented. The films created an image of manners and morals among characters who were usually upper class or wished to be, but it was an image which had no correspondence to reality, and then the filmmakers and participants in the movie community proceeded to live out the image of the fantasy as evidence of its validity. Between the seduction of intelligence the films themselves effected and the pulp propaganda that the media incessantly fed the public, the massive audience for this entertainment surrendered its own collective fantasy life.

The fantasies about love and sexuality were embraced by heterosexuals as well as by homosexuals, and perhaps their influence has been as deep for the former as for the latter, but the nature of the response is unrelated. Heterosexuals confronted their miseducations in experience; homosexuals confirmed it. Straight men and women soon understood the unreal world they admired when they entered marriage and the actualities of mainstream life. Homosexuals had no such opportunity for confrontation.

Despite that divergence, these fantasies of the childhood of my generation would later form a common bond, perniciously shadowing our ambitions and aspirations, fantasies that were lived out in work and love. No
other source of information was as potent, elevating, and unenlightening as
those generated in the gilded palaces of Los Angeles or in the Loews of
Brooklyn's ghettos. The same story and the same response created a bond
common to an entire foundering generation, a norm for its nostalgia.

I do not think that any other nation or culture or period can approach
what Hollywood provided for the universally deprived collective of depression and wartime America. It is staggering, the thought of what was ac-
complished, whatever was intended. Across lines of class, sex, religion,
perhaps even race, spread the sameness of experience. Only Elizabethan
London provides a reasonable comparison. It was irrelevant whether the
image and the story were real or unreal, were about our suffering or about
our wish to escape it. What mattered, between white satin sheets with
white chocolates to match, or in equally designed squalor, was the sense
that this was shared, that whatever awareness or sophistication we had was
not important to our responses. We were absorbed or we were not; that is
what good or bad meant. For once in Western civilization there was a
genuine egalitarianism of response to a fluctuating creation which varied
entirely in quality from memorable to incredible. Though art would come
later, and some of it—particularly from France and Italy—would provide
moments of extraordinary poignance, critical consciousness would already
make the difference: to know it was art was to know too much. Movies
became Film.

The substitute for art in the Hollywood movie was design. The world
it photographed was the unbridled creation of imaginations whose intent
seemed a lavish amusement, a campy exorbitant flagrance to a nation
nearly starving. Hollywood said let them eat cake, since it did not know
how to make bread. The price for such a diet seemed modest at the time,
but the final cost in our national health has been chronic: it was a diet that
nourished our cultural sexism, the lasciviousness that debases our sexuality,
and the sentimentality that sustains our infantilism and our moralism. And
the reward has been, in part, our tenacious romanticism, our unshakeable
belief in the fulfillment of the private life. Between the price and the
reward, we have been engulfed.

Glamour in movies exercised a kind of sorcery. Setting was almost as important as costume; where these fabulous people lived seemed as enchanting as how they looked. While setting was rich, it was also recognized as invention. Even if some people lived like that, their decors were not as radically influential as their appearance. None of us could afford to live in such style, but many could afford to imitate the mannerisms of dress and appearance that went with that setting. It was not merely an astonishing chic that movies showed women; it was a chic that implied behavior. One could tell by a woman's clothes what her morals were. It was and still is an economy of the costume designer to present the entire character in her wardrobe. The seductiveness of this stylization remains as potent as ever; it is the crafts of the costume and set designers that provide almost as much appeal as the skill of the director for contemporary audiences who are devoted to old movies. What is dated soon becomes a modern fad; the response to old films is partly made by the connection to surfaces. Certainly plots date in a way that is irretrievable; the ideas of old movies must be accepted with irony. But the implications about sexuality and gender, romantic behavior and adultness are still current, appearing precocious because the industry's codes demanded that these subjects be treated implicitly or euphemistically. Hollywood could say it all by gesture, and clothing was the principal signal to the audience of how it should understand the conventions. Because national decorum would not allow sexual mores to be treated with clarity, the ambiguity of the movies of this period sustains them as interesting and still educational. While it is not documented anywhere that I know of, it is pretty common knowledge that homosexuals were rarely permitted to direct or produce the films as much as they were allowed to design and wear the clothes in them. Thus, being homosexual was a tradition among costume designers, and it certainly did not create a handicap to becoming a performer. The telltale signs among the men were elegance and beauty, among the women a mysterious androgeny, at once deeply sexual but not recognizably feminine. That these traditions provided opportunities for gay men and women is an obvious asset, but that they also demanded closeted lives is a high price to have paid and to continue to pay. Despite the widespread common knowledge that homosexuals and lesbians are involved in movies and theater and always have been, there is still very little information aside from conjecture and rumor about who they are. For performers, the need to be closeted is as severe as ever for a successful career. Homosexuals' influence on the product remains subtle and difficult to document.

What the movie said directly, its story, was often the work of producers without special talents except to "know" what the public wanted; these men were often accurate in their assessment of what would be safe, for their roots were in commerce. But the way the movie looked and what it could say indirectly were often defined by homosexual designers and performers. That difference between intention and production is the foundation for the irony of experience that marked gay men so profoundly.

Movies as much as life experience were the source of information about heterosexual behavior, about romantic sexuality, information heterosexuals could verify and discard, but which gay men did not. The men who viewed that product, particularly as adolescents, perceived in it a message that was supportive at the very time when they began to experience their own homosexuality as deviant and alienating. For my generation, that message said there was a place outside family, school, and church, the three most oppressive institutions of heterosexuality, where it was possible to live another kind of life. Only when we discovered that the place was an illusion did the confusions about adult relationships begin to create havoc.

Some years ago, a film of major importance, Ingmar Bergman's *Scenes from a Marriage,* presented the very image of this havoc. Ostensibly an indictment of marriage, of modern heterosexual relationships with their unbearable complications and dishonesties, *Scenes* in fact makes clearer than any other work of art outside literature the appalling difficulty of all adult relationships, of any profound bonding in our times. The issues are sexism and romanticism, but the subject is no less than our immediate emotional futures, and a dismal choice between suffocating roles that are unviable, or waking from nightmares that show us handless and helpless before our new freedom. The film says that we awake at last, out of the hostilities and poverty of relationships that provide no intimacy but smug familiarity, to an immediate awareness of our loss. Freedom is experienced as being bereft of our conventionality. What else this freedom promises, besides a sense of loss and the nightmares of anxiety, is perhaps a truly honest optimism. It is Ophelia's mad certainty, "Lord, we know what we are, but not what we may be."

Bergman snares us with his persuasive discrepancies: the husband, emblem of academic pomposity and masculine rigidities, becomes the sweet, moving comfort in the middle of the night somewhere in the world. He becomes our adult lover, who offers nothing but that comfort which is everything. Marianne, dullish and trepidatious, sexually indifferent, discovers her athletic sexuality and dreams wild-eyed that she is maimed. If they both find adulthood, their definitions of self are diametric: he accepts his failure, foregoes his investment in success and virility, and achieves an extraordinary and mitigated humanity. She blooms into a radiant womanhood of thrusting and commanding erotic appetite only to be haunted at night. Amazing that *Scenes from a Marriage*, demanding and honest as it is, was made for Swedish television and for a popular audience. It seems almost miraculous that Bergman could transform the commonplace into these radical universals. Perhaps his eclectic audience only testifies to the universality of our deprivations in Western society, the ordinariness of neurosis, the predictability of instability, the expectation of compromise if not defeat. If Bergman is so completely the modern self, it is ironic that his modernity achieves itself in film, the very medium of culture where we lost ourselves to begin with.

However common the experience of gay men to others, there is also a particular response that differs from women's in meaning and in gratification. Gay men could hold a double moral sense about messages and endings.

While the Hollywood movie offered startling images of sexually and socially autonomous women in upper-class settings and repeated the image in stories of working-class women who were often more mobile and better rewarded economically than their men, the endings always showed capitulation. For love, for the love of men which demanded that women preserve male pride, women took to the bedrooms or the kitchens—indeed, if they wished company in the bedroom, the message declared that a man would only find his way there if beckoned from the kitchen.

While women must have been overwhelmed by such betrayal, and if not furious certainly confused and politically inhibited, homosexual men identified with both parties. The image of domestic submission for sexual love and the preservation of male pride were parallel fantasies fulfilled in the same banal moment. One result of this peculiarly efficient gratification of fantasy was to undercut women's resentment, making it seem less serious and they themselves unfeminine when they felt protest. The same orthodoxy about femininity could simultaneously divert straight men, depress women, and deceive gay men.

What did a homosexual audience get from it? Mostly, I suspect, a temporary relief from their anxiety about masculinity, and a momentary sense that the conflict was resolved even if the war was lost. The serenity of defeat was more bearable than the terrors of struggle.

In the early fifties in graduate school, I became a close friend of Sonia, a young Polish Jew who had survived the Holocaust. We struck up our acquaintance in the graduate reading room, where we discovered each other giggling with delight over the excesses of *The Maid's Tragedy* and *'Tis Pity She's a Whore*. In the course of our friendship I tried to explain that the campy qualities of seventeenth-century Jacobean drama were exactly like the conventions of Hollywood movies. The titles alone of the plays were sufficient hint: *The Fair Maid of the West, The Honest Whore, The Widow's Tears, Cynthia's Revels, The White Devil, The Broken Heart, Love's Sacrifice, The Dutch Courtesan, The City Madam, A Chaste Maid in Cheapside, Women Beware Women,* and *The Lady of Pleasure* are typical examples.

My analogy was dismissed as frivolous: one should not compare literature, even as inept as some of these plays, to movies, which were too shallow to be considered even debased art. The experience of the war in Europe had made it possible apparently to respond to ineptitude as a kind of metaphysical absurdity as long as the context of the drama signalled that the seriousness of plot and character was entirely metaphoric, that the literal was merely the occasion for one's response to more weighty thematic matters. No matter how empty Jacobean drama seemed, it could still be taken seriously by intellectuals as a mirror of its age, the manners if not the morals of its audience. In films, the style could be as sophisticated and pregnant as anything in Renaissance drama, but the style operated almost exclusively in images, its real rhetoric; film's language was entirely visual; movies could be banal, but not absurd. The literal was all there was. Psychological motivation didn't exist; only behavior. Manners were dictated by the decor and clothing which were the real story; morality was elementary. What gave interest—though they could not give depth—to movies were the astonishing men and women who were the living embodiments of the stylized vision of designers, among whom I count the producers and some of the directors. Taste rather than intelligence or even talent gave movies their distinction. That is why they are so popular as revivals among generations for whom these decades are history not biography. Wit and glamour do not date as ideas do.

My delight in Jacobean drama was the direct result of the kind of moral expectations created by movie melodrama. In *The Maid's Tragedy,* I applauded the heroine's cynical betrayal of the hero as expedient because she is the only character sufficiently developed to respond to and because all the virtuous figures are bores or fools. The social conventions demanded that the play end in universal catastrophe, a denouement of widespread slaughter, but the real moral was still clear, almost Brechtian in its utilitarianism: it is much better to exploit than to be used.

A similar moralism underlies all the vehement dramas of sexual discontentment favored in forties movies, particularly well done at Warner Brothers. If the characters played by Ida Lupino or Bette Davis were punished for their selfishness, their downfall was not a real moral issue. Our sympathy was committed to the energy, allure, and worldliness of these women. Because they were intelligent as well as neurotic, their willfulness seemed heroic and the lessons learned from them were the antithesis of the didactic sermons of the epilogue, often the puzzled commentary of the bystander. The suicides of Davis and Lupino were the understood convention; the wish was for their triumph. The heroines of *The Hard Way* and *In This Our Life* are both betrayed, but not by their unbridled ambition or their own sentimental and amoral passions as their Jacobean counterparts are. The modern heroine is made desperate by her folly: she trusts the wrong person, an unreliable lover or another woman who deserts her in the service of romantic infatuation. Just as I was pleased by the open villainy of the Jacobean heroine because it is heroic, so I was even more biassed against the soft women and their weak men in films, who survive at the expense of the true heroines, figures of neurotic strength and vigor.

Implicitly, the basis of movies' emotional seductiveness was the perception that all energy was libidinous, that ambition was really erotic. Davis and Lupino played male-identified women whose lack of sisterhood was their virtue; they would invariably lose in the game of sexual politics, but they would not be victims of their femininity. The moralism of movies was nonchalantly understood as hypocrisy. It was not how the plot worked itself out that gave the ethos, though that gave an ostensible one. What one saw as a child or adolescent at these movies was the *bad luck* that plagued the heroines, while one's moral identification created fantasies that drifted quite against the grain. In *The Hard Way*, Ida Lupino exploits her sister's musical talent and her own sexual permissiveness to climb out of the *Lumpenproletariat* of mining Appalachia. She is ruthless and invulnerable except for the intense tie to her sister. Though Lupino easily establishes her character's sexual promiscuity and her indifference to the piggish men who use and promote her, she is also sexually predatory when it suits her. She achieves, finally, a promised autonomy from even the cherished sister, but it is all snatched away by the ingratitude and sentimentality of that ingenue, who learns the lessons of hardness the easy way. If there was one lesson I learned, it is that even one's own flesh and blood is untrustworthy; Lupino was not ruthless enough. *In This Our Life* also deals with two sisters who are caught in sexual competition and whose names are Stanley and Roy. Bette Davis is even more luckless in this adaptation of Ellen Glasgow's novel because she is sufficiently ruthless for anyone's taste. Without any loyalties, she is dogged into disaster by circumstances alone. What is clear even to a child is that the sweet decent prettier sister is insignificant next to the nervy irresistible Davis, whose jumpy neuroticism enhances her sexuality to both the men in the film and the audience.

That Hollywood risked gainsaying the pieties except in the final triumph of convention is a testimony to the women-centered interests of this melodrama, an inheritance of romantic literary fiction and drama, and to the resources of actresses of extraordinary beauty, talent, and presence. Perhaps most of all it is a testimony to an audience that could still fall back on a literary response which permitted men to cross sex lines and identify with women.

When films dealt with women who reneged on their own aspirations, whether in remorse for their own aggressiveness or through the vagaries of love, the entire genre slipped toward a world of sentimental rather than melodramatic contrivance. A Joan Crawford story usually required that she be redeemed from her hardness by compulsive romantic sentiment.

Nothing of course was believable except the hardness. The implied exchange of her granite autonomy for sexual love was ludicrous, for Crawford was not sexual, and the men who inspired such a change of heart were
themselves sexless or silly. It was impossible to believe that anyone could
find himself infatuated with Crawford unless he was already beyond the
pale. Thus, in *Mildred Pierce*, Crawford is finally rich enough to buy a
playboy husband, and the relationship is convincing because it seems perverse: even the gigolo she chooses is effete.

There were autonomous women who were sexual, but they were
rare. Garbo was the classiest example. Unfortunately, her material was
either inferior to her talents or uninteresting compared to her presence.
When her material was serious, as in *Anna Karenina*, it was turgid with
melancholia. Once, in *Camille*, Garbo and her material fulfilled each other.
All sexual poise and inviolate passivity, Garbo displays the libertinism that
keeps her serious in the midst of the most sentimental romance. But her
beauty was too rare; it was hard for her to represent anything. Commoner
versions of autonomy were the urban girls like Jean Arthur or Barbara
Stanwyck, whose cleverness or slyness hinted that those ostensible submissions were so unreasonable. This resistance to the material was vivid in
Double Indemnity, where our emotional interest is invested in a heroine
who is unreliable. It doesn't matter that her last moments are steeped in
regret—the regret is for lost sexual pleasure. It is the same lesson Garbo
illustrated in *Camille;* she dies in a state of sexual excitement. It's the way
to go.

Perhaps only the tragedies of Christopher Marlowe set up so barren a
conflict between character and plot, between will and chance. With Marlowe, it is impossible to side with Barrabas or Tamburlaine or Faustus, but
they are preferable to everyone else. Marlovian tragedy is sustained by
gorgeous lyrical bombast, whose equivalent is the glamour of movie technology. The dichotomy between didactic action and the reality perceived
as character induces a strange sophistication in the audience, an ability to
separate the dramatic from the psychological, and to make two separate
moral responses: one ostensibly to propriety, and the other, far more seriously, to fantasy. Later, when we become aware of these conflicting
responses, each undermining the other, we call the material camp.

This duplicity of response, confronted with literature, inevitably distorted the material. Thus, *Madame Bovary*, when I read it as a freshman in 1950, left me with the unmistakeable impression of Emma as the author of the book. I simply did not believe what Flaubert said about her vanity or selfishness or destructiveness. I could already separate character and action; it was easier to ignore point of view. I was as myopic reading the novel as watching the movie made from it; in both cases, I sat too close.

Rereading the novel years later, I was surprised to find how little sympathy Flaubert actually invests in Emma. Charles becomes the protagonist when Emma's unmovable shallowness is stripped of our sentimentality. This occurs when we no longer see her as the victim of her education, and what remains is her beauty and her sexuality, both of which Flaubert genuinely admires. When we reread as adults, there is always a conflict with the nostalgic memory of our more innocent responses. It takes years to learn that the hero of *Anna Karenina* is not Vronsky but Levin. We may have to revise our estimate of Anna and confront Levin, but even when we willfully or helplessly misread Tolstoy we do not quite nullify his intentions as we do with Flaubert, because Tolstoy shares with both his naive and his adult audiences a deep compassion for his creation. Not that Flaubert lacks compassion, but when he finally displays any, it is for Charles and Berthe, not for Emma.

When *Madame Bovary* was filmed very opulently by M.G.M. in the mid-forties, it was given the studio's most careful attention; Vincent Minelli the director and Jennifer Jones as Emma were proven public favorites. The adultery was handled intelligently though touched with craven piety: in a prologue, James Mason impersonates Flaubert on trial for indecency, and art and truth triumph over prudery. However, though much movie art was involved, there was little truth. Strangely, the movie was very faithful to the novel; whole scenes, pages of dialogue, even parts of the narration were retained; Emma's famous seduction at the fair, with Flaubert's precocious spatial juxtapositions, was authentically enacted by cross-cutting. But the translation of the novel into film was an automatic distortion, an inevitable sentimentalization. Once Flaubert's acerbically understated voice is removed, the narrative spontaneously coarsens into Emma's own vision of herself, and her passion and beauty are as seductive for us as for her lovers. The camera is an irresistible liar: thus, Emma's adultery-as-folly is transformed into Anna's adultery-as-tragedy. The lingering loving camera is the surrogate for compassion, and we are mechanically infatuated by the camera that instantly denatures all the intelligence of Flaubert's irony. Minelli's direction and the writer's script were serious, literary, and adult in this treatment of a classic; how remarkable that it should have fulfilled my serious unliterary adolescent requirements.

The coincidence is a simple one: the camera bestows glamour which eroticizes everything exactly as fantasy does, and both processes are exclusively visual and unreflective. I am not suggesting that making movies is unserious; I suggest that looking at them seriously is not particularly adult, especially when that term suggests awareness. Movie-going is still the most pristine, least evolved aesthetic experience we can have. True, our taste changes, but our investment in movies is unique. We have no stake in sustaining our nostalgia in literature: who would want to reread what we once loved *as* we once loved it? Nostalgia in art is suspect, reminding us of past naivetés and rarely congratulating us on our discernment. Besides, it is too easy to remember the inadequacy of earlier judgments. Our youthful mistakes are really much less ridiculous than our present follies which are so unmistakeably neurotic.

Movies recreate the sense of the past and evade conflict with our innocence, because our early responses to movies passed no serious judgments, and because our hunger for glamour is unabated. The glamour at the heart of our bondage to the movies is a mystery. No one who did not go to the movies as a child, who did not have the duplicity of response I've described, is as permissive about film as that generation dumped at Loews twice a week for two decades. This same glamour is also a major source of our sexism, of the emotional support we lend to our own oppression. It is the most attractive image of surrender to the conventional expectations about romantic sexuality. Unlike literature, where the minimum requirement of literacy is itself a degree of intellectualism, movies do what the Puritans suspected theaters of doing: they are powerful agents of our corruption. When Huxley wrote about the "feelies" in *Brave New World*, he was very clever about the visceral pleasure of movies and their anti-intellectual gratifications. What is wrong with contemporary films is not their seriousness or even their loss of glamour, but their ponderous pretentiousness and their desire to imitate what is tendentious in literature.

The nature of the corruption of our values is suggested by the claim movies once made to give us images of love between normal, even ordinary people. We realized of course that they were neither, but then again, neither were we, yet we accepted their values as more genuine. Though in fact we soon understood that our only escape was deviation and we yearned for it, we were also deeply anxious. Our ambivalence teetered between the reluctant confession that self-discovery would show ourselves as queer, and willful evasion would certainly keep us depressed. One of the things Bergman reveals in *Scenes from a Marriage* is the peculiar plea-surelessness of fulfillment and the deep loss of no longer feeling ourselves to be like everyone else. It is ironic that Bergman should so profoundly deny movies the most potent of all their seductions: the rigid insistence on how men and women must regard each other and themselves.

How costly was it really? Compared to the damages of our rearings, the mess of our pasts, how pernicious could movies be?

Sonia, who survived Europe, who knew fully the pain of being the flotsam of Eastern Jewry, who had lost all conventionality, certainly all moral pieties and sexual hypocrisy, who was not beguiled by sentimen-tality, who had nothing to be nostalgic about but horrors—could not survive America. Though she could overcome conventionality and still retain a high moral sense and a high seriousness about literature, though she could sustain her own being in an amazing freedom from infantilism, she could not sustain her hardness in a culture that insisted on rekindling, in the institutions of marriage and motherhood, the desire for normality. America trivialized Europe's tragedies by coaxing its survivors out of their stoicism and proper madnesses into an apotheosis of romanticism that was never authentic.

In the late sixties when I first saw *Doctor Zhivago,* I thought Omar Sharif miscast and the film a failure. But I went with Sonia to see it again because she insisted that my adult censoriousness had blinded me. Through her eyes, the film was overwhelming—entirely illogical and completely heartbreaking. I suppose we could have analyzed how it happened, for she had had years of Freudian analysis and I was a virtuoso new critic and movie buff; but we realized that such a response to our response was improper. We knew we'd never really pierce that mystery, that we had better things to do with our waking lives. What the fantasy was and how it satisfied us were not so mysterious; why the fantasy was so satisfying to us both, why it was easy for her to teach me to regress from "literary" to preliterary values, is less clear. It is nothing to decide whether or not *Doctor Zhivago* is a good film; it is everything to surrender to it. But if the movies corrupted her and us, it is because we wanted, and want, them to. They are the visible agents of what is already internal; they make overt and political our nostalgia and fantasy.

Once my generation looked to movies to explain our behavior, and we thought that if we understood them we could explain ourselves. Later, when we thought we knew why we behaved or were past caring, movies were the best way to justify the extravagance of our desires. What they never taught us was what it *felt* like, that normality we had been so conditioned to desire. Movies made America forever a foreign country; they told us the only place to call home was the romantic and inviolate imagination, the utter reality of the self, and the primacy of the private life: the rest was someone else's fantasy.

4

If in popular culture, the stylizations of glamour veer toward camp, either melodramatic or farcical, in art it is another story. In popular culture, the examples chosen from fashion and movies, the style is the most creative and imaginative expression of sensibility. But in art, that issue is of less importance; art need not have a style that is elegant, witty, ironic, or even intelligent to move our feelings. Indeed, next to a raw power or an obsessive vision which can overwhelm us, a delicate knowingness is often mistaken for triviality or effeteness.

That was the reputation of ballet and dance when its audiences were dominantly upper-class afficionados, professional dancers, artists and intellectuals, and homosexual men. Of course, it was never trivial or effete, though some of the individual dancers may have been. In ballet and dance, the glamorous is used with a sad awareness about how we feel toward beauty and sexuality that is close to the feelings we have toward tragedy. While ballet and modern dance have been associated with homosexuality, it was the homosexuality of the male dancers and of a disproportionate sector of the audience that gave it such a reputation. In fact, dance has been dominated by women and by men in love with the beauty of femininity. The two greatest choreographers of the century, George Balanchine and Martha Graham, are notably heterosexual.

Ballet and dance offer a special case: their relevance to gay sensibility lies in their relationship to audience. In the business of clothing, homosexuals pursue their ambitions while enacting their fantasies. In movies, their activity is more difficult to discern; their participation in creating that image called Hollywood is really an exaggerated version of their place in the narrower commercial world of the fashion industry. But the effect of Hollywood on gay men as an audience was an enormously powerful miseducation of the imagination where extravagant investments in romantic love were authenticated.

In ballet and dance, the creative impulse is not significantly marked by sexual preference as much as by sexuality in general. Homosexual choreographers show themselves sometimes in the way they handle the dancers, since the *pas de deux* or its variations are always allusive, evoking the idea of the couple. But most homosexual choreographers are not distinguished in their work by their sexual persuasion. Unlike the effect of movies, the effect of dance on gay men is not to give misinformation. Rather, dance confirms another aspect of their experience in culture, and it does it in terms of social class. In this elitist diversion, an art which has only recently acquired a wide audience, the idea of refinement, of aristocratic taste is still alluring. More clearly than elsewhere, dance permits gay men to believe that beauty has a primary legitimacy, that they are privy to discriminations ordinary people are unaware of, and that their enthusiasm is different from that of the rest of the audience because theirs is so knowing.

I discovered ballet and modern dance in my freshman year: I was dating a very crazy girl, a Graham-trained dancer with Anna Sokolow's troupe, and she taught me how to sneak into the second balcony of the City Center or the Alvin Theater after the first number on the program. I was on the road to culture toll-free, since the previous spring I had stolen a student pass to the Museum of Modern Art, which I went to at least twice a week for the free movies. Occasionally I was shut out of the three o'clock showing and would idle my time until the five o'clock one by looking at a few paintings, but it took me a year to make it to the third floor. The second was prettier, and at least I'd heard of some of the artists. Eventually, things went from pure to impure, and I started visiting museums even if they didn't show movies, and it has never been the same since.

Though movies and dance and novels were the joys of my under-graduate life, my boredom threshold these days is very low for everything except dance. I have even started walking out on movies, though I admit I got the idea from Pauline Kael. Worse, I recently fell asleep in a theater, a phenomenon so shocking to me, who was taken to his first movie at six months and never cried once but has always cried profusely since, that I was haunted for days by this evidence of middle age. Dance rarely bores me, because when it is bad or dull or vulgar it infuriates me, and when it is what I want it to be I am moved, even to tears, in a way that little else still can move me.

Why is ballet traditionally an art that homosexual men have found involving? Part of the answer is obvious: why not? But I think there are factors beyond the suggestion that the ballet offers high art and a sophisti-cated moving experience. While I think homosexuals have tastes for every kind of entertainment and sport, ballet is one of the few opportunities where gay men are at home in the audience and with the experience. Other places, like sports arenas, often demand that they remain masked, that they inhibit their behavior because it seems inappropriate. Certainly, displays of affection or effeminacy are invitations to hostile confrontations, open competitions with heterosexual men. When San Francisco's gay community developed a baseball team to challenge the police department's, it was initially considered a joke, albeit a serious one. Gay men were saying that they could compete with straight ones, and with policemen, the strongest symbols of institutionalized heterosexual society. Even when the gay team lost, it was not a humiliation because it was still a challenge. But it is a challenge that says that gays can be as good as straights on the least rewarding level: they can be *like* heterosexuals. The appeal of such com-petition is felt by the most male-identified portion of the gay population, though there is probably a large segment that finds the idea campy, enjoy-ing it more as a coercion of the police into taking gays seriously as men than as a serious competition that could prove anything meaningful.

But at the ballet, gay men are neither challenged nor threatened by the experience. First of all, they are there in numbers and always have been; without their support, ballet would not have become the popular art it is today. Gay men have also used the ballet as a theater for disseminating their own values and for reinforcing the idea that their sensibility is unique. Ballet provides one of the few social activities which initiate younger men in a subculture that they are eager to enter but also anxious about. That the subculture is gay life and elitist art at the same time has been one of the strongest appeals of dance for homosexuals. Ballet in New York at least is no longer elitist, and that is sadly a mixed blessing, and as long as there are superstars like Baryshnikov, it will attract the curious as well as the serious, but traditionally, the performers who were outstanding have been women.

Like the romantic drama in the movies, the ballet is about the heroine; the hero is Prince Charming or he is a cypher. The heroine in the ballet is ultrafeminine, innocent, and presexual. Despite the fact that the commonest ballet convention is the *pas de deux,* it is not an ordinary couple who dance before us, a couple who clearly stand for a relationship in real life. Instead, there is the image of romantic yearning, male passivity, and female aloofness. The ballerina is to be served by her partner, but she need bestow nothing but her presence; her beauty and grace and distance are what is demanded of her.

Because it is an image of interaction between a man and a woman that is never consummated, it is an allusion that is experienced by gay men as a parallel to their relationships with women. And it also celebrates beauty as its own justification, which has its far less innocent correspondence in the values of gay subculture. Finally, ballet emphasizes asexual grace which is demanded of both men and women: the feminine ideal of grace transcends gender but does not nullify the requirement of strength. The male dancer with his feline character, lithe and strong, is not symbolically masculine. Only recently has virtuoso physical power come to be admired widely: Baryshnikov is more admired by the general audience for his prodigious feats of athleticism than for his art, and when he dances in a subdued piece like *Orpheus,* critics and audiences complain he is miscast. I do not want to dwell here on the deliberate attempt of some dancers, some of whom are gay, to herald the heterosexuality of male dancers as something middle-class audiences can comfortably take for granted. Despite such propaganda, sending one's young son to ballet school is not the favored idea for developing his strength among most families.

If homosexual dancers were criticized in the past for being effeminate, there was some logic for the objection. The effeminate gesture was distracting, drawing attention from the ballerina, and inefficient, since the grace required was neutral, without reference to any sexuality since the entire subject is intrusive.

The ballet then represented an idealized image of a romantic relationship that gay men did not find alienating because it had no correspondence in reality, an adoration of beauty which had a more powerful correspondence in their lives than in the lives of heterosexual men, and a celebration of feminine grace that ignored conventional masculine posing and could be interpreted as a justification for accepting one's own effeminate yearnings. And it also offered elating achievements, reaffirming heart and mind—in short, art of the highest order.

To see a Balanchine masterpiece, or the masterpiece I find supreme, *Concerto Barocco,* done as it should be, without a second's carelessness, with a partner who can lift with ease and dance with deference and a ballerina as beautiful and remote as Suzanne Farrell, is to be reduced, or enlarged, to helpless painful tears. It was Balanchine who first taught me about classicism, and that in classical art one can find the small perfections that are so sustaining and so rare. Though the work is danced to Bach's concerto for two violins, it is not really baroque at all. Abstract and formal, it takes from the Bach a mood of *politesse* and mirrors in the movement what the music also tells: that what matters in humanity is beauty alone. When the performance of the *Concerto* is "off" or miscast, then the relief of not having to feel so much is itself, oddly, a simpler pleasure. For when, after a few minutes, I can tell that the performance will be first rate, I'm stricken with anxiety about the audience's restlessness or the possibility of an accident on stage and greet the finale with relief. Such works of Balanchine's dredge up powerful responses: *Apollo, Agon, Serenade, La Valse, Symphony in C,* and *Symphony in Three Movements* are all astounding. Unlike painting, literature, or music, these works are fragile. When other companies perform them without Balanchine's direct supervision, it is as if we were looking at a forgery. Even Nureyev as Apollo or Baryshnikov before he danced with the New York City Ballet had inadequate support from their ballerinas: too stolid compared to the thoroughbred lines of Balanchine's ballerinas; when *they* suddenly turn into Apollo's horses, we all soar.

What Balanchine seems to do, especially in his collaborations with Stravinsky, is create works of such tightness and leanness that when they are danced by women whose training he has supervised since their teens we are left utterly gratified. Even when the pieces have an ostensible content, the apotheosis of Apollo, or the infatuation with decadence in *La Valse,* it is really the inimitable style that provides the substance for our gratification, a style that always abstracts Balanchine's perennial subject: the beauty of movement and music in the image of the beauty of women. The great works, like Mozart's or Shakespeare's, always identify taste and class as a single critical decorum.

5

For a lower-middle-class leftist adoring adolescent in the very provincial City College of New York, whose Ivy League-trained faculty in the late forties encouraged first-generation exuberance, going to the ballet was going from *prust* to Proust. Most of us in those days were too poor to have bad taste, which can be very expensive; we simply had no taste. Blank tablets all, we were perfect students: we knew scarcely anything about the world, and no matter how lurid some of our individual experiences might be, we remained collectively innocent, untouched but eager, as avid to be indoctrinated into genteel ways as we had been, some years before, into the Labor Youth League.

Nothing in literature or music or the graphic arts was safe from arrogant misreadings. I preferred my presumptions about James and Lawrence, loved Bartók and Stravinsky but had never listened to Mozart or Schubert, framed reproductions of Munch and Rouault and Van Gogh, thought them equally good for bad reasons, but dismissed Matisse as decorative. One might say, well, here were exercises in taste, and not bad considering that most of our homes played no serious music and had no books and only mirrored frames around parrots painted on velvet. One might say that, provided he came from a home with books and music and some connection with the range of Western civilization. But I was not sentimental about *kitsch;* I set about acquiring culture as greedily as others had tried to acquire goods, but for all of us there was the same hunger: to define oneself as American, to see oneself as the insider at last.

At first, the dance affronted my tastelessness: what did it *mean?* Only the theatrical was appealing; pretentiousness was something I knew a little about. I could argue with friends about the narrative of the dances, and a little later, about the dancers. The great favorites were Nora Kaye and Melissa Hayden, for both were always so expressive, and so neurotic and profane.

It was seeing Martha Graham dancing in her early fifties and still without any appreciable loss of strength that finally made clear that what I thought was psychological in the ballets of Tudor or Robbins was more accurately titillation, merely the daring of beautiful bodies miming sexual poses. It seems so remote now when so much of culture is either obscene or trite, that Todd Bolender's *Miraculous Mandarin* created a scandal, that *Life* ran a feature story on the sexiness of *The Cage.*

Graham exhausted the minor thrill of neurotic exhibition; she smashed the audience in the guts. She showed us sexuality more nakedly and more convincingly than anyone else ever had; she eroticized the audience. Only in her company are the men so emphatically virile, tense with an electric sexuality that the audience can take seriously. Whatever else Graham says about women, her subject is always their sexuality, their victory in the maze or the defeat in their voyages. Just as Balanchine always enhances the feminine, displaying it as his real interest, so the equivalent in Graham is the entrancing virility and beauty of her men. We are easily convinced of the passion of Jocasta or the madness of Medea because it is all substantiated in the priapic vision of her men. Interestingly, as Graham danced less and less, as she choreographed more and more for others seeing her partners without herself, they became more exposed, literally more naked, more sexually stunning. A weird voyeurism seeped into the experience: Clytemnestra and Phaedra became iconography: aging, all unslaked passion, obsessed with gorgeous younger bodies.

Graham told us so much about women, and so boldly; she disclosed what few men or women have the nerve to discuss, the carnality we are not supposed to see, so that we even close our eyes when we make love, and more, she got away with it. Instead of embarrassing us as witnesses to some violated privacy, she bypassed all the self-consciousness. When Greta Garbo in *Grand Hotel* looks up at Barrymore The Morning After (coincidentally, she is a fading dancer), the camera pans in for one of those enormous close-ups, and something shocking happens: we see quite plainly in her face the remains, the vestiges of sexual ecstasy. That was Garbo's genius, to show the camera what the rest of us feel in the dark. Martha Graham's daring was as iconoclastic and disturbing.

The connection of Graham and gay sensibility is that her concern in the dance is the same one that gay men have had in the arts and in their creative lives as homosexuals: the sexuality that is central to their lives, and the need to brazen it out before the world. In ballet, the counterpart to that brass is the classical adoration of beauty, essentially the same romantic idealization that has beset gay men in their sexual pursuits.

In the fall of 1978, I reviewed a collection of dialogues with famous gay men, *Gay Sunshine Interviews*. Initially, I was annoyed by the preface of the editor, Winston Leyland, and the blurb by Allen Ginsberg and was ready to do a ripping job. Leyland calmly claimed that the book "demonstrates the existence of a definite gay sensibility in the arts" and that it also "documents the impact of gay liberation on literature," both statements in the same short paragraph, and neither with a single additional word of substantiation. Ginsberg's praise seemed prattle; he called the book "a monumental piece of self-revelation . . . a fantastic revolution of manners. Won't it lead to Frankness for Centuries? Won't it change literature and politics forever?" What was he talking about? Did he expect everyone or just gay writers from now on to document who, when, and where they fucked (he is precise even about locale)? It seemed all hyberbole and self-congratulation.

Well, I loved the book. The sexual frankness in every interview (except Gore Vidal's) is the common denominator among eleven subjects, one of whom is a composer. What seemed at first just wonderfully indiscreet cumulatively had a more startling effect: this frankness is what is special to their gayness. What is brazened but acceptable in art, translated into fashion and glamour, is here set down nakedly. The sensibility that has its beginnings in shame is now shameless. The biology we have been politely told is awry but more often called perverse is celebrated as casually as if it were natural to do so. It is also at the heart of so much heterosexual distaste: Why do they have to talk about it? Who really cares what people do? Of course, everyone cares, they always have, they always will as long as the sexual life is darkened behind closed eyes, closed doors, and closed minds. Homosexuals apparently offend by being indecorous; behind that proper notion is an anxiety about sexuality that so many cannot confront. It is not homosexuality that is offensive; it is sexuality. When critics tell us that we are misusing the word "homophobia," which logically must mean "fear of oneself," they have inadvertently been prophetic. People, heterosexual men particularly, are homophobic not because they suspect their own hidden proclivity, though sometimes that is true; they are made acutely uneasy because they are provoked to examine their own sexual natures.

Now it is clearer: I care, I want to know, it matters to my life and work, and it is far more than gossip. If there is any relationship between gay sensibility and gay liberation, it is that now we are liberated to explore the meaning of the sexuality that has given so much definition to our lives. It is a meaning that has been left too often to those who define it disapprovingly or patronizingly. In our explorations, we can begin to discard the sentimentalities about homosexuality, such as the comfort of knowing Whitman and Wilde and Proust were all that finer clay we are the stuff of.

In the Gay Sunshine interviews, the finer clay of the twentieth century has been pummeled with heroin addiction, intermittant madness, cancer, obscurity, a schizophrenic adoration of brutality, alcoholism, terminal eccentricity, and unremittant triviality. Besides these disasters, what the men have in common is that they sexualized their lives and their work, that the meaning of their sexuality is the mirror of their lives.

The finer clay has indeed been the advance guard; too often it has been concerned with success without achievement, and that predilection has now become commonplace in the culture at large. Gay men have liked the legend of refinement and made the myth part of their history: Plato, Shakespeare, Michelangelo begin the list of names reeled off, though I do not think any of them display a sensibility to label homosexual, whatever their erotic preferences were.

Doubtless, the myth is part of our history, another illustration of oppression, though this example at least shows that the alienation from the social centers of power is no final handicap to wit and talent. As long as that sensibility was closeted by its interest in the feminine, society largely tolerated it as part of its own sophistication, perhaps its narcissism. Wilde's *The Portrait of Dorian Gray* is the best single work that lives up to that description, and in it, Wilde himself subscribes to the immoralism and corruption of homosexuals who succeed within conventional society. In life, when Wilde thought that his own success ensured his witty defense of homosexuality, the result was his martyrdom.

The idea of a special refinement among gay men as their best quality has been a legacy of conformity and acquiescence to the very class that would reward their arts and talents for their personal silence. If in the past the choice between silence and success meant exile or tolerance, one can understand their pragmatism. Those who broke the silence are still denied their frankness: Shakespeare in the sonnets and Whitman in his poetry are still the occasion for annual "evidence" of their heterosexuality by men who cannot reconcile their achievements with such a reputation.

Like other minorities eager for mobility and status, homosexual men have exploited themselves. Wilde's fate is an example of self-delusion, of thinking that scandal is ineffectual after one has proven himself to the world. Scandal is a limited damage, but prison is not. Nothing protected him, not marriage and family, not the genius he finally fulfilled in *The Importance of Being Ernest,* not the powerful friends in high places. He mistook tolerance for acceptance. When he tested out that mistake, he was allowed to destroy himself. It is a lesson: acquiescence is the price, and even if one is abjectly conformist, his place is never secured. No one's is. Privilege is fragile and unreliable if it rests on talent alone.

Now it is too late for collaboration; to mistake the comforts of the ghetto for the rightful freedom to self-determination is to ignore that the property is still enemy territory, that we are only in Vichy. It is also too late to ignore the enemy within who conspires to make us acquiesce in elegant bondage like the slaves who would not leave the plantation because they did not know where to go. Unlike the oppression of blacks and women in America, ours has been a diffusive and confused injustice. We share with them a history of emotional disability, like those who saw choice as a luxury and security as necessary. Gay men have yet to recognize the degree to which they have acquiesced, though I know of none who have not bitterly experienced the narrowness of their options. That acquiescence is collaboration, and it is most vivid in the unexamined values of ambition and romance so many homosexuals do not question. Indeed, too much of the energy for civil reform which gay liberation has spent is to ensure the unencumbered pursuit of romance and power, to convert past privileges into ordinary rights.

It is better to have rights than privileges. The fate of the Jews of Western Europe showed how capricious, how utterly unreliable gentile society was when the boots were on the stairs. Even for those most assimilated, most Aryan in appearance, there was little chance. I do not want to press the analogy too far: American homosexuals are nowhere as imperiled as the Jews of 1940. But like those Jews who refused to see or who could not understand until it was too late, homosexuals in contemporary America often behave as if the danger is always somewhere else. So far, gay pride has only been interested in assertion and not enough in what we are to be proud of. That assertiveness was and still is absolutely necessary, but the time is ripe to ask clearly what it is we are asserting.

Real security requires radical change: that the public and private life be allowed to integrate. This is decidedly not the time to rely on elitism, nor on the values of a society that divorces success from achievement. It is not a problem exclusive to homosexual men; quite the contrary, it is practically everyone's concern in Western civilization. There is little enough time left to realize that exclusivity is just another ghetto, no matter how gilded the streets appear. They may look paved with gold, but for gay men it is a short step to the gutter.

CHAPTER THREE

Passing or Memories of Heterosexuality:
Gay Men as Straight Men

1

Virtually all homosexual men and lesbians assume that they are heterosexual at some time in their lives. For some, the recognition that they are different comes early; for most, it comes somewhere in their early adult lives; for a few, it comes much later. Between believing that one is straight and discovering that one is gay, there is a gap, an ambiguous period of doubt, usually quite painful, which finally results in a confrontation with one's homosexuality. This is the primary experience of coming out; before one can proclaim he is gay to the world, he must acknowledge it to himself. Coming out to the world is a social, perhaps political, act with psychological consequences; confronting one's homosexuality is a private act of a different order. One recognition precedes the other: the public stance is always the secondary result of the private one. When the burden of secrecy becomes intolerable, the sense of isolation and hypocrisy too oppressive, one is compelled to act socially. Or one *chooses* to come out for moral reasons, a commitment to solidarity, or from anger at oppression. I think this is rare. Most of us come out for a complex of reasons, but the sense of personal rage and the hope of private support from other gays are part of the experience for most men.

Not everyone, however, comes out, nor is the time between self-discovery and public acknowledgement easy to generalize about. Some men never come out socially; they live in the world more or less exclusively as heterosexuals. Some men spend years living straight before they find it tolerable to live as gay. And a huge number of gay men, whose erotic lives remain a secret at work and among their families, lead large parts of their lives as heterosexual. For these men, marriage is the most effective camouflage; being divorced works nearly as well. Gay men who have been married may evade suspicion or detection far more easily than those who have not. What man over a certain age, say forty, regardless of his demeanor or testimony, who has never married, is not suspected of being gay? There are straight men who never marry, but their numbers are small and their reasons, excluding the priesthood, hard to ascertain. The wedding band or the priest's collar exempt one from suspicion of gayness or, what in the eyes of the world is almost as contemptible, asexuality.

Today, especially among younger men, living with women is nearly as good a disguise as marriage. Men who are suspected of being homosexual but are married or living in a heterosexual arrangement are usually tolerated more than open homosexuals, though the rationale for this is complicated.

Men living in gay ghettos can be open and political and libertine and anything they choose to be, but they have a minimal effect on society at large. Despite their segregation, it is these men who provoke the greatest anxiety among heterosexuals. Like prostitutes, who are most tolerated when they are off the street and behind red lights, homosexuals create anxieties of critical proportions when they insist on being seen and heard. Even people with no special distaste for gays ask why they have to be *confronted* with gay sexual lifestyle. I would guess that these people consider heterosexual displays in public just as vulgar and intrusive as homosexual ones. A longstanding tradition unites decorum and sexual oppression; some people don't want any dissemination of sexual information—of any sort, at any time—outside the bedroom. Their fear of sexuality may be far more intense than their fear of homosexuals.

The cycle of tolerance and backlash is tight. Homosexual liberation was created in the sixties and further spurred in the seventies by the demands from other groups, like blacks and women, for equality and justice under the law. Powerful right-wing forces have since discovered that the gains of the black and women's movements are difficult to rescind, although further progress can be made much harder to achieve. The Bakke decision, the growing support of anti-abortionists, the excrutiating slowness of the E.R.A. to muster its majority all testify that blacks and women may be lucky if they manage to keep what they now have. But these are class problems more than anything else: they affect working-class blacks and women far more than they do middle-class ones. For instance, middle-class blacks, though few in number, are in the most advantageous position in their history; if they have enough money to live like middle-class Americans, they don't have to worry about quotas. Middle-class women who can afford abortions can have them done safely. As yet, the efforts of the right have only touched the poor.

On the other hand, fear of sexuality, manifested as sexual hatred, cuts across lines of class, race, and gender. Nor is religiosity its only cause, though, God knows, it is a major denominator. There has always been a tradition of decorum in American Protestant culture that views sexuality as a subject analogous to bathroom habits. Both experiences are universal; dysfunctions should be left to the care of specialists, and the less said about it the better. (Though this is rather afield of present discussion, it is interesting to note that the suppression of sexuality in children and their toilet training occur during the same period.)

True, it is frightening to read of homophobic fanaticism and enraging to hear talk of abominations in the eyes of the Lord, but anyone who chooses an unorthodox sexual life style faces similar hostility. More pertinent here, sexual hatred serves as the greatest pressure on homosexual men to remain closeted. Militant gay men may hold themselves above such pressure though it is never petty, but militants are a small minority. Most homosexuals are more vulnerable to disapproval, the subtle, pervasive contempt of Protestant culture, than they are to fanaticism. They see themselves as ordinary people; if left alone, they would probably resemble heterosexuals socially and politically. The fanatic is dangerous but unpredictable and sometimes useful. Where is Anita Bryant now? *The New York Times,* however, or *The New Yorker,* among the most widely read middle-class publications, rarely acknowledge that gay means anything but cheerful except when they are quoting. These liberal publications, which are forthright about the legitimacy of women's rights, the problems of racial injustice, and even the inequities of capitalism, still regard gay rights as an "ambiguous" issue, an accurate assessment, to be generous, of the disinterest of establishment America in homosexual visibility, if not proof of its antagonism.

It is futile to argue that if all the homosexuals in America came out tomorrow their overwhelming numbers would make opposition useless. Homosexuals *won't* come out tomorrow because they have the choice to remain invisible, a choice denied to every other oppressed minority. What do blacks or women have to lose by increased militance? Closeted homosexuals, on the other hand, stand to lose all the privileges they have enjoyed passing as straight men. To claim that the psychic, social, or moral benefits of coming out will offset this loss of privilege, particularly the exemption from scorn, is arguable if not dubious. At present, coming out is a rite of passage undertaken alone; until gay men can offer one another the kind of support blacks and women are creating for themselves, they will have little to ease the trauma of going public.

After one is out, there are sources of comfort if one is lucky enough to live in or migrate to a community with a large gay population. But even here, one's friends usually cannot help to confront family or colleagues. One can hand them a book (there are so many now) explaining how everyone should behave, but that is emotionally evasive and only veils the issue which everyone can then choose to ignore. I know—that's how I did it; though in my own defense I wrote the book I handed them.

The reasons why gay men remain closeted are perhaps self-evident. At work they are vulnerable in a special way. And this threat should not be underestimated, even for hairdressers, interior decorators, and clothing designers. The myth that these occupations are dominated by gay men can easily be used as a pretext to demand that "equal opportunity" be offered to other minorities. At schools that have large third-world student bodies, such as New York's Fashion Institute of Technology, everyone is tolerant of gay professionals, but there is also a feeling that now it is someone else's turn, or at least that the turn should come around to third-world gays and women. No one can deny the pie is small. To identify oneself as part of the gay minority is to find oneself competing with other oppressed groups who have enlisted the sympathy of liberal society in ways that gays have not.

Coming out is an exposure; for anyone who has persistently deceived his family and friends it involves trauma. It is understandable then that so many gay men choose to remain invisible. The question is: what kind of lives do these men lead passing as straight?

2

Men who pass can be separated into two categories: those who pass by living with women (or as men who *have* lived with women) and those who lead lives "above suspicion." The latter are successful only as long as they are young and conform rigidly to conservative notions of masculinity. Their disguise is rented; sooner or later it will no longer fit properly. The former group raises another question. If one can function as a heterosexual, why categorize him as a homosexual? Why not bisexual, ambisexual, or any of the fashionable new labels?

Recently an informal group of gay writers discussed what it meant to them to call themselves homosexual or lesbian. One man said that if he were sexually incapacitated he would no longer consider himself homosexual. For him, the term referred predominantly to his erotic life. His sexual preference also made him political, but if he could no longer exercise that preference gay oppression would cease to be an issue concerning him. He explained that, unlike those who are born and die black or female, he had *become* homosexual; he could also "become" neuter or straight. He had indeed once thought of himself as straight; the process could be reversed. He admitted that it would probably be even more painful and difficult to try to change back again, but he did not think it impossible, only unlikely. He could not predict that he would die a homosexual, particularly since he had not resolved the question of fatherhood. He missed having or, more precisely, rearing a child. Because he was openly homosexual, it would be difficult to adopt, and he did not feel equipped to deal with the problems of raising a foster child, inevitably a boy, probably third-world, and undoubtedly the product of some years of institutionalization. He confessed he preferred girls, to whom he had always responded more spontaneously and simply. Somehow the idea of raising a son who might be heterosexual was too complicated to examine. This issue of homosexual fathering is the key concern among gay men who marry: to have children in a conventional family arrangement, whatever that means these days.

This man's views were singular and caused a younger man in the group to express astonishment. His view of himself was the result of very different experiences. He had come out within the movement. His first experiences had been at the Gay Activist Alliance in New York, and soon afterward he had moved into a couple arrangement that lasted many years. He claimed that nothing he did was unrelated to his sexual identity, which was both a statement about his personality and a point of view about the world.

The women in the group, all feminists, agreed that their lesbianism was not an exclusive sexual issue about erotic choice, though it had much to do with the idea of gender. They found it politically and emotionally unacceptable to divide their commitment to women into straight and gay concerns. The issues on which they focused their energies which appeared exclusive to gay women were in fact issues related to sexism. They maintained that the problems of lesbians are primarily women's problems, only more oppressive—especially those of lesbian mothers. Their choice to be open jeopardizes their custody of their children, but the difference between their predicament and that of straight women who offend the community is one of degree rather than quality. More lesbian mothers than straight women have been declared unfit and denied custody of children because the issue special to lesbians is that many communities equate being lesbian with being unfit to mother. But many communities do not. Probably more lesbians have won than lost their children by remaining silent about their sexual preference. The problem involves choice and militance. Women in conservative communities, like Fundamentalist ones, who insist on being openly gay must be prepared for risk; other lesbians find that risk too enormous to take and secure their children by silence.

The issue of custody is terrifying since it is always around The Children that the hatred of homosexuality is most fervent. I do not deny the special burden of lesbian mothers nor do I intend to treat their ordeals lightly. But their struggle isn't separate from the general struggle of women. When women's rights are truly secured, lesbian mothers will inevitably be protected.

In contrast, homosexual fathers rarely win custody of their children and often have to forfeit much more than heterosexual men do in divorce proceedings merely to get visiting rights. In England a group of divorced wives of homosexual men organized to air their bitterness about their predicament and the press gave them generous coverage; members of the group were interviewed for a television documentary, part of which was shown here on *60 Minutes* in the spring of 1978. The women all felt they had been deceived, even when their husbands had told them they were homosexual. They insisted that they did not really understand homosexuality, that they did not expect infidelity, and that when infidelity occurred they had hoped it might be a phase that a good marriage could resolve. None of the women sounded insincere or ironic.

I would guess that most women who marry men they know to be homosexual experience similar confusion. What motivates them to marry gay men is unclear, but they cannot be held fully accountable for their naiveté. Why should they assume that marrying a homosexual who says he wants to have a family is more of a risk than marrying a heterosexual?

At least the homosexual is unlikely to leave her for another woman. Perhaps to these women their sexual lives are less important than having families. Given the emotional responsiveness women have been led to expect of men, there is no reason to assume that gay men are poorer marriage prospects, in the area of either performance or communicativeness.

Of course, not everyone needs to live with his or her sexual partner; some people do not need sex at all. The French have an institution in which the partners remain chaste—the *mariage blanc*. The truth is that, until our own times, marriage was never intended primarily to satisfy erotic desire.

It is easy to see how women might rationalize marrying gay men and why gay men want to marry straight women—though it would be much more reasonable for them to marry gay women when they marry in order to have children. In such a marriage the limitations of fidelity would be irrelevant: monogamy would be "unnatural." The romantic needs of both partners could be met outside the home where it is already sought by so many couples, but the harmony of the family would remain undisturbed. Children would benefit from having parents less likely to sacrifice domesticity for a dubious romanticism. In such a marriage, the husband might well be more involved in the nurturing of his children than the father is in traditional arrangements. After one abandons monogamy, it is easier to question other conventions about the roles of husbands and wives. Such a couple, bound together as parents and treating each other with equality, could create a friendship that is both sustaining and profound, perhaps unprecedented. In many ways this would be the liberated family, a model for freedom and fulfillment even for heterosexual marriages, except that one would be living with someone who was not a primary sexual choice. But that happens in all types of marriages. Legally, neither partner would be more vulnerable if the marriage failed; fitness could be determined entirely on rational grounds, although women would probably continue to be favored.

And here is another reversal: gay parents would breed heterosexual children. There is a justice to it: most of us were bred and raised by heterosexuals. The few findings that exist seem to indicate that having a lesbian mother or a gay father does not affect the child's sexual orientation; it may even make of the child an unusual adult, one freer of sexist programming. Such families could help illuminate the origins of homosexuality. Those children who turn out to be homosexual would not necessarily be traumatized by their sexual identity, risk loss of their families, or suffer alienation from their straight siblings.

I like the plan, but I do not want to minimize the problems of such a marriage; in fact, I am not sure what all of them are. The marriages between gay men and lesbians that I know of have been marked by secrecy and duplicity; the children were always the last to know about their parents' sexuality. I do feel, however, that we have little to lose; we are certain to do better with one another than we have with heterosexuals, where marital disillusionment and bitterness seem almost guaranteed.

For such a marriage to work, both parties must be committed to a high self-consciousness: as little as possible should be implied or shadowy. To presume that one can enter marriage and raise a child, the very heart of heterosexuality, and feel and think as others do and still be homosexual is a dangerous paradox. Gay men will not be like other fathers. They may be better, for they will not take their paternity for granted. Indeed, it is a gift; I sense there are many whose barrenness, whose childlessness are deeply felt losses, and becoming a spectator, a perpetual uncle to the children of others is an inadequate substitute. The only redress for the alienation from the family one leaves to become an adult is to create another of one's own. There may be viable substitutes for parenthood, but there are no substitutes for lack of choice. For those who cannot compensate by creativity or work, or the pursuit of power and money, their childlessness at best is a dulled pain.

Sadly, those men who are determined to marry seem to prefer straight, usually conservative women with whom they can duplicate the very families that created their own conflicts about homosexuality.

3

As students in the mid-fifties, most of the gay men I knew thought about marrying, especially the first-generation working-class Americans. There were no bachelors among our European proletariat families, though there were "spinsters," aunts whose fate seemed the most pathetic lot of all. If very few gay men actually married, it was not for want of spending thousands of dollars and years in therapy trying to be straight. Both my roommates in graduate school were gay. Ben knew he would marry; my other roommate chose the priesthood.

Ben was a very wordly, rather snobbish Episcopalian who had converted from Catholicism. He arrived at graduate school with his own crystal and tea service, insisted that Italian opera meant Monteverdi and the rest were wops, reread Jane Austen every year to nurture his sensibility, and delighted in shy fraternity boys who wrote poetry. Ben yearned to be an Edwardian, though he was a Minnesota fireman's son. A veteran of the Korean War, he was slightly older than the rest of my class and claimed to be much more experienced and knowledgeable. He had more charm and brass than most of us and was not reticent about his history with women.

Early in 1953 I had fallen for a very butch, gin-swilling, nutty ex-jock teaching fellow in the English department. Our affair was barely two months old when we separated for Christmas vacation. Bob returned to school with a bride; within a few weeks it became apparent that he would have nothing more to do with me. I did not question Bob's right to marry; I was only hurt that he was now monogamous.

When spring term was nearly over, Ben became edgy and sullen and, to my surprise, confessed that he had just been dumped by Bob—with whom he had been having an intense affair. My rage doubled, at Ben's hypocrisy and Bob's perfidy. Eventually, Ben and I decided to live apart.

Our relationship resumed some years later. Ben, no longer a student, began courting Pauline, a recently divorced woman whom he had known for many years, and confided in me. I was flattered by his trust but had decidedly mixed feelings I wasn't eager to confront. I envied him. Pauline was an intelligent sexy woman and she had a son. By marrying her, Ben was not only getting a ready-made family, but he also seemed to be managing both his sexual worlds with poise and propriety.

The marriage worked nicely for more than ten years. Ben was a good stepfather; Pauline seemed content. Born a Jew, Pauline was now an ardent convert who could tell me without embarrassment that I needed Christ in my life. Ben had devoted himself to Oriental rugs, eighteenth-century antiques, haute cuisine, fine wine, literature, and partying. On all matters of sensibility, Ben offered himself as the quintessential finer clay. As he defined Pauline's style in dress, she became increasingly chic and glamorous while Ben began to look somewhat foppish.

He also made sure, when I played bridge with them or attended one of their elegant cocktail parties, to suggest to me the healthy, vital, ongoing sexual character of his marriage. He seemed to have put perversity behind him; I retaliated by bringing the most attractive and seductive men I could find as my bridge partners. Mutually but mildly hostile, our friendship remained shallow and outwardly unconflicted. Then one night I saw Ben at the Continental Baths. He didn't see me and I never mentioned the incident to him. But my attitude changed dramatically. I no longer felt comfortable seeing him with his wife. Soon, the bridge evenings stopped.

Two years ago Ben and Pauline divorced with much bitterness on her part and real regret on his. Ben had fallen in love with a young classics teacher at his son's prep school, who had given Ben an ultimatum: leave him or leave his wife. Ben came out of the closet. Pauline got a job in another city, taking with her all the antiques, the Oriental rugs, and her son. (Bob's marriage did not last either, but he has, to my knowledge, remained closeted. He developed a reputation for being a gifted teacher in class and a drunkard outside it. The last I heard, he had remarried and was teaching at a small college in rural Pennsylvania.) However grudgingly, I admire Ben's effort to come to terms with marriage, and I respect his failure. But there are men and women who want nothing from marriage except an alibi.

Charles and May met at one of Ben's and Pauline's cocktail parties. I had brought Charles; May was a colleague of Ben's, nearly thirty, a shy, plain woman who lived with her ailing parents and dated little. Charles was smart and good-looking and hated being homosexual. Neither their friends nor their families knew that they were seeing each other. When they announced their marriage, it was after the fact; there were no celebrations, parties, showers, or housewarmings. I suspected that Charles simply did not want May to meet his friends. Why May agreed to silence has never been clear. They lived together for less than a year; then some panic overtook Charles and he left May. They separated legally; Charles gave May all their common property, which consisted mainly of his wonderfully cheap rent-controlled apartment in the heart of Greenwich Village.

That was ten years ago; their status remains unchanged to this day. May does not seem to need a divorce, and it suits Charles to be separated. He is quite out of the closet socially, but not at work. His only regret is that the marriage was so wretched. May's life has altered more radically. She left Flatbush and the burden of demanding parents for a home that is practically a gift and a serious career in publishing. She likes being "Mrs."; it makes all the difference in a city where so many women are divorced. To fail in marriage is ordinary; never to have been asked is somehow not quite honorable.

4

About the time Charles and May broke up, I too became involved with a woman. I lived with her for nearly four years and we planned to marry. I was thirty-six. She was twenty-one, a feminist who had been on her own since she was seventeen, experienced sexually with both men and women, open to the experiments of her generation that enjoyed promiscuity and drugs, and totally uncritical of me (she had been my favorite student for three years). I discovered that drugs upset me in every possible way, I wanted a traditional couple arrangement, I had never explored my feelings about women's oppression, and I was totally delighted with her adoration of my intellectual superiority. Any sensible observer could have told me, and more than one did, that the relationship wouldn't work, but I managed to ignore this.

What had I to lose? I had been "out" for nearly twenty-five years and my record with men was messy. I was only in my mid-thirties; I still had time to change, to be a father, to avoid becoming an aging homosexual. If I was no longer young by gay standards, I was in my prime by straight ones. My taste in men had led me to experiences ranging from dismal to disappointing; my family had begun to view my life as queer even if they were not quite ready to call *me* that. My colleagues assumed I was gay, while my students paid me the compliment of thinking, as Marie later told me, that a mind as refined as mine was above it all, neuter.

Ever since I had been an undergraduate I had witnessed affairs between students and professors. When my fellow teachers indulged in them, especially in their offices, I objected, and not merely on the grounds of bad taste. I thought of the students as victims of that academic infatuation that seems to go back to the Greeks. The women's feelings may have been classical, but their instructors' were not. That the men risked little, given the academic hypocrisy about such matters, but had such formidable emotional power over their young lovers seemed grossly unfair to me. I reserved most of my contempt for the lunch table, where I exchanged witty comments with other like-minded puritans. Now *I* was having an affair with an undergraduate.

Marie was one of the best students I had ever had and exotic by New York standards: Southern, from a Fundamentalist background, quiet and ladylike, and a particular delight to an English professor of Renaissance literature because she knew the Bible so well; the writers whose work I taught often made no emotional sense to most of my class. Marie had left being a Christian behind her, but she remembered what it had been like. She took every course I offered and, when she ran out of them, elected a year's independent study with me. I had been to her home several times and liked the young man she lived with. Once when I was stoned, I had even dropped the fan a bit and *kvetched* about my love life, no revelation now since I had already told her I was gay.

Three months after we began our affair the man Marie was living with decided to close their open relationship. She relayed his ultimatum to me, and we decided to live together. But I insisted that we keep our relationship a secret from all but a few close friends until she graduated in June, six months away. I felt like a foolish hypocrite.

My relationship with Marie changed my way of living. I found myself unprepared for such an affair, confused about what to anticipate. I had never lived with a lover before. Somehow, I could not get over the feeling that Marie was a guest in my home, a feeling she perceived. Bachelorhood had made me rigid. I had the problem of living with someone who simply assumed that she did not have to put the ashtray back in the same spot I had placed it in. Nothing helped but moving to a new apartment. The difficulties of living *with a woman* were irrelevant; gender had little to do with our problems. In fact there was a wistful benefit, a sense of *déjà vu* when I'd find her pantyhose drying on the shower curtain, bringing back memories of my childhood among women, mother, sister, and grandmother. Living with Marie created unforeseen pleasures, a sense of the family returned, of continuity with my past, that I could not have expected from a male lover.

There were other advantages. I could try on her makeup, help buy her clothes and thus express how I would have liked to look as a young woman, have the laundry picked up when I was too busy to do it myself, share the shopping, and enjoy someone else's cooking. Marie only did what she had done for her former lover and all her life: take care of herself and defer to the breadwinner. She felt she had to do these things not because she was a woman but because I earned the money and she "merely" studied. I had never experienced this sense that my income created privileges. I would do the dishes if she cooked, and vice versa, but I need only thank her sincerely for ironing my things while she was doing her own. This conventional arrangement of roles suited me nicely; from these quiet comforts was born my idea that perhaps I should try fatherhood. I refused to worry about whether the affair would last. I wanted us to marry and have a child; then, if the marriage failed, I would have something, perhaps everything, to show for it.

This yearning was nurtured by all that happened to me socially, among my peers and within my family. When the news leaked out that I was living with a young woman, beautiful and smart, the English department's prize student. my colleagues responded with an attitude best described as professorial locker-room congratulations. No one quite knew what stance to take. I was too young to be called an old dog. The gay men on campus kept silent on the issue, but when I was asked by one of them just whom I thought I was kidding, I could say, with mixed feelings, "Certainly not you." The straight men responded in either of two ways, sometimes a mixture of both: with a kind of envy, for I was getting away with something they had to sneak and hide and lie about—and doing it with someone they would gladly try it with—and more subtle, with a kind of welcoming. The tension eased slightly in my relationships with my hetero-sexual colleagues. True, those colleagues who had laughed at my witticisms over pedagogical lechery at the lunch table disapproved, but not vehe-mently; it was clear that an exception should be made for me. I can only suppose it was like the feeling a practicing Christian might have welcoming a converted Jew to the fold.

I saw that I had been alienated from these colleagues more than I'd liked to admit. When they spoke of husbands, wives, and children, good manners forbade that I speak of my lover. Nevertheless, if I wanted to be crude, I could; I now had the choice. Better, I could marry; then no barrier would separate us. And I saw that much of my disapproval of sexual rela-tions between teachers and students had really been resentment that straight men could get away with something no gay teacher was willing to risk. While sleeping with undergraduate women was and still is nothing to brag about, it was not the worst of academic sins. Stupidity, bad teaching, irresponsibility to colleagues, troublemaking, and being a bore were much deadlier. Sleeping with undergraduate men was another story. No woman colleague was known to have done it; neither was there any rumor about the gay men on the faculty. It was assumed that in New York City such recourse was unnecessary. Gay men and straight women alike understood that *their* sexuality as an open issue was somehow much more indecorous.

It was, however, less easy with the women I had made friends with. As one of them said, "I had no idea you were so adventurous," a response that closed the issue but left it unresolved. She was one of a number of single heterosexual women who had admired me as I did her. Over the years, our friendship had been mutually satisfying as long as I was pre-sumed gay. Now that I was living with a woman young enough to be her daughter, I had created a situation in which questions could be pondered, even if no one dared to ask them. Was my sexual choice merely that of an older man preferring a younger woman; an ordinary phenomenon? Or was there something special about *this* young woman? Had I always been available, or was this a recent development? In short, if I could be "adventurous" with this woman, why had I not shown interest in others?

As it turned out, my sexual curiosity about women was far more complex than I had suspected. Perhaps because I had been so ignorant so long, my explorations were thorough. Marie told me that my interest in her biology as well as in her anatomy was unusual. Indeed, her biology was far more fascinating to me than her anatomy. I confirmed what I had always sensed: women were very different from men and quite mysterious. What was not different or mysterious was heterosexual fucking. That was literally more convenient; the accommodations were easier, but I also found that the easiest accommodation was often erotically less interesting. If the quality of my erotic experience was now different, it was because I was living with the person I was sleeping with, and with whom I was falling in love. That was not too surprising and very welcome. What I found astonishing was Marie's erotic experience. Whatever it was, it was very different from mine, yet I discovered a strange empathic envy. Female orgasms were a revelation to behold. That I was partly responsible for them had a curious effect on me as well.

Nothing illuminated the nature of my homosexuality more clearly for me than my excursion into heterosexuality. True, Marie and I lived together in a fairly conventional relationship. We planned to marry and discussed having children. Until the last year, I saw our lives together as ongoing. But I never thought of myself as anything but homosexual. At the same time I did not discourage others from thinking of me as bisexual. I knew that the problems I had had with men I would have with women, that the pleasures with men were not profoundly different from those with Marie. What I discovered was a peculiar maleness I had previously been uninterested in defining. My male sexual partners had often served as mirrors; I operated sexually on a simple premise: do unto others exactly as you would have them do unto you. I was often less rewarded for my virtue than I hoped, but I was optimistic. A selfish or inhibited partner might be encouraged by example; I could assume I knew what I was doing, that I could please men if I chose to. It was easy to understand their difficulties or reluctance; I had experienced them myself at one time or another. Dysfunction, dissatisfaction, dissimulation were par for the course; why fuss, when the next man might be better? I assumed that all my gay relationships would be open-ended; I had never believed in fidelity except as the most romantic fantasy, though that did not stop me from yearning for such an arrangement for a long time. My priorities had always been to begin with a good fuck and then see what the personality and character had to offer.

Marie was a foreign country. While I had freely entertained the idea of being a woman at different times in my life, sometimes imagining what my life might have been as a woman, sexually or otherwise, I now discovered how very male those fantasies were. I understood neither Marie's experience of life nor the quality of her sexuality. The more I questioned and the more I was told, the more I freed myself from anxieties about women that had held me back from experimenting before Marie, the more I felt that women were complex in ways that were beyond real empathy. All the excitement, the novelty, the gratification came from difference. I never lost awareness of that, and it was clear that that had not been true of my experience with men.

In retrospect, I see that much of the sense that I understood men proceeded from a rather shallow interest in them as individuals, that a great deal of my awe at the difference between myself and Marie was the result of our living together intimately. But it was not merely coincidental. Why had I never wanted to live with a man? When I agreed to live with Marie, I was not in love with her. She was in love with me; I wanted to see what would happen. I cared less that I might fail than that I might not try. In fact, I even anticipated failure with some sense of relief.

Ironically, one of my most pernicious problems with men was absent with Marie; after a few months, performance anxiety which I experienced with every new trick was trivial. My relationship with Marie was free of jealousy and possessiveness. I have never quite decided what this security stemmed from. Was it that I assumed she would outgrow me? Or was it based on the certainty that eventually I would return to men or at least be unfaithful? I knew I would sleep with men again, if only to test out these new feelings and ideas. Being a novice made it all uncertain. I could only know more if I could compare. I preferred fidelity; it was a relief to have the same sexual partner; familiarity had a new excitement. But I would not give up being homosexual. I could refrain from men, but I did not believe I should. I had been having experiences with men since I was eleven; abstinence only fed a sense of deprivation. In the beginning of my relationship with Marie I was enamored and did not want anyone else; falling in love was a complete occupation. But when the relationship "settled," I found my desire for men was more intrusive, as was my sense that it would be messy if not wrong to pursue them.

I also noticed other women. While I preferred to be faithful since the alternative was cumbersome, time-consuming, and stressful, when an easy occasion arose and I was interested, I took advantage of it. I assume Marie did too, at least after the first eighteen months. That did not concern me. I did not consider monogamy to be a moral issue unless the couple had agreed to be faithful. I did, however, want prominence. I congratulated myself not only on being broad-minded but also on being wise. It was the only way to make the relationship last.

By the time I met her, Marie had had a variety of sexual experiences including not only a wide range of lovers, but also some experience with women. She did not think of herself as bisexual. She merely thought it logical to express herself erotically in her close friendships with women, usually other undergraduates who were involved with women's issues. Her lesbian experiences were related to her ideas of friendship; her heterosexual experiences were romantic. However, it was through her feelings about women that she defined her dissatisfaction with her relations with men. When our relationship began to founder, it did so more on the basis of character than on the basis of gender: mostly her character and my gender. She discovered the literature and politics of feminism and began seriously to question her assumptions about sexual roles and love. Part of that questioning concerned her need for me, which she began to outgrow. As Marie changed, my ambivalence rose. The more I missed her waning idealization of me, the more I used casual sexual encounters to avoid confronting that loss. I did not want to ask what should happen next. I would let it "work itself out." I do not know whether I could have sustained the affair had I tried, but I know I did not try seriously enough.

When Marie finally left me, she left for someone else. It was a brief stormy affair, but she had also left her need of paternalism behind. When the new affair ended, she did not want to return to me; she wanted to be friends. We are still friends. Marie is grateful that I have forgotten my bitterness. She behaved, she confesses, badly with me, worse than she had with other men. But she had also felt more imprisoned by my hopes than she had ever felt before. I am grateful because I discovered more about myself than ever before, with more clarity and without complacency. By the time Marie and I separated, I had gathered my personal data and could verify what I had learned. I could function sexually with either gender if I was in the right frame of mind, and being high was often the best frame, but the conclusions were different from what I expected. Other women were less satisfying because Marie had been so satisfying; other men were now more satisfying because I was no longer the same man I had been.

Six months after Marie and I separated, I came out at work. I also threw myself into a budding new organization, the Gay Academic Union, where I met the man with whom I was to have the most important gay relationship of my life. That relationship lasted three years. I cannot say that it was less painful or more joyous than my time with Marie. The joys were different, the pains weighed roughly the same, the problems were almost completely uncomplementary, and the failures were equally excruciating. But the *consequences* were very different.

One of the benefits of passing as straight was the ease with which I could sidestep the sexual question with my family. In the second year of my relationship with Marie, I told them I was living with a woman. My sister and mother were surprised and relieved. It had been a number of years since either had presumed to ask me anything about my personal life. Until my early thirties, my sister especially had urged me to marry and start a family, then to settle down if I were not the marrying kind, then to at least date some of the women she thought I might get along with. My mother never asked or urged anything. Once I made it clear that my private life was to remain vague, suggesting that the less they knew the happier everyone would be, the matter rested. Now I was living with a young woman and willing to introduce her to them.

The meeting went quite smoothly and everyone was quite unhappy. My mother, a shy little woman, was frightened of this Junoesque gentile (Marie stood over six feet tall in high heels). My sister soon discovered that her daughter, who was three years younger than Marie, had more in common with my lover than she did. My brother-in-law flirted with Marie and treated her as if she were mindless. Marie was anxious: all those Jews, all those in-laws. Obviously I had not done it right. I was living with a woman who was too young, not Jewish, and, in my mother's eyes, not moral. But they were helpless to criticize. That satisfied me perfectly, and benevolently, I comforted everyone in his or her distress.

The news spread quickly through the family at large. I attended the next wedding or bar mitzvah, functions I had not gone to in years, with Marie. Initially, the family was more aloof than it had been before. Marrying a gentile was still a serious business among them. But the men, the usual assortment of philanderers, malcontents, and husbands unlucky in their choices, were envious. As the evening went on and they got drunker, they became lewder. I was again welcome in the locker room. Some congratulated me on waiting, on having had an exciting bachelor's life until it was nearly too late to settle down, and then, since it *had* to be done (what other choice was there?), on having done it with a woman whom it would take me yet many more years to tire of. By the time I got bored with Marie, I would be too old for it to matter much. Besides, one or two of them assured me, a properly trained *shiksa* would not be nearly as rapacious as the princesses they had married.

Such was Normality, the kingdom of heaven I had been exiled from. While I was pleased that their attempts at flattery did not diminish my contempt for bourgeois marriage, I did not challenge them on a single sexist, ethnic, or personal presumption. I accepted their vulgarity in the friendly spirit in which it was offered, feeling a tenuous bond with them. Our commonality was not that I was in a relationship with a woman, since I regarded most of their marriages as nightmares, but their envy of me, of having a young woman who loved me and would live with me without marriage. That envy went a long way. It soothed old sore spots, some of which I'd almost forgotten, as nothing else could. It was a triumph. If I chose to, I could have a better, happier, and probably more sexual marriage than any of my straight relatives; if I chose not to, they would never know why. I could not lose.

It was a singular feeling. I had always felt something of a loser with these men and women of my blood; to avoid that feeling I had avoided them, given them up before they might reject me, patronize or pity me. It was better to be alone, and I had been. Now I could choose. I was no longer walking on eggs; the ground was firm. I knew where I stood. I was different from them and always would be. I had experienced the world as a homosexual; if I stayed in the closet for the rest of my life, I would never see issues of sexuality as they did, and for that I was profoundly grateful. Now I understood the nature of my choices.

When Marie and I split up, I considered my next move. I was forty: a youngish straight man or an aging gay one; slim but bald and unathletic—irrelevant to women, handicaps among gay men. I could still make out in a gay bar, I was still negotiable, but the good gay years were over. It was too late for me to have hair down to my shoulders, develop an arresting body, dance all night on speed, or trick every day. But if I chose to be straight, if I continued to pass, I was a great catch. At forty, by straight standards, I was a very attractive and sympathetic man.

During my years with Marie, I discovered that I enjoyed the idea of women considering me available. Ironically, this gave me assurance with gay men that was also an asset. If I could take them or leave them, I was much less tense about either. And I had another choice: I could disregard gender altogether and be bisexual, though I didn't really believe there was such an animal. Suddenly there were lots of options. All I had to figure out was what I wanted.

And I wanted a romantic, ongoing relationship with a man.

5

My experience was not unique. One-fifth of the men interviewed by Alan P. Bell and Martin S. Weinberg in *Homosexualities: A Study of Diversity Among Men and Women* indicated that they had had some sustained heterosexual experience. That sampling was made in San Francisco. Would it be wild to guess that, in the rest of America, there are as many married men who are closeted homosexuals as there are openly gay unmarried men? Perhaps it is atypical for an experienced homosexual to experiment with the idea of living as a heterosexual, but the recent Masters and Johnson study, *Homosexuality in Perspective*, reveals that some gay men and women are dissatisfied enough to want to try being straight, even though this may be the worst time in history to invest in marriage as a viable institution offering a reasonable chance of fulfillment. But for gay men and women who want to try, this is the only time they have. For the few who are willing to risk straight marriage, there are increasing numbers of closeted gay men and women who are divorcing; it more than balances out. One group feels that their unhappiness is caused by their homosexuality; the other feels that passing as heterosexual is no longer tolerable. The issue is not changing one's sexual orientation, but *reasonable choice*.

How reasonable a choice is a closeted marriage? In a recent issue of *The New York Review of Books* (May 3, 1979), Andrew Hacker examined three new studies of marriage and divorce: *Husbands and Wives: A Nationwide Survey of Marriage* by Anthony Pietropinto and Jacqueline Simenauer, *The Extra-Sex Factor: Why Over Half of America's Married Men Play Around* by Lewis Yablonsky, and *Current Population Reports: Series P-20* by the Bureau of the Census. These studies confirm what we all suspected: something drastic is happening to conventional marriage. According to which set of statistics you use, either 40 or 50 percent of the people now marrying will divorce. In Utah, fewer than 20 percent divorce; in California, over 80 percent do. Infidelity is more common than fidelity; among those who stay married or remarry, the difficulties and problems remain acute.

One might argue that since heterosexuals do not seem to manage marriage well but enjoy some of its benefits, homosexuals might do just as well; that at a time when no one is sure *what* constitutes a good marriage, homosexuals may have a better chance of succeeding in a closeted marriage than ever before. In addition, unmarried women exceed unmarried men in number; a husband's homosexuality might not be regarded as the same kind of handicap it has been in the past.

I do not think so. Let me give another example. Fred has been out less than six years. He is forty-eight years old; his marriage of twenty-seven years is over and he is trying to get his bearings in gay life. He has five children, three daughters and two sons, ranging in age from twenty-five to ten. His income is moderate (he is a high school teacher); with all his financial responsibilities he will not be able to enjoy the selfish pleasures of New York City or even to indulge without thought in the ones many gay men take for granted: entertainment, dining out, clothes, and travel. Fred's wife has had to find a job, but it is low-paying and clerical; she would prefer to return to college and train herself in some occupation besides motherhood. Of course, Fred left her the house, since three of his children still live there, the car, and most of their meager assets.

Fred has no problem about custody or visiting arrangements. His marriage broke up because his wife discovered she is a lesbian and no longer feels she can live with a man she does not love or live without the woman she does. Both women are mothers and plan to combine their households as soon as their divorces are final.

Although Fred would have preferred to remain married, he is optimistic about his future. I hope he is lucky, for he has frail grounds for optimism. He looks every minute of his age and, while he is homosexual, he has never been gay; he knows nothing of gay life style except bars and baths, which had been humiliating experiences for him. I told him of a number of organizations, alternatives that might provide him with a chance to meet men more humanely. But he is shy about going alone; each new move is burdened with anxiety. Most difficult of all, Fred's homosexual experience has been very limited though he is eager to expand his range. He wants to enter a long-term monogamous gay relationship, but he will have to find someone patient and undemanding, someone who is not hung up on looks and/or youth and who is willing to understand the importance of Fred's children in his life.

Fred's prospects are poor if not dreadful. His wife refuses to continue a marriage which fails to answer for her, though it might be very supportive for him. At the moment when he is most fully acknowledging his homosexuality, he is least willing to entertain the idea of another marriage. He is enjoying his privacy if not his loneliness. When he thought of himself as straight he was content with marriage; even while he was furtively experimenting, his relations with his wife did not alter as far as he could see. The changes happened to her, not to him. Fred understands that he is now paying the price for wanting to lead a "normal" life. He loves his children. Dealing with their mother's lesbianism is not easy for them; as a result, Fred does not feel he can be open about his homosexuality. He enjoys their sympathy but feels guilty that it is based on false premises. He says he would choose to lead the life he has led if offered the chance to do it all over again.

Is Fred worse off than other gay men his age? In a sense he is much more vulnerable; he has optimism without youth, eagerness without experience. Are there men who will support him in this difficult time? Yes. Are there men who will fill his romantic aspirations and share his longing to recreate a stable domestic life? I doubt it. Despite my envy that he has five children, I certainly do not envy Fred.

Fred is not an extraordinary man. He is not militant; he is not gay and proud. He is merely a man who wants to find someone to love and live with. Activism is foreign to him; it might serve to give him some exciting engagements, might even provide him with an opportunity to meet a lover. But it has taken him decades to discover that he is homosexual. He is not ready to leap into the limelight. Until his opportunities are clearer, he is puzzled about what he should have pride in. Everything he used to define himself by is now a lie.

He says he is ready to come out. He has told his closest friends, all straight, and they have been sympathetic. He isn't afraid as much as he is uncomfortable with his ignorance about what to expect. Gay life offers no clarity about what substitutions to make. Luckily, his prospects are uncertain: poor, if he insists on simply changing the gender of his lover and trying to lead his old life; better, if he changes as he discovers the limitations of his options. For a new life, there must be new values. He passed successfully; now he runs the risk that he may fail utterly.

CHAPTER FOUR

Friendship:
Gay Men and Straight Women

1

One of the least examined aspects of gay life is the long tradition of friendship between homosexual men and heterosexual women. The emerging political alliance of gay men and feminists is the outgrowth of this undeclared social adaptation. In the past gay men have married straight women, but usually those men present themselves as heterosexual. Besides, marriage is rarely friendship. The tradition I refer to is platonic friendship between men and women where sexual issues remain ambiguous and complicated.

Friendship between people of the same sex is quite different in character. The clichés about male bonding and sisterhood among women are no doubt grounded on truths, though I do not think they have been deeply explored. Close friendships among straight men are modeled on fraternal relationships; when that locker-room intimacy that is more than or different from brotherly feelings arises, the phenomenon suddenly becomes questionable. Some people, especially homosexuals, see the physical familiarity of this camaraderie as evidence of a suppressed eroticism. Others don't know what to make of it. Whatever it is, it isn't simple: people who relate to each other on the basis of gender operate partly out of their ideas of what constitutes masculinity and femininity.

Until recently, associations among women evoked suspicion. Many women distrusted each other and had, in fact, been brought up to do so.

Single women were supposed to be in competition for men, or, if they were married, envious of the status of each other's husbands or the achievements of the children. We now know, mainly as the result of the ongoing work in women's history, that while there certainly has been a legend of bitchiness between women, there were other kinds of relationships, supportive and intense, that were seldom documented in literature or popular culture. The evidence of a strong tradition of close friendship among women points to the need to reevaluate stereotypes. What is significant is that until feminists began to explore the documentation of women's culture for a revised history, the idea of female bonding was ignored or examined entirely in terms of the family. Doubtless, this has been the result of the lack of interest in the subject by those who have written social history, namely men. But evidence of such bonding is apparently abundant and has always been available, although women have been secretive about this part of their world. While they have shown no reluctance to testify as mothers, wives, daughters, and lovers, they have been relatively silent as friends.

Friendship between heterosexual men and women has been seen as rare, nearly impossible. Those involved are either inhibited lovers or, more suspect, psychological siblings, whose actual lovers distrust or resent this undefined intimacy. Men are often uncomfortable about publicizing such intimacy; it has always been thought "unmanly." Both men and women face the frequent assumption that the relationship is part sham, that they either are lovers or wish to be. I am not doubting the existence of these friendships nor their genuineness; I only think that they are rare and find scarce social accommodation.

Homosexual men pose a special case. I will offer a gross generalization I subscribe to: gay men can be divided into two camps, those who would not mind if they never saw another woman, and those for whom women are absolutely necessary. Of the former, there are plenty: gay male ghettos, even with their small minority of lesbians, exist in New York, Los Angeles, and San Francisco. On Castro and Christopher Streets, the population looks cloned. Some gay men, a minority, structure their lives so that they never have to relate to women, which means confining themselves almost entirely to such ghettos. It is an impoverishing choice: their psychological space is as constricted as their geography. However, it is a choice, although one I'm not here concerned with except to add that this aversion is an extreme variant of heterosexual woman hating. Straight misogynists are stuck with their sexual orientation; they may pretend women are unimportant or mere objects, but a vital part of their lives is spent with women, their sexual and family lives, where the consequences of misogyny are acted out. Gay men who dislike or fear women simply avoid them. They live as nearly as possible in a world where women do not exist, except perhaps as men in drag.

For other gay men it is different. Deep friendships with straight men are unusual. Some retain friendships from when they were heterosexual; some sustain relationships with men who marry, enduring the same limitations of a single person involved with a couple. There are exceptions, but as straight men find themselves under fire in their relationships with women, they stay even more distant from gays, who they feel are exempt from these anxieties. As they are forced to question their own roles, the priority for examining their feelings about homosexuals falls even lower than in the past.

The glaring omission in this categorization has been the friendships between gay men themselves. For some, these are the most lasting relationships of their lives. The commonalities of homosexual life, the stresses of oppression, the internalized fears, and the disappointments of gay life itself are extraordinary mutual grounds on which to build a relationship. Nor are these friendships fragile, although they are often unexamined, vulnerable, subject to envy and hostility. When a gay man finds a new lover, the importance of romance is taken for granted, exactly as in heterosexual ritual. Like straight women, gay men are thought to be bitchy with each other, envious of the erotic success of others, and hostile when shut out by a new romance. Like women, gay men are accused of being in competition for other men. Some of this is quite true.

In the last ten years, there has been a lot of talk about breaking the old molds, particularly among younger men who are much less adept at camping, a mode of behavior that characterized gay relations for generations. Ideas like "fuck buddies" are certainly novel, the liberated result of wanting to experiment sexually with someone who is erotically if not romantically interesting. But most homosexuals still draw rigid lines between men with whom they sleep, the temporary relations, and friends with whom they do not, fearing that such intimacy will alter or damage the friendship. Some gay men seek support groups in an effort to avoid the problems and demands of paired relations.

My premise is that the richest, least infantile, and most moral relationships gay men form are with women. Eroticism is converted into something else, and those emotions adjunct to sexual attraction share in the metamorphosis. These men and women do not compete for the same sexual objects though both are attracted to men; there is little source of envy since their lives are often invested in exclusive institutions, work and marriage, yet both are oppressed in those places. I would like to explore this idea by comparing two important friendships in my own life, one with a gay man and one with a straight woman.

2

I have known Wally for thirty years, since high school, but we have been close only since our early twenties. For over two decades, we have stood mutual witness to failed affairs and the humiliations and tensions of work. I have watched the silent rage of a gentle and considerate man at the barbarousness of others, which he never fully understands. I have sympathized with his arduous voyage through psychoanalysis, and he has done similar duty for me.

Any time one of us needs help, the other never denies the request; we also know the limitations of what kind of help to ask for. He is liberal with his compassion, his time, and his money. His loyalty to me is preceded only by his concern for his lover and his obligation to his family; if these should end, it is assumed I would take up the slack. We joke comfortably about our old age together, beyond affairs that fail and families that no longer matter or exist. Our past together will alleviate the future. This option against loneliness is a mitigation of other problems and makes the present time between us unstressful and casual. If we cannot see each other today, or this week, or for a few months, that is temporary; we believe we have found a lifelong continuity.

We often talk of the disappointments that we never seem to accept with equanimity. At our ages, work seems to have reached its plateau; our ambitions are finally circumscribed and fairly realistic: we both suspect we know how far we will go and how much to expect back. We are not colleagues. I am more interested in his work in films than he is in mine as a writer. I enjoy excursions into his more glamorous world, but a little goes a long way. He reads what I write and is generally admiring, but the feedback is terse. He cares more about the reception of my work and how it gratifies me than about its content. I have no quarrel with this; it is close to my own attitudes about his career.

Lovers are lovers; one waits and watches. Our values are identical concerning tact. In the midst of romantic difficulties, neither takes sides; loyalty means to listen carefully, not to judge blindly. When a relationship is irrevocably over, there is some room for criticism if it is not careless. These agreements were hard won after a number of clumsy confrontations when we were younger. We have come to respect each other's limitations; they no longer rile. Extraordinary familiarity risks some contempt, but whatever there is left of that is no longer important between us.

He is not my brother. He has a brother and I a sister; we know positively that we have no such feelings for each other. We are not surrogates for the families we are now distant from. I am comfortable with his family when I see them; he does not see mine, mostly because I do not.

We agree about the common decencies and share a certain rigorousness about sentimentality, self-pity, and narcissism, three detestable distortions that have played havoc in our lives. With our lovers, we ruefully recognize a kindred masochistic strain of delusive optimism that things may work out when common sense tells us they won't. We are both judgmental though he is far more puritanical about sexual matters than I. He prefers fidelity though he does not always practice it; he advocates a conventional idea of monogamy. He has striven to replicate in his homosexual life what he might have had in a heterosexual one. When he realized that he would never marry, he grieved over the children he would not have.

The wholesome comfort of our friendship rests on tact. There are issues we do not discuss much, like the quality of our lives with our lovers. Of course, we keep in delicate touch; we have subtle signals that indicate some probing would be welcome rather than wearisome. We have tacitly agreed that the real comforting should be reserved for the real heartaches, and we are pleased as we increasingly refrain from the low-keyed complaining that turns dreary so quickly. We are least interested in confirming for each other that life is a nasty business. When we spend time together, we try to forget the angers of the day; if such amiabilty is impossible, we cut the evening short. We cultivate decorum with each other; the thank yous may sometimes be perfunctory, but they're not forgotten. We try not to act as if we can take much for granted. Though we dislike raising the question of "our relationship," when things are awry between us, they must be aired. Those times are infrequent and always very tense.

The friendship is far from simple, yet simplicity is what we desire. The sad lapses, the flare-ups of irritation, or the easy occasions to use our intimacy punitively or to test each other happen unpredictably. We have no insurance that times will not come when we will behave badly, but we trust we can mend our bridges. As much as we trust anything, we trust each other.

I met Sonia twenty-five years ago, but our friendship ended when she died in 1968. Since then, our relationship has become one of my psychological legends. I am still unsure whether grief and time have made it seem so nearly perfect or whether it really was. When we met, we were both in graduate school, but at different universities. She was one of those few people who mastered English in her late teens and was now so proficient she could compete with native speakers in literary study. She was two years older than I, old enough to have been very aware of what was happening when the Germans invaded her native Poland in 1939. She lived in a *shtetl,* a small town, and thus avoided most of the initial chaos. By 1941, she and her family were ghettoized in a town near Lodz. Her family had been somewhat assimilated; she had attended secular schools and was fluent in both Yiddish and the national language and was beginning to study Russian well. At the time of the invasion, her most upsetting experience was the interruption of school, which she loved. That was soon superseded by the ominous anxiety of the adults in the ghetto, and that was overshadowed by the onset of hunger and sickness. Until 1943, her ghetto survived, despite quotas of Jews being shipped out regularly, selected by category: young men, professionals, young women, and so on.

One day, her mother heard a rumor about an imminent deportation of children. As the eldest, almost twelve, Sonia was packed off to survive in the surrounding forest, a gamble her mother could not have taken with her younger children. Sonia hid in the woods for two days, listening in terror to the distant fire of machine guns. It was not a children's round-up; the Germans were murdering the entire ghetto.

She survived in the woods for eighteen months by attaching herself as a kind of mascot to a small group of Jewish partisans. When the Russians liberated Poland, she was sent to an orphanage in the Soviet Ukraine. She was content there; she was kept clean and fed, and she could study again. In one of those flukes of the times, one morning her sole surviving relatives, a cousin and her husband, arrived at the school and simply walked away with her.

The war was over. Eastern Europe was rubble. They joined the flotsam and jetsam of thousands of refugees, walking from Russia to Germany, sneaking across borders, stealing their food, bartering what they could. They arrived in Hamburg and from there contacted their American relatives, who sponsored their emigration. Sonia was now fifteen; the onset of puberty also invited sexual molestation; her cousin's husband seduced her.

When she arrived in America, there was little she had not seen except the death camps themselves. She was sent to an uncle she had never met before. He was kinder than his wife and daughters, who were impatient with the problems of a young refugee. When she was a senior in high school, her uncle died. Rather than leave New York to live with her remaining relatives, she applied to Jewish charity, which placed her in a special residence near Brooklyn College designed to harbor young refugee women who could not live with the families that had brought them over.

When I met Sonia, her life struck me as tragic and she herself as heroic. She was living with two women near Columbia and having an affair with a young sociology professor. He was serious, but she had had many lovers already, and her priority was scholarly work. At twenty-three, she was more worldly than anyone I'd ever met, entirely free of moralistic attitudes about sexuality. Compared to genocide, she thought the question of sexual propriety less than trivial. While her roommates were also liberated young intellectuals and radicals, their sexual lives were much more tempestuous, fraught with rebelliousness or guilt or doubt. Sonia had different expectations.

She had been greatly influenced by novels: she sought from her lovers those experiences that would make her feel romantic. She was not interested in marriage, in domestic stability, or in a family of her own. Foremost, she wanted to spend her life studying and teaching. Of course, she also wanted to be in love, either with this lover or with the next. Her affairs, like the one with the sociologist, terminated when the men became demanding, wanting some long-term commitment, at which point Sonia declined firmly and ended the affair, often in a manner her friends thought ruthless.

She claimed she understood herself. Some years in therapy had helped her manage her life. She said she was resigned; her losses were without compensation. Work and romance were the only proper distractions; friendship was the only abiding relationship. While Sonia had much sexual experience, she was basically monogamous and faithful to the man of the moment. I preferred to keep my sexual history cloudy. I did not know what others thought, but I assumed they must suspect "the worst." In 1956, the subject of homosexuality was still taboo in mixed company of any sort.

When Sonia broke with her lover, she went through a chronic period of depression and physical illness. She could not eat, or when she did, she could not hold her food. I would cook for her, lend her books, take her to movies, and spend time in endless talk mostly about literature. I soon found that my sympathy for her was more intense than any I'd felt for the men I'd been in love with. I was not conscious of much sexual interest. Her experience, sophistication, and neediness were greater obstacles than I could overcome.

But the sexual tension between us grew, silent and palpable; when I hinted more boldly that I was queer, she was unimpressed. She remained a European living now in a country whose vulgarity amazed her and whose culture she was indifferent to. Having endured the worst of civilization, she dedicated herself to what she believed to be the best of it, its literature. She was entirely adult in the sense that there was simply no social vestige of the child left in her. Her past and her character combined to give her personality a magnetism and strength I marveled at. She saw the familial as the last source of pain; she looked to friendship for all she hoped would be nurturing. Yet she understood as little about male homosexuality as she did about Oriental religion. She saw it as a flaw of character, an eccentricity like Hamlet's indecisiveness. It did not occur to her that my sexuality might be exclusive; she understood *that* to be the preference of men who lived without women entirely.

I was certainly not that. Despite our pessimism about romantic love and our idealization of friendship, we ignored the risks and tried to become lovers. The failure was excruciating. We were both hurt and angry and humiliated, but she insisted we salvage what we could. The tears and recriminations were bitter but brief. She said she would never again raise the issue; it was finished. We had been foolish, she argued, to hope for everything. We would make our sexual lives irrelevant to each other. After all, were we not in the same boat? We were damaged and demanding; our romantic chances were poor. We envisaged a parade of lovers, small failures, little deaths of the heart. But such a prospect had its gratifications: it confirmed that ordinary happiness, a normal life, was not for us, but we could choose a stylish dignity for our unhappiness.

With the ordeal of sexuality over, we found a new exhilarating frankness. There were unquestioned demarcations; I did not go into details with her about my erotic life any more than I would with another woman, and she never spoke of such issues. Over the years, we found a rare consolation with each other that I have never duplicated. We regarded each other as entirely safe; together, we expected to be momentarily happy, beyond demands we could not meet, beyond even our own wretchedness (when we were really sullen, we did not meet). Somewhere we decided that this room in the house of our lives would be the brightest. Our friendship was reserved for the best of ourselves; the rest was good enough for the world. And the best was, of course, our intelligence and our compassionate irony.

Fortune was a brute: the war had ruined her chances for normality; homosexuality had ruined mine. The friendship validated my disappointment; from her, I borrowed a dignity for my unhappiness that seemed to free it from self-pity, and more, give it a meaning. Instead of a victim, I was, at best, like her, a survivor.

We were younger than we thought. We wanted of our lives the beautiful self-abnegation that seemed so fine in the literature that we loved. Our romance was talk; in the endless talk were imbued all the feelings we could not enact; all the intimate aura lovers exude we simulated in talking. It was our surrogate for passion, and finally its pleasures made us love each other more than we could our lovers.

One solace from seriousness was laughter; we were both quite funny. When she would fall into a strange nostalgia for the fields of the Ukraine upon seeing the daffodils in Central Park, or when I would melodramatize my wastrel life, we relied on the other's sense of the absurd to chasten our sentimentality. To yearn after the past, for it to have been different, to remember our regrets and mistakes was a stupidity that would cripple us, victimize us with self-pity. As survivors, we were determined to be loyal to the present and resigned to the future. Whatever we needed to flee our pains we accepted uncritically, as we accepted the follies of our pleasures.

In our vicariousness, we idealized values we learned from books. Our elitism we cultivated from literature; our education was in fine distinctions. We felt a smug awe for our own self-creation. Neither Semeshlanu, her Polish village, nor Flatbush was an impediment in our study of refinement. We were haughty about "things" and often about other people, but surgically precise about moral excellence.

She had difficulties with the world she claimed were insurmountable; she could not work without duress. Oh, she could earn a marginal living teaching part time, but writing her doctorate was unremittingly painful. The inadequacies of her teachers she could not forgive. In contrast, I was competent and cynical. Work was difficult for me because it was often meaningless and usually boring, but I could do it. I did not mind being shallow if I could be fast. Academic work seemed fraudulent; if there was no one I could respect enough to try to please, I pleased myself by getting rid of the work as quickly as possible. It is unclear what would have happened to our alliance had nothing changed. The pains in her life were furies; mine were phantoms. As often as I was bored, she was tormented. And I had diversion; despite my contempt for my promiscuity, my remorse did not begin until the adventures were over.

"He's someone who will never hurt me," she said, doubly astonishing me when she confessed that she was going to marry her current lover. I had no idea this man was special, nor could I credit that she believed such a promise. Her marriage created many petty problems for me, and for her, ultimately fatal ones.

She consulted one of the leading psychoanalysts in the country, who told her plainly that only a full-time lengthy psychoanalysis would help her. The more stable experience became for her, the more she would seek ways to destroy that stability. Every claim to conventional life would send out waves of anxiety and guilt. I accepted the diagnosis as accurate, but I resented the struggle. Why did she have to have that life? She claimed she was tired; the marginality of poverty was growing narrower. She needed someone who would take care of her, who would do it lovingly. The premise of our friendship seemed challenged. She was going to defy the destiny of her neurosis and her past. If she could try, then certainly I could. But if I were to try to be heterosexual, shouldn't that attempt be with a woman I was already more bound to than anyone else? I felt caught: for me normality would mean giving up both my homosexuality and my relationship with her.

I had invested so much. Compared to the complicated hostilities of my life among gay men or even the ordinary angers of everyday life, this relationship seemed innocent and dulcet. I did not care if I were naive; that seemed unimportant when I could verify my own niceness with her. Reflected in her affection, I felt decent, adult, stoic, and sane. I did not feel, as I often did elsewhere, gypped. Such friendship was too valuable to risk. I accepted the marriage and her husband, whom I could not really like, and I rejected therapy merely for the sake of changing my sexual orientation. If she needed the trappings of normality to survive, how could I resent it? It struck me as both crazy and heroic that she should try by sheer determination to salvage her life through marriage and motherhood. I felt that like myself, she really did not have such resources, but she had an amazing willfulness which perhaps would be enough.

It wasn't. Maternity was fatal for her though she did not die in childbirth. In fact, she adopted a child, a luminous little boy, and for two years it seemed that she might have turned the tide of her own self-destructiveness. She became a superb housewife; she returned to European and Yiddish ways. The texture of her home was both lovely and foreign. She had disliked cooking and had always found American food inane. Now she discovered she was a gifted cook. She recreated childhood dishes by remembering how they tasted. She returned to her past, to her sunny village and the kitchen lessons of her mother.

On Friday nights, I often had dinner with her and her family. She lit Sabbath candles though she did not believe in God; the evenings gleamed with tradition. I was nourished in her home, and if I was saddened by my own exclusion from such a life, I accused myself of envy. Instead of feeling as I had with her before, sensitive and boyish, I now felt duplicitous, hiding wolfish resentments I was ashamed to speak of.

Imperceptibly, I began to guard myself. I became more discreet about my private life. Where in that setting could I even mention the experiences of my nights? In this ugly new decorum which she accepted because she felt guilty over abandoning me to my unnaturalness and which I sustained defensively and no doubt punitively, I did not understand what was happening in the last months of her life.

She was losing weight; I knew her insomnia was a plague alleviated only by barbiturates. She said she was at the edge of some sort of breakthrough in her therapy. She now knew she should no longer be her husband's burden. He was not a saint: there was a limit to what he could do for her. He was tenaciously ambitious about his work; the illusions and romanticism that had led him to believe he could bear the burdens of both their lives were over. It was no longer possible for him to live his life as a character in someone else's tragedy.

Instead, he became a bystander; I became a witness. The morning of her suicide, he was immersed in his work two rooms away while she silently overdosed. His reaction, after the initial shock and grief, was to deny the meaning of her death. He saw a possibility that it was not suicide, but what is legally called misadventure; perhaps she had taken too many pills in confusion rather than deliberation. To my horror, this idea comforted him. An accidental death was bearable. If her death, like her life, was only misadventure, he was exonerated from the suspicion of collusion or even from suspecting his own relief that the marriage was over. He could demand pity untempered by guilt.

For me, there was plenty of pity and guilt. I had broken my most solemn promise: I had let the bonds grow slack between us.

3

I had glamorized deprivation, and I found the consequences criminal. Since then, I have been careful in my own recognizance. Now when I feel the ties of friendship with women are fostered by a disaffection with life, I do not convert that into another kind of affection.

When I tried to dramatize my guilt, to make stronger claims than I was entitled to, for my importance in Sonia's death and, therefore, in her

life, Frances, a mutual friend, said, "No one rescues anyone else. There are
no rescue operations. They are all highly suspect." It is still hard to give up
the fantasy that rescue is at hand if we want it. Frances advocates comfort,
but she does not confuse it with rescue. Comfort demands a momentary
selflessness and ends when one stops listening. Rescue implies future care;
one is accountable for what one has presumed to do. To intrude into
someone else's life, even if the motives are not confused with egotism and
expectations of gratitude, is to act where moral consequences are unpredictable.

It seems now that those painful questions about my importance in
Sonia's life, my rank in her affections, were not an isolated egotism or
jealousy. They were part of a pattern of insecurities; about myself as male,
of my powers of assertion in the world, of my priority. Where I stood in
her life was a question that never arose until Sonia created a family, presenting herself as a person with a right to normal experience, which I
perceived not just as alienating but as disloyal. Had I not been ashamed of
such smallness, I might not be living with the remorse of my evasions.

Is such a conclusion at odds with the thesis that gay men and straight
women share the richest, most adult, and most moral of friendships? Perhaps the last of these qualities is the least disputable. From the beginning, it
was the person of the woman that I was to find so important. Whatever
symbolic or idealized meaning I gave her in my life were tangential to my
recognition of her integrity. Only when I felt threatened by her need for
conventionality did I begin to objectify her and our friendship. Because of
our confusions, our youth, and our pain, we could not free ourselves from
postured notions of what men and women should be for each other. Perhaps such powerlessness is the worst consequence of oppression. What
failed in the relationship was our ability to live up to a morality we valued
more than anything else in each other. In that sense, it was also an entirely
adult relationship. Despite the fantasies, it was essentially in the arena of
the adult life and adult awareness that we struggled. "Adult" is a term
suggesting approbation; "infantile" or "childish" is somehow contemptible
or pathetic. To fail to be adult is cowardly if it is a *choice,* though I think it
rarely is (then we call it "playful"); if one is childish because he cannot
help it, then it is a form of pathology, psychological or social or both.
When I claim the relationship was adult, I mean that the needs of the child

within were less demanding than they are in sexually intimate relations, where often they are not questioned seriously or at least are patiently endured. And because it was moral and adult, it offered the richest possibilities for self-illumination and self-approbation. I came to know myself more clearly here than I ever had before; though I did not like, indeed ultimately found most painful, some of what I learned, the gift of friendship was to refrain as much as possible from the kind of judgment of self that is devoted to deprecation and self-dislike and finally converted into self-pity.

It seemed to me that these values were markedly different from those that governed experiences connected to sexual availability. The question of whether men were sexually available, possible prospects, arose, was confronted, and was resolved almost before I needed to think about it. The groin determined everything. Desire is irrational and in the true sense indiscriminate: it overrides all the other discriminations that seriously concern people.

With Sonia and other women, the idea of sexual use did not arise until they were already important beings to me, an experience that I find women accept as customary, but men rarely do. Recently, a close woman friend, a lesbian with whom I enjoy a great deal of frank exchange about sexual matters, asked me whether I thought that gay men have different attitudes about erotic arousal from those of straight men. She really wanted to know how gay men could manage their legendary promiscuity, which puzzled her more than it made her envious. Did I think that if straight men had no strictures placed on their pursuit of women, they would be equally libertine? Would they be as casual about intimacy? First, I properly said I really did not know what straight men would be, but I hardly finished with the propriety when I said that, yes, yes *of course* they would. Male sexuality is barely disturbed by orientation; all boys grow up with the same understanding of what society expects men to be.

Recently, I read of a response to the prodigality of gay promiscuity that I thought provoking. In *The Spada Report,* one man said he considered it a "compensation for the injustices society has wished on us." This struck me as more than just defiant. It implies that sexual obsession is not devoted exclusively to sensual pleasure but is much involved with an individual's sense of powerlessness. Don Juan and Casanova are heterosexual myths about men whom women find irresistible, for whom women could be

slavish because those men had mastered the secrets of giving others supreme sensual pleasure, yet who are insatiable themselves. The great lover
is the great pleaser; his power over others is earned by the pleasure he gives
them. But the pleasure they return is primarily his sense of power, and
such a need is never satisfied. That is why Freudians suspect that sexual
obsession is theatrical, an acting out of something else and an action that is
illusory and impermanent, in constant need of repetition. But that still does
not take sufficient account of the special nature of the drama.

Some homosexuals do behave exactly as if they were heterosexual
except that the object of their choice is male, just an irrational, primitive
preference: "That's what I like." This bespeaks a self-centeredness so
monumental that no quality of the sexual object, the thing that allows
erection, is relevant except as it promotes desire. Or it is woefully superficial. If it were merely a question of taste, there would hardly be a fuss.

Most gay men are very conscious of their homosexuality when they
deal with others. It arises with other gay men, with straight men, and
certainly with women. Perhaps it is least complicated or interesting with
lesbians. Perhaps also that is why gay men and gay women have been
unable to say exactly what they have in common and why they have had so
much difficulty working together.

Before Sonia's marriage, when I felt that the burdens of my past were
hardly worse than hers and those of the present were equal if different
handicaps, there was little embargoed between us. But a husband is not a
lover; he is head of the household, breadwinner, father—in short, the social
man. Husband I have never been and the husband I loved most and knew
least was my mother's. These attitudes about masculinity are evidently
patriarchal if not Oedipal, but I have subscribed to them, and I have discovered that understanding those attitudes always concerns women, especially the mother and the motherly.

The specter of heterosexual men has always obtruded in my other
friendships with women. If we are alone together in public, we somehow
become a couple rather than two people. Other people respond to what we
appear to be, which is understandable coming from waiters and other
strangers. But among acquaintances, usually the woman's, there is a faint
unease. No matter how stolidly I present evidence to the contrary, some
erotic possibility lingers unresolved. As it arises, provoked by a constant

barrage of suggestion from the example of other couples, from films, from
every intrusion of the culture, it is the gay man who declines the choice.
And rather than contend with the hurtfulness of individual rejection, it is
sometimes easier to let it all be subsumed as some sad heterosexual default.
I am homosexual because I could not or would not be heterosexual. Some
women are sympathetic to that default; given their experience with men,
they can easily understand the fear and anger toward institutionalized
heterosexuality.

These days, the problems of gay men and straight women are alarm-
ingly alike. If desire is apotheosized in gay culture, the same idolatry is now
widely proselytized in society at large. When a straight man leaves a stable
relationship because it is sexually stale, and if he leaves for a younger
woman and the age difference is wide, he is regarded as a fool. People
assume he is buying youth or beauty with experience and status, but that
eventually he will pay more; depending on what he has left and for whom,
he is seen as shallow or sick, selfish or silly.

But when the gay man breaks up a long relationship for a younger
man, explaining that the "marriage" was a sham because the couple no
longer desired each other—or worse, no longer slept with each other—he is
seen as making a sad but sensible move. Why not try again for that ungovernable excitement? Who knows how long one will be able to sustain
it, find it possible to believe in, or fearfully, to feel it? The majority of gay
men assume that all sexual relations have a natural duration, but the prison
of legalities and obligations is not as binding for them. There are no children between the men, no property that is really disputable in the law. His
is his, and his is his. Who packs up is not even the question: usually one
name is on the lease. The tyranny of desire is only rivaled by the tyranny
of God. The object that creates desire, inspiring in men the erection so
increasingly unreliable, is to be venerated and, by some, worshipped.

About sexual experience, the world has been verbose; about relationships of kinship, there has been even more discussion. But about relationships where mere companionship is everything, the testimony is sparse. In
literature friendship, and always between members of the same sex, has
been either sentimentalized or idealized. It is depicted as the experience of
children or innocents, antecedent to maturity, something that is ultimately
replaced by more serious bonds of sexual or filial love. There are excep-

tions in certain aristocratic circles and in the long story of camaraderie among men in male institutions like the military, a story that Western civilization never tired of repeating in the settings of the classical world or the chivalric age. But aristocratic society is idiosyncratic about its intimacies, and those comrades who died in arms were often in the arms of each other. No scholarship that I know of has ever suggested that the feelings of a Roland for his friend had any source in eroticism.

Between men and women, gender raises the sexual question inexorably: yes or no? Sadness or relief, the issue is felt if not confronted. I think all gay men wonder at some time in their relations with women whether they might have loved them had they been heterosexual, and some consider whether they can love them as homosexuals. In these friendships, once the relationship has matured, the erotic is transformed yet subtly retained. Presuming those involved are old or wise enough to refrain from experimentation for its own sake, the friendship then becomes imbued with a tenderness that is borrowed from romanticism but purged of sexual tension by resignation if not regret.

My own experience says that the confusions of sexuality are so powerful that they obscure too much; in that obscurity of vision, one can behave carelessly, hurtfully, taken by surprise by unforeseen panics. Because gay men have a history of oppression from the larger society and from their own tribalness, the attractiveness of women suggests a possibility of rescue from heterosexual scorn and from the undignified prospects that age promises to homosexuals.

Initially, the woman one approaches is only companionable: the feelings are safe; the empathy a gay man brings to his friendship is unusual and seductive. That rare empathy begins in deprivation. Gay men are deprived of the knowledge of women that their heterosexual counterparts seem to possess. Straight men replace their mothers and their sisters with wives and lovers and daughters. The continuity of women in their lives is unbroken. They leave the family to start a family. For gay men, the loss of family is sharpened by entry into a culture that is centrally sexual and exclusively male. Friendship then offers one of the few compensations for that loss.

But that empathy only begins with the need to link the child's past to the adult present. It is created, for better or worse, by the long identification with women; gay men have not only been fascinated by the idea of the feminine; they have also wanted to define its style. But it is on the common ground of femininity, which modern women are angrily exploring, that the special understanding of women and gay men is cultivated. At some level, both recognize that they have been exploited by this idea: women by having to struggle to define ideas about womanhood free of servility to men, and gay men by having to recognize that if forced to choose (and they are), they are more feminine than masculine.

Right now we are witnessing among gay men a faddish macho style which is already under attack for making its practitioners look ridiculous, but the extremity of the fashion is the fear of the effeminate. It is ironically a failure. It began as a statement that claimed gay men could be as manly as straight ones; it is now a signal that men who are exaggeratedly manly are probably gay. Women and gay men both have to come to terms with what society demands of them as manly or womanly; both are struggling with their feelings that they can no longer conform to those notions. Women are in rebellion against them, and gay men have felt fraudulent practicing them.

While the idea of the feminine has only recently become a universal political subject, gay men have understood its subversive potential much longer. Women have united the surfaces of femininity with their own psychology, rooting it to their sense of being, and thus at least it is theirs, for their happiness or their discontent. Gay men have known that for them it can never be connected harmoniously with their idea of maleness. But it can become an elaborate holiday from the discomforting weight of pretense, a holiday in drag or in camping that are ancient rites, or it can lead to behavior more alienating, to transvestism and transsexuality. The easiest vacations, however, are in flights to the imagination. To camp well requires flair and wit; to dress in drag requires effort and courage, but to fantasize requires only solitude.

It is from their fantasies of the feminine, learned early from mothers and sisters and aunts, that men find relief from posing and posturing, and it is from such long experience that their deftness with women develops. Gay men have observed women more closely because they are intrigued, for a purpose straight men have ignored or found dull or fearful: what does it feel like to be a woman? Heterosexual men, of course, have been exploring that question incessantly in their relationships with women, in their work on the subject of women, but their explorations have been self-serving more often than not. They ask, as Freud did, what women want, because women are their wives and the mothers of their children. Unlike Freud, most men begin with the answers rather than the question. Women themselves are not sure of the answers, and that uncertainty is provoking an unparalleled anxiety. It is easier to make up the answer, to tell women what they want.

Gay men have another use for their observation: it is information they need for their fantasies, their psychic identification of themselves as mirrors of women. That is why gay writers such as Tennessee Williams, who have made women their main subject, are accused of disguising their homosexuality; their detractors say they are really writing about homosexual men or homosexual issues. The accusation is true in one sense: gay men and straight women have an enormous tie in their need of men. But Williams, for example, is certainly not writing about a man in drag with such characters as Blanche Du Bois or Amanda Wingfield. Try to imagine those roles played in drag by men and you have parody. Shakespeare's Cleopatra has been played in drag, but not Blanche Du Bois. Williams' treatment of her is deeply informed by his homosexuality, but it is a woman's experience he is trying to render, one in which notions of femininity and sexuality and romance have entangled themselves into a net of madness. In *A Streetcar Named Desire,* the confrontation of Blanche, crazed with her failures, and Stanley, the *uhr*-male, raises all the questions we are still arguing. Blanche loses because it is good theater and because Williams does not think that Stanley can be defeated, but who did thirty years ago? Williams' drama is still with us; he even predicted that rape would be the act that defiant women would protest most furiously. Blanche is nearly crazy when she is raped; then, everything that has been driving her insane is confirmed: the world is exactly as brutal as she thought it was. Williams also begins Blanche's madness in her guilt over her homosexual husband's death. She provoked it, and it is good grounds for her self-destructiveness.

I do not think that gay men ever want to be women, with the rare exception of the transsexual. Though it may sound obvious, why would they, when their sexual interest is in their own sex? When they play out the fantasy of themselves as women too dangerously, one of the first things they do is avoid women. Some homosexuals prefer sexual contacts with men they call "straight," but whom everyone else has named "trade." Why they believe that their partners are heterosexual because they substitute gay men for straight whores is an elaborate delusion I do not fully understand. But "trade" is an interesting idiom; what is being bartered? Which of the men is being serviced? And which service is more meaningful and powerful?

4

Gay men need from straight women what they need from no one else: not their sexual partners, their male friends, or their lesbian ones. That special need gives a character to their tenderness, which is like no other—perhaps like one other: the tenderness toward a former lover whom one no longer desires. It is a frail nostalgia for what might have been that is easily swept away, a lingering sweetness that is quickly evanescent. Like the peculiar English habit of serving a "savory" after the dessert to clear the palate so the meal will not end cloyingly and the final taste of sweetness is mixed with salt, so the attractiveness of women is intermixed with sweetish wish and salt resignation.

For example, last summer I visited Anne, a woman I do not see often because she lives three thousand miles away, but with whom I have a long close friendship. She was and still is in a difficult marriage with a strange man, emotionally unpredictable but intelligent to the point of genius. When we were younger, in graduate school, I spent more time with them than with anyone else. I became inordinately involved with her son; I was around all during her pregnancy and in fact, since I had a car, brought her and the baby home from the hospital. It was a nasty, snowy Michigan day, and she sat next to me in the front with the baby while her nervous husband and her irritating mother chattered in the back. I was concentrating on driving in the sleet, but I was also conscious that I wished the child were mine, that I were the husband and father rather than the "uncle." It was a sad small wish prompted by my real affection for her and a need to feel sorry for myself.

Suddenly Anne began quietly to cry. I knew instantly her tears were about her confusion and fear, about her postponed career, about their genteel poverty and the loss of liberty the baby would bring. I also knew I could not help her with those tears; her husband and mother might understand the pain less because they were more involved with the child, but they could comfort her better than I. Understanding is not loving; being loved does not entail being understood. I would be a good friend; I would help her with the child because I was grateful for Anne's friendship. I would babysit and stroll with her and give her time; it was all I could do.

When her husband and I finally eked out our doctorates, we left for different coasts. The separation was a wrench because it was the first time I was leaving a friend whom I did not want to leave, and I knew our lives would never again be so familiar to each other. Wonderfully, our reunions are easy; within hours, a day or two, we find where we have hidden our former feelings. True, there is so much now we do not know; in fact, after fifteen years of living separate lives, we are strangers to each other's histories. What is her marriage now? her career? her sense of herself as a mother? While I find myself without information, it is more of an oddity than an impediment.

When we were young, we often spent time frivolously, compared with the drudging seriousness of scholarly students. We were both disillusioned with graduate study, but I was at least getting my degree while she was waiting until she could return to her studies. She wanted her degree, to explore literary matters in a professional way, to enter academia; I wanted the degree in order to teach. I preferred to read rather than study; I did not understand the mandarinism of critical and scholarly work, which I failed to connect to the literature it purported to illuminate. It seemed to be written for itself. Anne found it more interesting; even when she was skeptical she thought it was genuine: she wanted to *know*. Meanwhile, we dawdled through the years; our most pleasurable diversions from the grind of school for me and the confinements of childrearing for her were each other. We chattered about Victorian novels while we shopped for cheap Mexican vases, talked our way through the farmers' markets while we selected fifty-cent seedlings, wandered through the elegant gift shops, occasionally stealing a porcelain ashtray or a silver bangle while we took turns carrying the baby who was nearly as comfortable in my arms as he was in hers.

Fifteen years later, the baby was in Harvard, the marriage was awry, the past a grayness. I was a tourist on a trip to her life, and we spent our time learning the landscape that we were no longer familiar with while she showed me San Francisco, Sausalito, Marin County, and the Big Sur. Near the end of my lengthy visit, I wanted to buy her a present. She loves *chatchkas,* Chinese and African baskets, pottery, old farming tools, campy small advertising signs in tin, but I did not want to give her something for the house. In Sausalito, where we were browsing after a lazy lunch, she saw a dress she wanted to try on. Anne had always been the most beautiful woman I knew, sensual and delicate at the same time. She had been full-figured, but her arms and hands, her legs and ankles were slender and as graceful as a dancer's. Now she bordered on the voluptuous; her hair was shot with gray; she no longer tried to look exotic. The propriety of univer-sity life and the prudery of her sons had inhibited her taste, and she found it easier at home to look plainer, more ladylike. The dress was very flatter-ing and made her look sexy, baring her shoulders and emphasizing her breasts; it was a summery thing flowing in muted flowers. While she modeled it for me, the saleswoman turned to me for my approval; her assumption was unmistakable and mistaken: I was the lover. Anne decided to have the dress; while she changed, I quickly put it on my credit card. The saleswoman wrote up the charge quickly, speeding through the credit check on her machine, pleased to enter into this little lovers' exchange. When I gave Anne the box as her gift, she kissed me chastely and thanked me, not particularly surprised. We left the store feeling close and senti-mental. Anne had not noticed the response of the saleswoman, had not felt her interest in us. At first, it occurred to me that she was just too engrossed in how she looked in the dress, but that wasn't it. Had the situation been reversed, she would not have noticed anything either. It was something that would not occur to her. Who we were in the world never crossed her mind as it did mine.

The subject of my homosexuality was no longer taboo. When it a.ose, provoked by the obtrusive gayness of San Francisco, when she was curious about the kind of gay life I led, I could tell her what she wanted to know simply and usually with ease. I wasn't defensive or eager to explain. She was much shorter about her own sexual life; it had been generally satisfac-tory; it still was. The problems of her marriage were not in the bedroom. Anne had always been assured in her dealings with men. She had been puzzled when we first met as to why I showed little sexual interest; she was always a bit flirtatious, and I was unresponsive. Even before she understood that I was homosexual, she gave up pursuing explanations. If I were uninterested that was my affair; she found herself content with friendship since she was rarely without a lover before her marriage.

In our mid-forties, we met again as adults whom the intervening years had done much to define. Motherhood had been the central experience of her life; homosexuality had been mine. But we did not dwell on what neither could really understand; we had rediscovered our sympathy for each other, and it made us tender. People mistook that for romance because it conformed to their notion of what tenderness must mean between men and women.

Though it mattered less than it ever had before, rousing less confusion and anxiety, my homosexuality was a context always with me. Anne was not curious about why we had managed a friendship of enduring feeling despite the obstacles of distance and time. We interested each other, we provided amusement, we did not rasp the nerves, we were together for comfort and pleasure. For her, what more was there to ask?

Toward the end of my visit, Frances arrived. Frances, Anne, and I had all been close in graduate school. Frances lived in New York and I saw her regularly; she had not seen Anne much over the years. Anne and I decided we would treat her to the spectacle of the Big Sur, taking three days to explore Carmel and the beaches.

The weather was normal: foggy and cool with moments of sunshine. After we walked the gorgeous sunless beaches, we would return to the state-owned Big Sur Lodge, located behind a high hill that blockaded the fog and that was always warm and sunny. The best of our times was an afternoon walking upstream to find the source of the Big Sur River, which in August was barely more than a brook. Midway to the source, the land rose and the water cascaded over small boulders creating safe little eddies and miniature waterfalls. We were wearing sneakers in order to wade the rocky stream bed, but we had not expected to swim. Now we were in an irresistible spot of sunshine, redwoods, and rushing water that was bearably cold, unlike the frigid Pacific. We cavorted like delirious children. I wedged myself between two boulders while the water gushed around me and the women sat on the slippery stones, thigh-deep in the stream. It was a golden moment; two New Yorkers escaped from the dog days of August in a green frolic of light and water. Anne found us infectious, and we all surrendered to a blessed childlikeness.

The next morning we started back; we decided to picnic at Point Lobos if we could get there before the fog. At one of the coves, so beautiful that it is a signature for the California coast, we ate our fruit and cheese and cold meats. We were lucky; there were few people on the beach. As we lay in the sun content with the food and the weather, happy with each other, we began to reminisce. Remember this? Remember that? we said, regaling each other with the follies of our twenties, our bright-eyed cynicism, our old snotty arrogance that seemed so silly and rather harmless now.

It was Anne who brought up Sonia. She had been one of the women who lived with her at Columbia and had adored her; Frances had become a close friend in the years before Sonia's death. Out of touch with us all, Anne had less understanding of what had led to her death. It was Frances who answered most of Anne's questions: Frances, who had been so lucid about the improbability of rescue, who saw Sonia's misery and her death with a painful clarity. She said the neurosis was inexorable; married to Sonia's iron character, like her social marriage, it had been deadly. Frances reported that Sonia had stopped seeing her some months before the suicide, which I had not known before. Anne said that she and Sonia had been distant even before she came to California, that somehow she was frightened of the sickness, that she wanted to flee it. She had hoped their estrangement was temporary, and that they would resume a friendship when the agonies were spent.

Anne fled the sickness, Frances had found it impenetrable, I had glamorized it, and we all had failed her and lost her. Anne and Frances were sobered by their memories: sad and quiet and helpless to connect the feelings for that death and the serene beauty of the Pacific and the happiness just moments ago. But I was plunged back into grief. It was still there, a miniature of what it had been ten years ago, only dormant, always latent.

They also had their regrets, but they were not like mine: they regretted that they had been unable to help, too frightened or too distant, too ignorant of what was happening to Sonia. But her death was past for them, a major loss in their life, an unmendable rent, but something to live with or live without. Time had done its proper work.

Why hadn't it done its work as well for me? Why had I cherished the grief? Frances and Anne had loved her; her friendship had been a profound relationship in each of their lives. But I sensed they had not celebrated, as Sonia and I had, a conspiratorial evasion of the world, committed to enshrining the disasters of the past. We had all scorned the world and been frightened of it, but Anne and Frances were determined to live in it, to secure what they could for themselves. Sonia and I had never resolved our ambivalence; we had never felt entitled enough to the world, little as we liked it, and thus, somehow we had not been entitled to our lives.

CHAPTER FIVE

The Flesh as Fantasy:
Gay Men as Women

1

One evening in June 1979, I was bored with the late movie and turned the dial on my television set, which is connected to a cable that gives me channels A through J as well as the customary thirteen. On channel C, on a program run by a woman who calls her show "I Can Do Anything," was a tape of a transsexual operation in full progress. Later, I saw that the film belonged to Columbia Medical College, but until the credits, I watched the gory, horrifying, fascinating emasculation of the patient and the reconstruction of his genitalia to resemble a vagina. The voice of the operating physician calmly outlined all that he was doing with a minimum of medical terminology; I could understand most of what he was saying. But I really could not understand at all what he was doing. When the film finished, the narrator commented with satisfaction on the appearance of the two month postoperative vagina splayed before the viewer. He noted the texture and the color of the organ, which he had constructed so artfully that even another physician might accept it as genuine. Nowhere in the film was the image of a full body. The screen filled with a torso from navel to mid-thigh; the self had become the sexual organ, the final transformation of sexual obsession into thing.

When the tape was finished, I was faintly nauseated and wide awake. I think I would have been upset watching the gore of any operation, but the technicalities of the emasculation were more gruesome because the image and the issue are so provocative for a gay man, one like so many who has thought what his life might have been like had he been born a woman. I was also bothered by the casual obscenity before me, inadvertently stumbled upon by flicking the dial of my Sony. Perhaps there still is mystery about privacy, but obviously little about what used to be called private parts.

I thought how astonishing were the changes about sexual publicity in the last decades. Here I had witnessed a procedure on a human being that Mary Shelley could not have imagined when she wrote *Frankenstein,* but the procedure was the enactment of that gothic fantasy written a hundred fifty years ago. Even twenty-five years ago when I began to explore the gay world of bars and parties, overt displays of sexuality bordered on the scandalous. Close dancing, surreptitious kisses, and covert fondling were the limit in public; after that, one sought privacy unless he were deranged or the party was an orgy.

My first gay party was also the first time I saw men in drag, two of whom were professionals, the third an amateur transvestite. The profes sionals looked like hookers; their wigs were cheap, both platinum and coarse; the makeup to hide the texture of shaved skin was thickly applied; the clothes were sleazy evening gowns. One of the men looked preposterously tall, well over six feet in his heels. He tried to seem willowy, but he was clumsy; the other had a good figure and shapely legs, and while I do not think anyone would have mistaken him for a woman, he did suggest a tawdry aura, a tough bar floozy. What bothered me was that neither man thought he was ridiculous or comic; both took themselves quite seriously. But the men at the party did not; snide cracks about the ineptitude of their drag were giggled over as soon as they were out of earshot. After an hour or so of milling, during which time I sensed the party was waiting for something to happen, the host announced that we were all to keep quiet while Flo made her entrance. He put out the lights, flung open the door, and there was a pretty young woman with two handsome escorts. Flo swept into the room very theatrically, blowing kisses to this one and that, and came up to me to give me a hug. Then I realized it was Larry, the man who had invited me to the party.

Larry fooled me, and he could have fooled anyone if he hadn't behaved so campily; his appearance was impeccable. His dress was from

Bonwit Teller, a tasteful black cocktail number made of heavy silk taffeta with a wide skirt and modest neckline. He wore expensive black velvet pumps with three-inch heels that he navigated in with ease and some ladylike jewelry, a bracelet of silver and dainty matching earrings. Larry was a successful hairdresser; not only had he the money to spend on good drag, but he was also skillful enough to arrange his own hair in a modish fashion: very short hair then was the latest look for women. What he had daringly done was to cut the back of his hair so that it no longer came to a "V"; instead, it lay in an even sprayed swirl. I wondered how he would get away with it; how would he manage to explain his haircut to people when he was out of drag? In 1950, there was so much that could show one was queer: clothes were easy betrayals, and one was always on guard about his perilous mannerisms. To be caught swishing in public was an invitation to humiliation, if not violence.

Comparing Larry's fantasy with the torso on my television screen, I fumble for explanations that will link his girlishness and the fantasy of flesh that Columbia Medical College filmed for the world to see. Larry played out his drag at a gay party, in an apartment whose drapes were tightly drawn, before men he knew well and who would applaud his skill and his bravura in actually leaving his own apartment to come through the streets dressed as a woman. Sensibly, he had two escorts as a precaution. The patient on the table two months after the operation, whose vagina was now probed and manipulated for the benefit of the camera, has in common with Larry a willingness to be shown as an object for the curiosity or edification of others, but on other issues of sexuality, they seem opposed.

Larry was so convincingly feminine that none of the men at the party dreamed of asking him home. Going to bed with Larry as Flo was unthinkable; he certainly didn't expect anyone to want to. He wanted to be the belle of the ball; when he wanted to pick up a man, he naturally wore men's clothes and tried to minimize his effeminacy. The transsexual wants to disappear into secrecy, and the ordeal of his mortified flesh enables him to sleep with a man convinced that neither of them is homosexual.

The transsexual, like the drag queen, is the emblem of the oppression of homosexuals, though they are opposing reflections. The drag queen is the heroine in a dark farce, a comedy *noir*, but at least he knows what the nature of the play is. The transsexual is the protagonist in a modern gothic melodrama; she or he is indeed the bride of Dr. Frankenstein. For the record, I do not mean that I am unsympathetic to nor do I want to patronize the agony of the men who undergo gender reassignment, but the very term I have borrowed from medicine to describe "neutrally" the transsexual change sounds like doublespeak from Orwell's *1984*. I think the man who needs to be emasculated and reguised as a woman expresses the direst pain, since any other explanation must be his madness. Indeed, the operation is probably the alternative to psychosis. The testimony of transsexuals before their surgery is urgent and desperate. Insanity or suicide are likely alternatives to the operation, and if not, an acid self-hatred still has to be lived with. A viable alternative to changing the body to fit the mind is of course to change the mind to fit the body. Ironically, it is cheaper, easier, and probably less painful to change the body than to undergo the kind of therapy needed to reconcile the transsexual to himself and to maleness. And surgery is final in a way that psychotherapy can never be.

"I felt I was a woman trapped in a male body" is the standard testimony, now an orthodoxy before doctors will accept a prospective client. Oddly, these men are sometimes in heterosexual situations, married to or involved with women. Logically, they should then feel emotionally like lesbians if they make love (which they do infrequently), but none of the men raises such an analogy. First, lesbians don't count; second, women's sexuality doesn't count; third, these men who claim to be psychic women in the wrong bodies have very special meanings for the word "woman." Most of them insist with vehemence that they are not homosexual, that even the idea of such experience is unattractive, without erotic appeal, and frequently some talk of it with a disgust that rivals that of the most fanatic bigot. Yet the two commonest occupations transsexuals enter postoperatively are housewife and prostitute. Many were prostitutes before the operation, ostensibly to pay the astronomical medical bills, but there is little data about why they return to prostitution except that they prefer to. Most transsexuals are interested in entering the mainstream world in some relation to men, affirming their femaleness as women have traditionally done, by some deeply important relationship to men. The information on this subject is thin. Logically, a new identity would dictate discretion. The public careers from Christine Jorgensen to Renee Richards are beset with smirks and anger. Even a biography as intelligent and eloquent as Jan

Morris' *Conundrum* tells us it is about confusion. When Rebecca West reviewed it, she described how appalled she was by the anguish and how unconvinced she was of the solution. Outside of physicians and their clientele, few people are advocates for transsexuals. No small factor for this indifference is the bizarreness of the transsexual's situation: the surrender of maleness is simply incomprehensible to most men, straight or gay.

Many former males are completely successful appearing as women in the world, usually quite conventional women, since those doctors in charge of the sexual change demand that the patient pass for a lengthy test time, sometimes years, while they are on hormone treatment. Though surgery can provide a sensitive organ that closely resembles a vagina, it can only create a cosmetic clitoris. Yet some postoperative transsexuals claim to have orgasm within weeks after recuperation. These statements are provocative, raising questions about the reliability of evidence, about the nature of gender and sexual experience, about the limits of self-determination.

2

The question of orgasm is a precise and controversial one. The penile tissue used to construct the vagina is carefully relocated so that the nerve endings and the capacity for sensitivity are preserved, but the descriptions of orgasm by transsexuals are hard to evaluate, in contrast to the descriptions of sexual excitement which are not. Perhaps, some skeptics offer, these former men join a sisterhood of women for whom the orgasm is not the center of their sexual lives: eroticism and romanticism are experiences that do not depend on the completion of orgasm, whose nature no one has ever measured satisfactorily.

The idea of orgasm as distinct from the experience of it has been much discussed, and that idea has been a crucial measurement for notions of successful masculinity or femininity. The man who is not orgasmic is thought of as unsexual, particularly if the absence of orgasm is the result of the lack of tumescence. The man who stays erect but cannot come, a rarer but not unheard-of impotence, can be regarded as competent by his partners, and if he fakes orgasm, he may even be held satisfactory. Women have used such pretense to please their partners throughout history. But the issue is not the same for both sexes: women are expected to please, men are expected to perform.

Even in sophisticated literature like Hemingway's *The Sun Also Rises,* the issue is distinct: the hero's incapacity for orgasm makes the heroine's intact capacity irrelevant. His wound makes his life and the life of the woman he loves a complete mess. I never liked the novel, but I could not help admiring it. Hemingway's anxiety about masculine performance came too close to home but seemed somehow wrong-headed. I knew there was something wrong with it even before one of my students, slightly smashed, muttered aloud in class while we were discussing it, "Aw, why doesn't he just suck her off." The class tittered, but the discussion, the novel, maybe Hemingway, was over for me. Why indeed?

The answer is Penis: Peter Pecker Dick; the cock, tool, prick. Without it, the best mouth in the world is just another hole. Whether or not it is even used, it must be there, otherwise there is no legitimate sexuality for men, and for some women. And as long as it is there, even if sexually useless, the transsexual must be rid of that mark of maleness before the body is no longer felt as alien. This concept of the genitalia as the heart of sexual being is mysterious and atavistic, a savage remnant, as arrested as infantile fears of darkness, and as omnipresent with men in modern technological society as it was in totemic culture.

Those inches of flesh between the legs, not even clever, say, like fingers, or nice like hair, another of nature's endless absurd amusements before the cosmos, is humanity's smallest and most powerful tyrant. What we lack in testosterone compared to the lower species, society makes up for with its incessant indoctrinations. The penis is ever the problem. First, it is uncontrollably obtrusive and embarrassing; then, it becomes the alter ego; finally, it is unreliable and disloyal. I was recently at a bar on Long Island Sound whose patrons are professional fishermen and boatmen, working-class middle-aged rural men, all heterosexual to my knowledge. They were making up nicknames for their penises: Sweet William who used to be Wild Bill, Red Snapper, Sleeping Beauty, Deadwood Dick. They were witty and easy, sad and bemused, but they were not indifferent, disinterested, or past caring.

The lore of the penis has been a history of male penology. In literal imprisonment, the penis may be the only solace; in the psychic imprisonment of men's obsession with their own or the organs of others, it is anything but solace. Women often complain when they are treated as sex objects; they find it debasing to be equated with their breasts and buttocks and vagina, and it is even more enraging for them that there is no comparable experience for men. Men who dress to provoke sexual comment or interest are hardly insulted nor do they feel debased when they get them. But that box men fondle so assuringly and casually as their most blatant sexual signal, "Do you want it?" where "me" is transformed into "it," is Pandora's box.

The history of masculinity is one that is symbolized and sometimes reduced to the meaning of the penis, and only in its sexual function: the erect penis exclusively. Untumescent, it is a modest bud under the fig leaf, not even a significant distraction on the idealized statuary of the classical world.

In myths, it is magical. Fearsome matriarchal cults emasculated the corn king annually, and the spilling of his blood renewed the land, blood as semen, spawning new life in mother earth. That the fruitful wound is from the torn genitalia rather than the heart tells of the potency of penile emission. Totemic tribes also worshipped the penis enlarged to a phallus beyond use or human proportion, and Japanese pornography has made of that adoration a special art. The penis as phallus becomes a supreme weapon, its powers magically lethal, vaguely divine.

In our individual prehistories, the penis is one of the first male masteries, autoerotically providing some pleasure distinct and autonomous from mother and the femaleness of orality and breasts. It is an early experience, the autoerotic as autonomy, and it later comes to color all the joys and fears of phallicism, from Oedipal castration and performance anxiety to pride, or shame, in size as proof of virility.

In *Civilization and Its Discontents,* Freud makes one of his astonishing boggling little suppositions, dropping it into a footnote. It is worth quoting in its entirety. Freud is talking of the unprecedented achievement of primitive man in his evolution toward civilization by his acquisition of power over fire, and the long footnote is an amusing aside:

> Psychoanalytic material, as yet incomplete and not capable of unequivocal interpretation, nevertheless admits of a sur-

mise—which sounds fantastic enough—about the origins of this human feat. It is as if primitive man had had the impulse when he came in contact with fire, to gratify an infantile pleasure in respect of it and put it out with a stream of urine. The legends that we possess leave no doubt that flames shooting upwards like tongues were originally felt to have a phallic sense. Putting out fire by urinating—which is introduced in the later fables of Gulliver in Lilliput and Rabelais' Gargantua—therefore represented a sexual act with a man, an enjoyment of masculine potency in homosexual rivalry. Whoever was the first to deny himself this pleasure and spare the fire was able to take it with him and break it to his own service. By curbing the fire of his own sexual passion he was able to tame fire as a force of nature. This great cultural victory was thus a reward for refraining from gratification of an instinct. Further, it is as if man had placed woman by the hearth as the guardian of the fire he had taken captive, because her anatomy makes it impossible for her to yield to such a temptation. It is remarkable how regularly analytic findings testify to the close connection between the ideas of ambition, fire and urethral eroticism.

Whether this is poetic surmise or intuitive anthropology is not of concern here. But this is an example of a mode of thinking, the psychoanalytic, which has become a powerful premise for modern thought, as well as a sample of the intelligence of one of the most formidable minds in human history. Some close attention to Freud's assumptions and analogies is useful. He begins with the idea of the mastery of fire as the first step in human culture, the beginning of civilization. In the myths about fire, its acquisition is always at the price of hellish suffering, though not always man's own. Prometheus is eternally tormented for his gift of fire to mankind; the gods are affronted that humanity has acquired an instrument that will make it less slavish, terrified, and brutish. The hostility of authority is taken for granted; the gift than enables mankind to rise above its insignificance is miraculous.

Then Freud makes his wonderfully fanciful conjecture about peeing out the fire. That man who first refrained was promethean. Analogously, the fiery passions also had to be mastered before mankind was free of brutishness. Freud goes another step and connects the material and the symbol. The passion that primitive man first had to control in order to master fire was homosexual in character. This homosexual rivalry about masculine potency is inherent in the race even if it is infantile. It belongs to a time in mankind's development when phallicism is a primary symbol, equating virility and animal strength as the actual means of asserting mastery over others. Man must first forego his rivalry with the flames and with other men in order to advance: the progress of course is toward the greater domination of others, immediately the domination of women, whom Freud remarks men make guardians of the hearth: the primeval domestication of women. They are put in the place men have made to keep the weapon of their passion. Domination or ambition, homosexual eroticism, fire: all mysteriously enflamed.

Freud's assumption that erotic homosexual rivalry is spontaneous and natural, even instinctual, is not elaborated, just assumed. Civilization is that stage when such behavior and feeling is relinquished in order for man to effect his drive to dominate the world, beginning with the end of his homoeroticism and the onset of the subjugation of women. Once primitive man is free of his need to compete phallically and he has secured women, he is ready to confront nature and subdue if not destroy it.

Freud implies that homoeroticism is infantile and natural and, like many infantile and natural pleasures, must be put aside to fulfill needs more "useful," more adult and more "masculine," like ambition or the need for domination. What Freud does not pursue is what happens to those feelings when they are put aside or repressed, though he is quite clear about his pessimism. The price of civilization which men have created to give unbridled scope to ambition has been both their own personal misery and the imminent destruction of the natural world they have wrested civilization from.

The civilized is the antithesis of the natural; in other words, it is artificial. None of this terminology would be more than descriptive if society had not made it proscriptive, insisting that "natural" is the synonym for "good"; logically, everything civilized would have to be bad. The discontentments that Freud refers to in his title are the exactments of civil society as well as the failures of its achievements. Not only is society the major source of human misery, an illogical irrational creation that is perpetuated by the part of us that is least attractive, our aggressiveness, but also the other sources of misery, nature itself and the knowledge of mortality, are not lessened. Even the most technologically sophisticated civilization, like our own, has done little to alleviate natural catastrophe, and Western civilization's contribution toward reconciling us with our own deaths has been ineffectual. Christians are just as reluctant to die as others are, and when they are not, as in cults like Jim Jones', they are regarded as duped or mad. Religious belief has only rarely managed to ease the terror of dying.

Centering around these confusing and contradictory ideas of natural and unnatural occur all the issues of sexual oppression and the hatred of sexuality. If the control of phallic sexuality is the hallmark of progress, then the failure to control such impulse threatens to return us to a sinister barbarism. On the other hand, the suppression of sexual aggression and the failure to transform libidinous energy into something constructive results in much of our social hostility. Some say nature takes care of those impulses in women by maternal instinct. In legend, women's sexual aggression is less threatening because first, it leads to generation, which is inevitable and destined, and thus it is "good," and second, women are less powerful, so even if their sexuality is harder to control, the consequences are not as significant. It is in the area of sexual behavior and feeling more than anywhere else that ideas of the natural and the good and the natural and the bad exist simultaneously.

In classical mythology, the tales of male sexuality focus on desire run amok, rape. Leda and the swan, Europa and the bull, Philomela, Daphne and Apollo—the list is very long. In most of them, divine rape transforms the woman into a victim of bestiality. When she is saved, as Daphne is, she is turned into a tree, losing her vulnerability in losing her humanity: if she will not submit, she must give up both her sexuality and her humanity. When she is not saved, she is mutilated like Philomela or she becomes the mother of suffering, like Leda, whose daughter Helen is the occasion for the fall of civilization. Male sexuality uncontrolled is tragic in its consequences to those it falls upon, but somehow the onus is connected to the woman who inspires the desire rather than to the god who fails to control it.

The myths of the sacrifice of phallic sexuality, the legends of transsexuality, are alternative visions of violent phallicism. Tiresias is probably the

most famous of these figures, though there does not seem to be a real
distinction between sexual transformation and androgyny. However, it is
clear that after Tiresias is no longer male, he becomes privy to mysteries
hidden from men, embarking on his career as mystic seer, votary of the
gods, and prophet of doom. Having sacrificed sexuality and the natural, he
is given access to the supernatural. These mystic powers are recorded
cross-culturally in all the legends of sexual transformation, from those of
the American Indian to those of eastern Asia. The American Indians have
a number of precedential institutions. The Indians of the Mohave who
were destined to be shamans ritually pulled their penises between their legs
and claimed that they were women. In the same culture, some boys who
were chosen to live as women became the *berdache,* a word whose meaning
variously is someone who changed his gender, a man-woman (the an-
drogyne), or the person who had no sexuality, neither man nor woman.
What it did not seem to include was the idea of the exclusive homosexual.

If tribal society saw in sexual aberration a condition inspiring more
awe than fear, it is partly because the sacrifice of masculinity was so momentous, rather than monstrous. Among the tribes to become a *berdache*
was often a choice freely offered: if a boy or young man did not want to do
man's work, warrior's work, he was offered the life of a woman. That
choice was irreversible, since to live as a woman forever disqualified him
from maleness. But once the choice was made, the boy was dressed as a
woman, a husband was found for him, and the tribe made an honorable
accommodation. His transition was marked by solemn ritual. The symbolic
act was enough; there was no need to make it surgically literal. Modern
anthropologists still have not decided whether such men were homosexual
transvestites or were acting a role that has no analogy in modern society.

The momentousness of phallicism as masculinity has not lessened in
technological society; instead, it has become a subject for the doctor rather
than the priest. One of the oddest expressions of this is the construction of
pseudopenises for female to male transsexuals. Nearly all this discussion so
far has pertained to male change, but there is as long a history of women
who chose to live as men. But it is only recently that the story has become
freakish. I do not want to speak at length about what women want, for it is
no doubt presumptuous, even when the women in question are so male-
identified that they want to become men. Also, there is less data on women

transsexuals; among those who undergo surgery the ratio of women to men is 1 to 5, and among women, there is much more reluctance to speak out. Female transvestites have sometimes legally passed as male and then lived with men's advantages, but those women usually lived in intimate relations with other women; they were, simply, lesbians. In the transsexual situation, both the patient and her lover insist that they are not lesbian. Sometimes that insistence relies on acquiring an appendage that can pass as a penis though it is not capable of erection. Without going into clinical detail, I understand that the relocated flesh covers the clitoris and can sometimes accommodate the insertion of an object, that is, a phallus, to harden it. Some approximation of heterosexual intercourse is possible, as is orgasm, since the clitoris is stimulated by friction even when permanently covered in flesh. When women are apprised of the severe limitations of this procedure, of the extensive hospitalization and repeated operations, they often still insist on its necessity, though the results will serve "little, if any role in sexual activities" (John Hoopes, "Operative Treatment of the Female Transsexual," *Transsexualism and Sex Reassignment*, ed. Richard Green and John Money, 1969). Dr. Hoopes draws his conclusions about sexual utility from a purely physical model; what might be psychologically necessary for imagining one is engaged in heterosexual intercourse is more complicated and not easy to verify. Interestingly, these women make a better adjustment to their new status even when they do not have active sexual lives. They claim they are happier now, reasonably content, free of the fear of detection with the pseudopenis. The phallus represents power; it is what they have wanted. Their male counterparts are often less fortunate postoperatively, unhappy or dissatisfied. The men have given up phallicism for the vagina that promises the bliss of romantic love or of sexual allure. For men, surgery can create a reasonable facsimile of a vagina but not guarantee the sensitivity of the organ; for women, there is no necessary sacrifice of orgasm; the changes externally are cosmetic.

Male transsexuals report that after recuperation they experience female orgasm entirely as the result of the redistributed penile tissue; for them vaginal orgasm is no myth. In the May 1979 issue of *Playboy*, Wendy Carlos, the composer of the record *Switched-on Bach*, gave a candid and lengthy interview. Like Jan Morris, Carlos is educated, articulate, intelligent, and successful. Her responses are more complicated than what is usually recorded by doctors for medical records. The photographs of Wendy Carlos show an attractive middle-aged woman with no visible masculine characteristics. Two statements are striking. She emphasizes that the entire experience for her was one of self-creation. She is what she made of herself, a point stated repeatedly. Second, her contrast between her pre- and postoperative sexual life is enormous. As Walter Carlos, life was almost asexual, the only experiences were dissatisfying heterosexual ones, and those were tried after the decision to become a transsexual as a test to see whether there was any genuine masculine heterosexual feeling. After the operation, there is frequent and satisfying sexual experience starting with masturbation, which she never attempted as a man. The masturbation is medically prescribed to keep the vagina from closing. She is clear that as Walter the abhorrence of the genitalia was so intense that even autoeroticism was out of the question. She claims she is luckier than many who end up with fine cosmetic results, but who are almost numb. Then she describes her present sexual life and her capacity for multiple orgasms. Here the testimony is confusing. She first describes the physical basis for multiplicity as clitoral, saying those sensations are more capable of sustained intensity than penile sensitivity. She also says the operation was only a vaginal reconstruction, yet she concludes that her orgasmic experience is female in character if not in nature. During the interview, the only time she becomes angry is when she is asked how she felt about being castrated. She angrily denies the appropriateness of the term: she had corrective surgery. Unlike Jan Morris who described only the social changes in her life, Carlos is one of the few transsexuals who is candid about sexual experience. Despite her frankness, what that experience is like remains unclear.

Recent efforts like Masters and Johnson's to document the quality of sexual experience are still basically quantitative and about function; they leave the reader as uninformed about the emotional character of experience as he was before when he had to deal with tables, graphs, and statistics. Doctors Money and Green of Johns Hopkins Medical Center have given more data on the subject than anyone else. When they record the differences in sexual behavior before and after surgery, they sometimes comment in an aside on the patient's testimony. They say that "there is considerable doubt" that the patient has ever achieved orgasm because the description of sexual sensation belies the claim.

Such evidence tells more of the sexual ignorance of the patient than of the nature of transsexuality. The patient's claim is discounted because the description of experience is not recognizably female. In one of the cases Money and Green record, a young actively practicing homosexual with an exclusive preference for passive anal intercourse was rejected as a prospect for sexual reassignment. He said, "I'm just a homosexual and I want to be something else," which was insufficient grounds for surgery. To be unhappy with one's sexual identity is not enough; one must claim that he or she has *no* sexual identity. In such a case, medicine will provide one. As a postscript, Money and Green tell us there is no comparative testimony from transsexuals on the differences between experiencing anal and vaginal intercourse, nor have they asked women who have practiced both to describe the differences as a control testimony, though obviously it is the descriptions by women of vaginal and clitoral orgasm that set the standards for veracity in accepting the reports of postoperative transsexual success.

Surgeons and doctors are rarely interested in the quality of sensation; it cannot be measured. Psychoanalysts and therapists are, but they are not involved in the transsexual phenomenon since few of them accept it as legitimate. Instead, there is an alliance of medical and religious authority to establish the reality of the transsexual claim. I do not mean that there is no extensive psychological counseling before a candidate is accepted, but the battery of tests is primarily to determine that the client is not psychotic and that he or she will psychically survive the trauma of the change. Nor is all religious authority acquiescent. Orthodox rabbis and Catholic priests have been most critical about the compliance of medical men: both the doctors and the patients are immoral, since, as the rabbi explained, normal men are under the religious mandate to beget children, so the operation should be prohibited, while the priest explains with some sense of who his audience is that the surgery is immoral because it reverses the proper therapy: to make the mind sound rather than to mutilate the body.

The response of physicians is to educate the layman to rid him of his notion that the operation is outrageously meddlesome, and part of that campaign is the recent publicity that institutions performing the surgery now allow. Johns Hopkins spent time and money interviewing (by a mailed questionnaire) hundreds of clergymen. The majority reluctantly approved the procedure; to be transsexual is preferable to being homosexual, which most of the clergy assumed was the alternative to treatment. The sinful nature of homosexuality is beyond dispute, while the ethical status of the transsexual is still open to question.

In the case histories of male transsexuals, the cumulative picture is one in which the symptoms are almost identical with the stereotypes ascribed to homosexuals: excessive "blissful" physical and emotional intimacy between infant and mother, usually without the distraction of siblings; evidence of strong dissatisfaction with her role in the mother's own history, as shown by an early premarital tendency to prefer boys' clothes, be a tomboy, or be "intellectual"; a passive or absent father; an angry but stable marriage: distant father, close binding mother. The difference between this classic therapeutic diagnosis of homosexuality and transsexuality is that in the latter case, the individual abhors the idea of being homosexual and often detests homosexuals as well. A typical statement of desperation is that the operation must be performed because without it life is not worth living. Such despair unquestioningly equates sex and love. Many transsexuals insist that they are not homosexual and often not sexual. Some claim that they may have been bisexual. But since they cannot find a suitable sexual partner in their present condition, they cannot find love. It is the simplest romantic vision of the meaning of life. Without sex, one is without love; without love, life is not worth living.

Thus, the collusion of church and medical authorities fortify the obsession not only as real but as reasonable. They confirm that there is a preoperative condition which is truly distinct from homosexuality and transvestism, and then they test out their diagnosis to fulfill their definition of the true transsexual. Once those criteria are met, it is only humane to operate to fulfill the diagnosis. However, the definition of transsexuality relies heavily on distinguishing it from homosexuality and transvestism. Such a comparative definition would be entirely valid if the men who did the defining knew anything reliable about either of the other conditions.

It is a contradiction in modern medical science to seek the authority of the church to approve a procedure that is in the service of civilized unnaturalness. The dogma of religious belief and the purpose of medical science are often to bring people into conformity with what is natural, howsoever that is defined. But when it is convenient, such a criterion can be ignored. This evasion does not seem to trouble the diagnostician or moralist, because what hovers as the logical alternative is to reconcile the patient to his body and his feelings, to his repressed and detested homosexuality. It is convincing that transsexuals cannot function happily as heterosexuals with their given bodies and minds, but little effort is made to see whether they could function as homosexuals. Instead, a bodily change is created to allow them to believe they are heterosexual, though that belief is rarely accepted by either heterosexuals or homosexuals as anything but delusion.

Recently there have been some startling exceptions: men who became transsexual women and then insisted they are lesbian feminists. The feminist criticism of transsexuality has focused on the reactionary insistence that male candidates first pass successfully as feminine women. Many of the men are excessive in their notions of what femininity requires, and the result is that they appear less like ordinary modern women than as some Hollywood idea of ladies. Money and Green remark that in these cases some elementary tutoring by counselors on makeup and clothing and deportment usually helps tone down the frilliness.

Now a very small number of transsexuals have appeared at lesbian organizations and feminist groups and have asked for recognition and acceptance. They are quite contemporary in dress and demeanor, eschewing the style of ladylike subservient femininity. Their presence is always the occasion of debate and rancor. It is extremely difficult to be dogmatic about their demands when these transsexuals claim that they have had surgery performed because they love women so much they wished to become them and then love them as women. Like other transsexuals, they abhor masculine genitalia, but any resemblance to the usual aspirations of postoperative patients ends there. These new women cannot be categorized easily. The medical texts on transsexuality do not speak of them, nor are they discussed by other transsexuals.

The best known case is that of Sandy Stone, formerly male, and a recording engineer for Olivia Records, a feminist enterprise. In the early summer of 1977, a number of feminist musicians and technicians protested to Olivia Records in an open letter in *Sister,* a California newspaper. They objected to Stone's presence in a woman's organization, at woman-only events, to Stone's failure to disclose that she was a transsexual before her employment, and to her taking work away from women sound technicians in a field where there were few opportunities for regular employment. The letter was not interested in discrediting the company nor was it at all interested in Sandy Stone; the protestors did not accept Stone as a woman, nor were they concerned with her motivation in claiming to be a lesbian. One woman wrote, "I feel raped when Olivia passes off Sandy, a transsexual, as a real woman. After all his male privilege, is he going to cash in on lesbian feminist culture too?" Another adds, "All transsexuals rape women's bodies."

Olivia Records defended Stone's employment. They cited that the operation alone was not the single determinant that made a transsexual a woman, since all candidates live as women for a considerable period of time, sometimes years, before surgery. They denied that transsexuals had special privileges, except for rare cases like Renee Richards. On the contrary, since Stone had given up a male identity and now lives as a lesbian, she faces not only that oppression, but the added one of rarely being accepted by other feminists. The women at Olivia Records also reported that they found Sandy Stone was "a woman we can relate to with comfort and trust" and one who was training other women in technical skills difficult to acquire.

The women at Olivia Records responded supportively and compassionately despite the criticism which continued with some acrimony. In their statements, they did not take a position on transsexuality except to note that it is a transitional state and one about which little was known. They preferred to address their arguments to the individual case. It was a sensible if evasive response.

The case became a topic among lesbian feminist groups, some of which were faced with the same demands. "Women only" meant just that; there was no confusion about the term "woman," and the argument used was genetic definition. When other women responded that even if transsexuals were not genetically women, biology was a dangerous argument as the final authority for what a woman is, the debate deadlocked. Janice Raymond, a radical feminist, who stridently attacks the medical profession in *The Transsexual Empire,* insists on using the term She-male for transsexuals and sees those who claim they are lesbian feminists as still aggressive and oppressive males usurping the energies and legitimate concerns of feminist women. "They exhibit stereotypical masculine behavior. Signifi-

cantly, such transsexuals have inserted themselves into positions of importance and/or performance in lesbian feminist circles." Raymond's
arguments are the most extreme I have found, and while nearly all that she
attacks in the medical profession and much of her skepticism are attitudes I
share, her tone and her contempt for the men who become transsexuals are
often unbearable. In her extremism, she concludes that the investment of
the medical profession is part of patriarchy's scheme to destroy dissident
women and replace them with docile facsimiles, "to wrest from women the
power inherent in female biology."

I can't say I'm convinced, but these are times when hostility between
men and women is more acute than ever before; who knows, she may be
right. But it is hardly important. Even if there are presently some thirty
thousand transsexuals in America, five thousand of whom were formerly
female, that cannot pose a threat, nor will these "she-males" replace biological women as mothers. The bothersome assumption is that women are frail
and lesbians so weak that the presence of one person whose gender is
confusing may be seriously harmful. How lesbians and feminists are to
handle this disturbing presence is for them to decide. Nor do I think the
debate a waste of time or the usurpation of proper feminist concerns. If
ideas about gender, sexuality, biology, and social role do not concern feminists, what should? If the evidence of individuals like Wendy Carlos who
are obsessed not only with the wrong body but with the passion to create
themselves is not significant to oppressed women and to homosexuals, what
subject is more appropriate?

Almost as unexpected is the decision in October 1979 of Johns
Hopkins to stop transsexual surgery. Dr. Jon K. Meyer, a staff psychiatrist,
completed a study that claimed persons who were operated on at University Hospital were no better adjusted afterward than those who had been
denied the surgery. The report was immediately challenged by a fellow
psychiatrist at Stanford University whose hospital now performs more operations than any other. The Hopkins study indicates that at least more
thought as well as more testing is necessary; the Stanford response men-
tions the backlog of cases, the thousands awaiting surgery. Hopkins now is
cautious about the future; Stanford is committed to the urgent demands of
those whose lives in the present seem untenable.

The transsexual is the object of creation; whether he or she is the physician's creation or whether the physician is the instrument of the transsexual's own creation is an unresolved issue, and probably academic. They are men and women who have refused to accept themselves as they have been taught they must; their defiance is often expressed at enormous price, but their protest is not trivial. It is the same protest women and men are making everywhere when they say they cannot live by the old definitions. If they appear grotesque to some, it is a good analogy to how grotesque militant homosexuals, lesbians, and feminists appear to much of conservative America.

3

If transsexuality represents a new and confusing statement about what men and women really are, an older fantasy of homosexuals is an illuminating contrast, the venerable tradition of cross-dressing, officially called transvestism and more familiarly called drag. Heterosexual cross-dressing is generally regarded as fetishistic. Most straight transvestites wear some article, usually underwear, of the opposite sex while otherwise conventionally clothed. It may be safe to say that this fetish is singularly male, since fashion for women permits them to dress almost any way they wish, and convenience or comfort are reasonable explanations for unfeminine attire.

Secretly, some of the men may dress entirely in women's clothes, and some have joined clubs to exhibit their preference together. The gratification they describe is somewhat erotic and often related to their sexual lives, but no one has yet generalized what the nature of that vague gratification is. A common explanation for men is that it provides relief, a sole relief, from the demands of masculinity which they cannot find in other areas of their lives. These men are usually conservative about sexual matters, and conventional in the rest of their lives, married and parents, apparently ordinary members of society.

In contrast, homosexual cross-dressing is not erotic, creates an aberrant life style even within gay subculture, and demands an extraordinary alienation from mainstream society. There is a divergence of attitude about sexual behavior: professional drag queens tend to be conservative; street queens tend to be radically unconventional.

In Esther Newton's *Mother Camp, Female Impersonators in America,* the subtitle is the thesis: drag is an impersonation that is the quintessential camp statement of homosexuals. Not only is the professional drag queen impersonating a woman, but as a homosexual he is simultaneously impersonating a man. One impersonation is the variant on the other; one questions the legitimacy of traditional ideas about gender, the other about sexuality. The essential awareness for the drag queen is that his performance is always parody and that he must convey that to the audience at the same time that he asks for their disbelief. Professional drag queens or stage impersonators deplore hormonal and surgical therapy; they insist that the whole point of impersonation depends on evidence of maleness. Without it, where is the irony, the commentary, the camp? Without it, what is amusing or entertaining or artful? For them, impersonation is a statement about homosexuality in the world. Those performers who begin treatment are called "hormone queens"; they are advised to get out of gay life altogether. If they want to be women, they have no place there; they should go straight.

This attitude is logical, but it is not without self-interest. In performance, even the impersonator whose style is "glamorous" rather than comic reveals at the end of the act, often a strip tease, that what might have passed for a woman beneath the sequins and feathers is actually a man: the performer wisks off the padded brassiere to reveal a flat chest. The performance is all bravura, a weaving of fantasy and irony, during which there are moments when the drag queen invites the audience to suspend disbelief so that he can finally confront them with their seduction and with his illusion. It is a momentary holiday from rigid responses to masculinity and femininity, and for the audience it gives relief from the tensions that homosexuals historically bear in their impersonation of masculinity. The drag queen shows no special dislike of his homosexuality nor is he self-hating. Instead, he yearns for a professionalism and a status among other theatrical performers which acknowledges his skill.

But the performer is a special case. Amateur drag is another kind of experience. Cross-dressing has usually been regarded as a homosexual indulgence, and when it was not homosexual, it invited an equal if different contempt. Social attitudes have varied. In licentious Rome, aristocratic life welcomed a number of amazing diversions. In Renaissance England, the upper classes avidly approved foppishness in men's clothing. The young lord with his elaborate coiffure curling down his back, his earrings, tight hose and gaudy garters, bejeweled rigid satins and silks was the counterpart to the young noblewoman whose costume was even more baroque. Despite the courtier's lush feminine tastes in costume, his stuffed codpiece was often prominent. Of course, dress as recorded in portraits was ornately rich as a symbol of the sitter's status; nevertheless, there is a decided ambiguity about Elizabethan propriety. The poetry of the period praises male beauty and elegance, not handsomeness or strength.

During the early decades of the seventeenth century in London, a series of pamphlets appeared which have never been reprinted. Their titles indicate that they were published as part of a debate about propriety in fashion. The first is called *Hic Mulier: Or, the Man Woman, Being a Medicine to cure the Disease in the Masculine Feminine of our Times*. It was answered by a piece called *Muld Sack: Or, the Apologie of Hic Mulier to the late Declamation against her,* and another defense appeared the same year called *Haec Vir: Or, the Womanish Man, Being an Answer to a Late Booke intitled Hic Mulier*. Without extensively digressing, a brief summary of the initial attack argues that men dress effeminately because women are so unfeminine. It is basically an attack on women who cut their hair short and whose costumes were deviant, those who wore a kind of pantaloon, perhaps for riding or even simple convenience. The anonymous author says that such women usurp masculine modes of dress which encourages a converse perversity in men, effeminate fashion. The two responses defend the new styles; one is by a woman (though the writer could have been a man), and one by the frankly womanish man. The texts are difficult to follow, somewhat illegible, and local in their allusions, requiring some first-rate scholarship to be fully understood.

What I saw in these arguments about masculinity and femininity seemed very contemporary, except that the butch woman and effeminate man could boldly defend themselves in print. The history of deviance is a sketchy document. I would only add that it is a history belonging to a class: Jacobean costume with its ambivalences was an aristocratic luxury, and what is permitted those with money and power is often the exception rather than the rule of social convention.

It is not appropriate nor within my skill to examine the history of a complicated society whose resemblances to our own are conjectural, but I do want to place the issue of social drag in a context that shows it has long roots. In contemporary American society, the most radical statements about clothing and gender as sexual issues are not upper-class explorations, but lower-class, *Lumpenproletariat* ones. It is the street queen of New York and San Francisco and every gay community who defies all the proprieties, even those of traditional gay drag.

No one deplores the street queen in his drag more than the theatrical transvestite. There is the disdain of the professional for the amateur, and also the disapproval of conservative men with rigid definitions of the propriety of drag for those whose lives are governed by impulsive feeling. However, the greatest gap in understanding between those who make their living from drag and those for whom drag is their lives occurs in their attitudes toward being homosexual. The stage queen needs to institutionalize his desire to dress in drag, to give it both form and some dubious status, if only among gay men. He accepts the marginality of gay life, and his sole protest is in the complicated camp meanings of dress that he exploits. He is a minor commentator on modern ideas of gender, acquiescent about masculinity and satiric about femininity. The stage queen dramatizes his awareness of his own effeminacy, protesting in camp his society's contempt for him. He converts behavior he has not really chosen into criticism: he says I am this way because I cannot help it, but your contempt is unfair; would I not have been otherwise if I could have helped it? When the performer stands before his audience still in his makeup and four-inch heels, mesh opera stockings, sequined G-string that utterly suppresses the genital bulge, but bare and flat-chested with his wig in his hands, he says of course I am really male if not masculine, but he has also submitted to the authority of conventional ideas about gender. His professionalism demands it; the performance must come to an end despite the nuances of the script. The protest lasts only as long as he performs.

But the street queen has no propriety or decorum or definitions at all. He lives by powerful feelings he neither denies nor limits to an occupation. His drag is his sense of self. Like the transsexual, the street transvestite creates himself in drag, and his costume is as original as his self-concept. There seem to be two types of street queens, pre- and post-Stonewall. The former were often lost in self-hatred, abandoned to masochism; their only hope was to become transsexuals. They were nelly, often hustlers, and a few could pass as female prostitutes specializing in oral sex. The life was transient, drug- and crime-infested, despairing and often short.

The new street queen is post-Stonewall. Much of the life is still the same, except the despair is now informed with rage, as shown in an interview in *The Village Voice* with Marsha P. Johnson, née Malcolm Michaels. Marsha or Silvia Rivera are men whose lives are implicitly political and defiant and who are the *sans-cullottes* of gay liberation. Marsha P. ("Pay It No Mind") Johnson can usually be found somewhere near Christopher Street or the West Street docks, usually impoverished and aggressively sure of himself. He sometimes hustles for his money while Andy Warhol's silkscreen print of him sells for $1,400 in Christopher Street galleries. Unlike Holly Woodlawn whom Warhol also helped to infamy, Marsha is always broke and never elegant, soignée, or glamorous. Marsha was one of the original founders of STAR (Street Transvestite Action Revolutionaries), and when that group became defunct, he carried a banner in the Gay Pride Parade that read Gay Poor People. Recently, the banner has been an innocuous Gay Love, as if to tell how tired Marsha is of a struggle that is usually as violent in confrontation with other homosexuals as with heterosexuals, though more than a hundred arrests in seventeen years is nothing to dismiss lightly. Marsha's confrontations are often with gay bartenders who refuse to serve him in gay bars in Greenwich Village, and these are not just the leather bars with their strict dress code requirements. Homosexuals detest Marsha, and the irritation he provokes is as likely to be among political militants as among the politically indifferent. Feminists and lesbians object to all men in drag as offensive to women, which I think is the least thought-out and most priggish of statements. Militants who are proud of being gay are not proud of Marsha.

But he is the sum of oppression and alienation in America: poor, black, homosexual, deviant by any standard, but defiant and utterly unremorseful. He cannot even pass: his six-foot frame is well-muscled, his large features undisguisable by makeup. For Marsha, there is no alternative to homosexuality and to his own statement about maleness. In his refusal to do anything but what he chooses, except when he is at Rikers Island or Bellevue, he is completely nonconformist. Neither masculine nor feminine, he makes his living selling sex; he is famous and destitute; he can always be found in the gay ghetto, but he has no home. He has disavowed every social idea of masculinity, conventionality, normality, and success, and his existence disquiets nearly everyone. But he refuses to accept the limitations for blacks, for men, for black men, for homosexual men that we are all supposed to come to terms with. It is no wonder some in the gay culture wish to canonize him, not because he is a martyr but because he has survived.

The insistence of such a person is more than an eccentricity of urban life; his biography is a history of the breakdown of social convention, and while it is a life whose drama makes the street its stage, it is a revolutionary one that says one cannot end the performance for the convenience of the audience.

Marsha and other street queens like him lead lives antithetical to those of transsexuals who accept their society but not themselves, though both have in common their passion to create themselves, one defying nature and the other defying civilization. In none of their lives is the message clear for the rest of us, except that as things have been, life is not reasonably supportable.

One of the most moving of Jan Morris' statements in her autobiography is, "I wear the body of a woman." This seems to concentrate layers of meaning in both its simplicity and pathos. It is the frankest confession of the kinship between the transsexual and the transvestite for whom having the appearance of a woman is the central ambition. For one, success is achieved through costume, but for the other, the body itself becomes the costume. It is entirely accurate that the image of this struggle is an idea of clothing which itself is a prominent symbol of civilization, of social man, whose contrast is the natural naked savage. In clothing we express gender, the sense of our sexualness, our sensibility and taste, our class or ethnos, and often even our occupation. Is there anything as expressive as clothing for most people?

Most of all, in clothes we tell the world what we think of it and of ourselves in it. For most of us, clothing is an area of our lives where we are least likely to be nonconformist no matter how unconventional the rest of our lives may be. Thus, feminist women may suffer the return of high heels, gay liberationists sheepishly don the uniform of the moment. How we dress tells instantly what we think of ourselves, of our affection or self-dislike. To wear the right clothes sometimes seems the only reliable reconciliation with society; in such conformity, at any cost of price and pain, is a relief from the ultimate suffering of feeling alienated from the world which too often is translated and experienced as the belief that one is alienated from oneself.

CHAPTER SIX

Where Have All the Sissies Gone?
The New Masculinity of Gay Men

1

One week after Labor Day 1977, I made a trip to the Anvil Bar, a gay club in New York City. For a long time I had wanted to know whether the legends of debauchery one heard with some skepticism were accurate. No one I knew was a member, and I had been told by those who claimed to be informed that I was not a likely type to crash successfully. I presumed they meant that my only leather jacket, tailored like a blazer, would not pass muster. Then a close friend became enamored of a go-go boy who danced there, joined the Anvil, and took me along to meet Daniel.

The bar nearly lived up to its fame. The boys do dance continually on top of the four-sided bar; they do strip naked, not counting construction shoes or cock rings. There is a back room where no-nonsense, hard-core porno films silently and continually flicker, shown by a mezmerized projectionist wearily perched on the ledge of the back wall. A small pitch-dark cubicle called the fuck room opens off the rear wall. In the middle of the front-room bar is a stage raised five feet where fist-fucking demonstrations used to be held at 3 A.M. if the crowd was enthusiastic, but those spontaneous shows were stopped when they began to draw tourists from the uptown discos. Now it is used by the dancers who take turns exhibiting their specialities in the limelight. The boys range from extraordinary to middling, from high-schoolers to forty-year-olds, from professionals (everything) to amateurs who move awkwardly but who are graceful and stunning when they don't move at all. There are types for every taste and some for none. Hispanic and black, WASP and Italian, the boys dance three hours of a six-hour stint for $25 a night, three or four times a week. There are always new faces, and the management is liberal about letting anyone with a good body try out. Usually, there is one dancer who has had some ballet training and is naive enough to make that clear; he is invariably the least favored by the clientele.

My friend's Daniel is unusual. He is one of the few boys who can use the trapeze bars bolted to the ceiling with real expertise. Without breaking the rhythm of his dance, he leaps for a trapeze and spends four or five minutes hanging on or swinging from one bar to another in the most daring manner. When he alights, it is with a sure flip back onto the bar where he continues to dance with an unbroken stride. Daniel has never fallen, as some of the boys have (a broken nose or a fractured arm is not unheard of), nor has he crashed into a customer since he holds his drugs well.

His other speciality is his ability to grab with his buttocks the folded one- dollar or five-dollar tips the men at the bar hold between their teeth, a variation on the skill of the Cotton Club girls of Harlem in the twenties and thirties. His perfect behind descends in time to the music over the customer's uplifted face, and there is a round of applause when the money disappears into those constricted rosy cheeks.

Like most of the clientele, Daniel looks like a college athlete or con-struction worker, two favored images these recent seasons. Clothed, he wears the uniform of the moment: cheap plaid flannel shirts and jeans, or if it is really warm just overalls, and boots or construction worker's shoes no matter what the weather is. With the first signs of frost, boots and heavy leather bomber jackets are *de rigueur*.

Daniel is also typical of one type of club client in that he is a maso-chist, a "slave" who sleeps with other men only with the permission of his master (who instructs him to charge a hefty fee). While Daniel's maso-chism has taken a pecuniary turn, he is not really a whore, for he is indifferent to money, keeping only what he needs for his uppers and pop-pers, his grass and coke. He dances frenetically four nights a week and does what he is told because he finds that exciting. There is little that he has not experienced sexually, and at twenty-two, his tastes are now as perverse as the possibilities Western civilization has devised.

To look at him, one would hardly suspect that this Irish kid from Queens with his thatch of reddish hair, cowlick and all, this sweet-faced boy built like a swimmer in his blue-collar uniform, lives a life more sexually extreme than anything described by the Marquis de Sade. When he discusses his life, it appears to be an endless dirty movie, but the anecdotes tend to leave his listeners in a moral vacuum. While it is possible to become erotically excited hearing his adventures, it is difficult to judge them without feeling prudish. Conventional moral standards are tangential, psychological ones almost as irrelevant. One is not really shocked; rather, he feels adrift, puzzled, perhaps bemused. Most of all, this nice boy seems very remote.

The values of his generation, acted out as theater of the absurd, are even more histrionic in Daniel's life. Just as one does not view experimental theater or avant-garde art expecting it to live up to the standards of naturalism, one does not try to understand Daniel's life from the lessons of one's own experience: the collective sanity of the past is momentarily dumb.

What one struggled to learn and call "adult" as the final approbation now looks somewhat priggish. If one wanted to use such standards, why go to the Anvil at all? But once he *is* there, or at the Mine Shaft or any of a half-dozen bars just like them, what does he use to understand this spectacle of men? Some like myself are clearly audience at a drama where only the actors understand the play. Intuition is not trustworthy, and easy judgments make one feel like a tourist. But whether or not one wishes to refrain from judgment, one thing is clear, if not glaring. The universal stance is a studied masculinity. There are no limp wrists, no giggles, no indiscreet hips swiveling. Walk, talk, voice, costume, grooming are just right: this is macho country. It is a rigorous place where one destroys himself in drugs and sexual humiliation.

The same impulses are evident in other scenes. Fire Island Pines is as besotted and extreme as the leather and Levis world, and often they overlap, but the Pines is playful. Like its shabbier neighbor Cherry Grove, the Pines enjoys the long legacy of camp. It loves to dictate next year's chic to café society, for novelty, flair, and sophistication are as paramount in this scene as they are in the world of women's fashion. For a time, the place seemed to veer toward egalitarianism; only youthful beauty was required if one were not rich. But with inflation, the freeloading beauty has to be spectacular indeed. The dance halls of the Pines and the Grove, like the waterfront bars, are filled with handsome men posing in careful costumes, and no matter how elegant or expensive, they are all butch.

As a matter of fact, young gay men seem to have abjured effeminacy with universal success. Muscular bodies laboriously cultivated all year round are standard; youthful athletic agility is everyone's style. The volleyball game on the beach is no longer a camp classic; now it takes itself as seriously as the San Francisco gay softball team. Hardness is in.

But talk to these men, sleep with them, befriend them, and the problems are the old familiar ones: misery when in love, loneliness when one is not, frustration and ambitiousness at work, and a monumental self-centeredness that exacerbates the rest. These have been the archetypes of unhappiness in homosexual America for as long as I can remember.

What is different from anything else I remember, however, is the relentless pursuit of masculinity. There are no limits; the most oppressive images of sexual violence and dominance are adopted unhesitatingly. Though the neo-Nazi adorations—fascinating fascism as Susan Sontag termed them—are more sinister than the innocuous ideals of the weight-lifting room, they are equally mindless. The offense is not aesthetic; it is entirely political. The homosexuals who adopt images of masculinity, conveying their desire for power and their belief in its beauty, are in fact eroticizing the very values of straight society that have tyrannized their own lives. It is the tension between this style and the content of their lives that demands the oblivion of drugs and sexual libertinism. In the past, the duplicity of closeted lives found relief in effeminate camping; now the suppression or denial of the moral issue in their choice is far more damaging. The perversity of imitating their oppressors guarantees that such blindness will work itself out as self-contempt.

2

This is the central message of the macho bar world: manliness is the only real virtue; other values are contemptible. And manliness is not some philosophical notion or psychological state; it is not even morally related to behavior. It lies exclusively in the glamorization of physical strength.

This idea of masculinity is so conservative it is almost primitive. That homosexuals are attracted to it and find it gratifying is not a total surprise. Gay male sexual preference has always favored a butch boyish beauty, and only in artistic or intellectual circles has beauty been allowed a certain feyness. Butchness is always relative; the least swishy man in the room is the most butch. It usually meant one looked straight, one could pass. In the past, an over-enthusiasm for butchness translated itself into a taste for rough trade. Those who were too frightened or sane to pursue that particular quarry could always find a gay partner who would accommodatingly act the part.

There is a special eroticism in the experience of pretending to be degraded that is by no means rare in adult sexual behavior of whatever persuasion. The homosexual whose erotic feelings are enhanced by the illusion that his partner holds him in contempt, who is thrilled when told his ass or mouth is just like a cunt, is involved in a complicated self-deception. What appears to be happening is a homosexual variation of masochism: the contempt of the "straight" partner emblazes gay self-contempt, which in turn is exploited as an aphrodisiac. Why this process works is less clear than how it does.

The complex tie between the need for degradation and sexual excitement has never been satisfactorily explored, though Freud began the effort over eighty years ago and writers and artists have always intuitively understood it. It seems to be prominent in societies that are advanced, where sexual mores are liberal or ambivalent, and where intellectual life is very sophisticated. In times like ours, when women are redefining their roles and images, men must also redefine theirs. As women forego in dress and appearance the *style* of their oppression (it is the easiest to abandon and thus one of the first aspects to go), and as glamour falls under a suspicious light, men, increasingly accused of being the symbol of sexism, are forced to confront their own ideas of masculinity.

While straight men define their ideas from a variety of sources (strength, achievement, success, money), two of those sources are always their attitudes toward women and toward paternity. It is no coincidence that the same decade that popularized liberation for women and announced that the nuclear family was a failure also saw men return to a long-haired, androgynous style. If straight men are confused about their maleness, what is the dilemma for gay men, who rarely did more than imitate these ideas?

It is no accident that the macho gesture is always prominent in those gay bars and resorts where women are entirely absent. Certain gay locales have always catered exclusively to one sex: porno movie houses and book-stores, baths, public toilets. The new bars are often private clubs as much for the sake of legally barring women as for screening male customers. Their atmosphere is eerily reminiscent of the locker room. And, of course, while they are there, the men live as if there were no women in the world. This is a useful illusion. It allows some of them to get gang-banged in the back rooms and still evade the self-reproach that derives from the world's contempt for homosexual men who behave sexually like women. If there are no women in the world, some men simply must replace them. With women absent, whether one is sexually active or passive is no longer the great dividing issue.

In fact, some of the men who look most butch are the most liberated in bed, the least role-oriented. While there is still much role preference for passivity, it no longer has the clear quality it had in the past. Then, gay men made unmistakable announcements: those who liked to be fucked adopted effeminate mannerisms; those who were active tried to look respectable.

Quentin Crisp in his autobiography *The Naked Civil Servant* epito-mized these attitudes. He documents the anger of an acquaintance railing over the misfortune of having picked up a young soldier who wanted to be fucked: "All of a sudden, he turned over. After all I'd done—flitting about the room in my wrap . . . camping myself silly. My dear, I was disgusted." Today, to replace the usually reliable information that straight or campy behavior conveyed in the past, gay men at the leather bars have taken to elaborate clothing signals: key chains or handkerchiefs drooping from left or right pocket in blue or yellow or red all have coded meanings. Occasion-ally, some of the *cognoscenti* lie and misalliances occur. Of course, one could ask a prospective partner what his preferences are, but that is the least likely behavior between strangers.

If I am critical of the present style, it is not because I advocate a return to the denigrations of the past. Quentin Crisp's rebelliousness testifies to the hourly misery of gay life when all the sexual roles are petrified. He considered all his friends "pseudo men in search of pseudo women." That is not an improvement on pseudo men in search of nothing. Nor is his sense of inferiority: "I regard all heterosexuals, however low, as superior to any homosexual, however noble." Such estimates were commonplace for men subjected to lifelong ridicule because they could not or would not disguise their effeminacy.

But camping for Crisp and for the entire homosexual world until the end of the 1950s was not just the expression of self-contempt by men pretending to be women and feeling pseudo as both. Camping also gave homosexual men an *exclusive* form of behavior that neither women nor straight men could adopt. Some women and straight men are camp, but that is another story.

Camping in the gay world did not mean simply behaving in a blatantly effeminate manner; that was camp only when performed in the presence of those it irritated or threatened or delighted. Swishing is effective only if someone else notices, preferably registering a sense of shock, or ideally, outrage. In discreet bars like The Blue Parrot in 1950, men impeccably Brooks Brothers and as apparently WASP as one's banker could, in a flicker, slide into limpness. They had available a persona that mixed ironic distance, close observation, and wit, all allies of sanity.

Camping did express self-denigration, but it was a complex criticism. For example, the women whom these men imitated were themselves extraordinary; androgynous idols like Garbo or Dietrich symbolized an ambiguous and amoral sexuality. But more important, in their campy behavior, gay men revealed an empathic observation of women and feminine interests.

When camping also released for gay men some of their anger at their closeted lives, it became a weapon as well as a comment. The behavior chosen for imitation or ridicule was usually evidence of sexist attitudes, of positions women had taken or were forced to take that had effeminized them out of their humanity. It is for this reason that feminists object to drag queens who still try to resemble the slavish emblems of the past, and their criticism would be valid if the imitations were sincere. But men in drag are not swept up in the delusion that they are women; only insane men in drag believe that. The rest are committed to ambiguity; they are neither men nor women and are only rarely androgynous—the aura of drag is neuter.

When a gay man said, "Oh, Mary, come off it," he was sneering at pretension, self-deceit, or prudery. That it took the form of reminding one's fellow faggot that he was in reality no better than a woman, and often not as good with his "pseudo" sexual equipment, is not politically commendable, but why should gay men have had a special consciousness about sexism? At least they had a sure recognition of it: they imitated women because they understood that they were victims in sisterhood of the same masculine ideas about sexuality. Generations of women defined themselves entirely in men's terms, and homosexual men often seemed to accept the same values.

But there was also a chagrined recognition that they just could not live up to expectations. They could not be men as heterosexuals defined manhood; most of all they could not be men because they did not sleep with women or beget children. No amount of manliness could counterbalance that. Between the values of virility that they did not question and their rage at having no apparent alternatives, gay men would camp out their frustration. It was not a particularly effective means of ending oppression, but it was a covert defiance of a society that humiliated them.

With the political and social changes of the sixties, a new androgyny seemed to be on the verge of life. Heterosexual and homosexual suddenly became less interesting than just sexual. Getting out of the closet was more than announcing one was gay; it was a pronouncement that one was free of sexual shame. The new mood fostered this: even straight boys looked prettier than girls. The relief at seeing male vanity in the open, surrendered to and accepted, made it possible for homosexuals to reconsider some of their attitudes toward themselves. It was no longer extraordinary to look effeminate in a world where most sexual men looked feminine and where sexually liberated women were the antithesis of the glamorous and fragile.

Sexual style had become a clear political issue. Conventional manliness was properly identified with reaction and repression. The enemy had a crewcut, was still posturing in outmoded chivalric stances, while his wife and daughter and son embraced the revolutionary notion of rolelessness. To some extent, this is where American society still is: searching for a sense of what roles, if any, are appropriate for adult men and women. Only the betrayed patriarch still refuses to acknowledge the permanence of these changes, since for him they are pure deprivations, erosions of his long, long privilege.

3

"Feminist" is a term that increasing numbers of gay men apply to themselves as they come to recognize the common oppression of homosexuals and women. The empathy of gay men in the past is the foundation for this newer understanding, and it is heartening to discover that a mutual sense of victimization need not always lead to self-denigration. If in the past women were less likely to feel self-contempt at being women than gay men felt at being homosexual, it was partly because women were rewarded for their acquiescence and partly because they did not have to experience the sense of having betrayed their birthright. Homosexual men usually gave up paternity as well as other prerogatives for their gayness and too often felt gypped for what they got. They exchanged the simplicity of being phallic oppressors for advantages much more dubious, and the sense that they had betrayed their best interests was haunting. As more gays come to realize the bankruptcy of conventional ideas of masculinity, it is easier for them to forego the sexism they shared with heterosexual men.

Unfortunately, heterosexuals cling to their sexual definitions with even greater tenacity. For example, the Save Our Children slogan is not as banal as it sounds; the phobic hostility behind it expresses a genuine fear that some children will be lost, lost to patriarchy, to the values of the past, to the perpetuation of conventional ideas of men and women. There is a fear of homosexuality that is far beyond what the surface can explain.

Many gays, especially apolitical ones, are dismissive of Anita Bryant and what she represents. Remarks like "Straights will just have to hope that heterosexuality can hold its own on the open market" express a contempt for the fears, but not much understanding of them. It *is* puzzling: where does this idea of the frailty of heterosexuality come from, the assumption that a mere knowledge that teachers or ordinary people are gay will automatically seduce children? It comes from the panic about new sexual ideas, but most of all, about the identity of women.

It often sounds absurd when conservatives accuse feminist women of attempting to destroy the family, though it does not stop them from making the accusation. It is easier to appear sensible talking about the seduction of children by homosexuals. I suggest that much of the recent vehemence about the children is deflected from a much more central rage against women who are redefining their ideas about childrearing. The political issue is always hottest when women and their connection with motherhood is raised. Thus, the issues of childrearing and anti-abortion gather a conservative support that puzzles liberal America. What these issues have in common is the attempt of women to free themselves from conventional roles, crucially their roles as mothers. That liberation is the first wave; the secondary one, far more perilous, lies beneath the surface: it demands that men liberate themselves from their notions as well, since the central ideas about masculinity have always been related to the unquestioned responsibilities of men as husbands and fathers.

Curiously, lesbians are never mentioned when child molestation is raised as an issue, and when lesbians are attacked, as they were at Houston, it is in relation to their militant feminism, not in relation to their being school teachers. Lesbians have usually been exempt from heterosexual fears about seduction, partly because they are women and, like all women, traditionally powerless. When they are attacked, when the press notices lesbian issues, it is often in connection with custody cases. There the issue of saving the children for heterosexuality and precisely for patriarchy is clear. These lesbians who once lived as straight women, who married and had children, are objects of the most extreme wrath, and one which has used the judicial system as its instrument to punish them.

But most lesbians are not mothers, and most lesbian mothers do not end up, thankfully, as victims in custody hearings. Lesbians are usually dismissed as unimportant, as nuisances. It is the lowest rung on the ladder of social contempt. But gay men who have abdicated their privileges, who have made sexual desire a higher priority than power over women, are indeed not men at all.

Bryant's keynote is that homosexuals should return to the closet. That would solve the problem for straights, since it is *visibility* that is terrifying. To be openly gay without contrition or guilt or shame is to testify that there are viable alternative sexual styles. But the real alternative for the children is not necessarily homosexuality; it is to reject the old verities of masculine and feminine.

Ironically, the men at the Anvil have not rejected those verities at all. Their new pseudo-masculinity is a precise response to the confusions of a society venturing toward sexual redefinition. But it is in its way as reactionary as the hysteria that Anita Bryant's campaign consolidated.

The men of the macho bars will not buy Quentin Crisp's book, or if they do, they will not read it sympathetically, whereas they are part of the audience that made David Kopay's story a best seller. I do not want to belittle Kopay's modest effort, but its success depends more on his image than on his courage. Effeminate men like Crisp who have the courage to defy society are eccentric; butch men are heroic. Of course, what is left unsaid is that Kopay could have passed: no one would have known if he hadn't told them, and having once announced it, he can still pass. What could sissies like Crisp do even if they didn't flaunt it? Quentin Crisp's *life* is an act of courage.

Leonard Matlovich is also a respectable image. When media reporters treat him and Kopay just like the mainstream Americans they have always been, they make a point many gays approve of: homosexual men are really like everyone else. If beneath Matlovich's conservative, bemedalled chest beat aberrant yearnings, the public, if not the army, can accommodate them. What makes Kopay and Matlovich seem acceptable to gays and straights alike, while the Quentin Crisps remain pitiful?

Crisp was defiant and miserable, an acknowledged victim, and unrepentant: it was all agony, but it couldn't have been any other way. Even more, Crisp made his sexuality the obsession of his life. His whole existence was devoted to proclaiming his homosexuality; it is the meaning of his life. Today, his heir is Daniel, who is as absorbed in the same singular definition of himself. Daniel's life seems consecrated to pleasure while Crisp's was miserable, and that is an enormous difference. But the source of his pleasures in sexuality is as extreme, as dangerous and defiant as the quest for pleasure in Crisp's life. I may feel that Crisp is morally superior because he has suffered and Daniel refuses to, but that is only a sentimental notion. What is stunning in both their lives is the exclusivity of sexuality, and while Daniel is not heroic, his life demands that one refrain from easy judgment. The drama of such displays is filled with meaning for them and us. These lives are not like others'.

Kopay and Matlovich are fighting to be like everyone else. They claim that they are just like other football players or professional soldiers, and I do not dispute them. Compared to their conventionality, their homosexuality is almost incidental. Neither of them has gotten off quite free, nor have they seemed to expect to. For reasons they articulate with unquestionable credibility, they could not tolerate the duplicity of being conservative, rather ordinary men and secret homosexuals. Ironically, to some extent they have now become extraordinary men if somewhat common-place homosexuals.

The men in leather watching naked go-go boys and having sex in back-room bars are not like Crisp or Daniel whom they regard as a kind of erotic theater; they are much closer to Kopay and Matlovich with whom they can identify. The rock-bottom premise of such sympathy is that all forms of traditional masculinity are respectable; all symptoms of effeminacy are contemptible. Real sexual extremism, like Daniel's, belongs to a nether-world; it is not regarded as liberated but as libertine. Daniel is the complete sexual object, and his presence makes the bar world the psychological equivalent of the brothel for the men who watch him. He turns them on, and then they can play whore or client or both.

Most men who are ardent for leather defend it as play. Dressing butch is another version of the gay uniform. What is the harm of walking through the world dressed like a construction worker? What does it matter what costume you wear to the ball? Go as Cinderella's fairy godmother, and you may break the law. But go as Hell's Angels, and you risk breaking your own spirit.

It is not coincidence that in the macho bar world and the libertine baths the incidence of impotence is so high that it is barely worth remark-ing, or that gay men increasingly rely on the toys and trappings of sado-masochism. It is not irrelevant that the new gay image of virility is most often illustrated in pornography.

Manly means hot, and hot is everything. Why then isn't it working better? Men tell me that I do not appreciate this new celebration of mascu-linity, that I am overlooking the important "fact": "We fell for masculinity when we were twelve; there must be something to it because it made us gay. Most of us didn't become gay because we fell in love with sissies; we became sissies because we fell in love with men, usually jocks."

It sounds familiar. And so what if one chooses to make one's life pornographic? Isn't that only the most recent version of sexual devotion, of incarnating Eros in one's life? Besides, it's too late to be a do-gooder. Obviously, as soon as one sets up notions of propriety, no matter how well intended, they will be preempted by the worst, most coercive forces in our society. One is then forced to accept all choices of style; the alternative is to find oneself allied with oppression. In the arena of sexual politics, there is the left and the right. Those who think they are in the middle will ultimately discover that the center is the right.

But my feelings tell me that there is another version; that macho is somehow another closet, and not a new one—many have suspected that it's the oldest closet in the house. Macho cultures have always had more covert homosexuality. Without belaboring the analogy, there is one consistency. In those cultures, homosexuality is not a sexual identity; it is defined as role. Only the passive partner, which means anally passive or orally active, is homosexual; the other role is reserved for men, because one either is a man or he is not; that is, he is a woman, and a woman who cannot bear a child and attest to a man's virility is beneath contempt, at best a whore.

The men in the macho bars are not like this. They have adopted a style and abandoned its psychic origin in sexual role playing. Apparently, they have rescued the best and discarded the worst. But it is an appearance that resonates with unexamined yearnings. It says I am strong and I am free, that gay no longer means the contemptibleness of being nelly, which is the old powerless *reactiveness* to oppression. In so far as it does that— strong is better than weak, free is always good—it is an improvement on the past. But it claims more: it says that this is a choice, a proper fulfillment of those initial desires that led us to love men, and even at its oddest, it is only playful.

But it is not free, not strong, and it is dangerous play. It is dangerous to dress up like one's enemy, and worse, it can tie one to him as helplessly as ever. It still says that he, the powerful brute, is the definer, to which we then react. It is the other side of nelly, and more helpless because it denies that one is helpless at all. Effeminacy acknowledged the rage of being oppressed in defiance; macho denies that there *is* rage and oppression. The strength of those new bodies is a costume designed for sexual allure and for the discotheque. Passing for the enemy does not exempt one from the wrath. Men in leather are already the easiest marks for violent teenagers on a drunken rampage in Greenwich Village or on Mission Street on a Saturday night. Macho is another illusion. The lessons of Negroes who disliked blackness or Jews who insisted they were assimilated, really *German,* are ignored. To some whites, everything not white is black; to Nazis, Jews are Jews, sidelocks or no. Telling the enemy one is as good as he is because one is like him does not appease; often it makes him more vicious, furious because somehow his victim seems to approve his scorn. And the freedom—that too is illusory except as sexual taste. In that area alone, there has been real change. Compared to their counterparts in the past gay men today have found a freedom to act out their erotic tastes. But taste is not a choice; usually, it is a tyrant.

Homosexuals at their most oppressed have not been in love with men; they have been in love with masculinity. The politics of the New Left and the sexual aesthetics of androgyny have not lasted, but they seemed to be offering alternatives that were authentic, better choices than the ones we had. The new style seems both inauthentic and barely better than the old options. Sometimes it seems worse.

That is what is disturbing and enraging: to find it the growing choice in the 1980s. Does it seriously matter that some men choose to imitate their worst enemies? What is remarkable about such an old story? For one, it is so unnecessary. For the first time in modern history, there are real options for gays. The sissies in The Blue Parrot had little choice other than to stay home. They could only pretend their lives were ordinary. That pretense was survival, but one that led fatally to rage and self-contempt. The theatricality of camping helped keep some santiy and humanity because it was an awareness of one's helplessness. Macho values are the architects of closeted lives, and adopting that style is the opposite of awareness. Whatever its ironies, they are not critical ones.

Happily, gay men are less helpless than they have ever been before, and because of that they are more threatened. What is worth affirming is not bravura, but political alliance with women and with a whole liberal America that is dedicated to freedom of personal choice. *That* is worth celebrating.

CHAPTER SEVEN

Sexual Pioneers or Uncle Tom's Bondage:
S-M, F-F, ETC.

Ten years ago at Fire Island Pines, Ethan, one of the men I shared a house with, began to experiment with fist-fucking. Ten years ago, in the waterfront bars, gay men began to adopt a sinister allure with the trappings and toys of leather, the look of Hell's Angels. Ten years ago, the riots at the Stonewall Bar also inaugurated gay liberation. These events are not coincidental; in fact, the experience of political liberation has been translated into sexual terms, stimulating new explorations of perversity among homosexuals. It is too simple to call it a precocious backlash, but the first significant steps gays have taken toward the political and social control of their lives have been shadowed by experiments transforming fantasies of power and powerlessness into new sensual experiences, ones in which the need to feel utterly passive and thus without moral or psychological responsibility have acquired unprecedented erotic interest.

Sadomasochism has been a seductive subject for psychologists and intellectuals since the eighteenth century. Fist-fucking, known affectionately as fisting, hand-balling, or punching, has emerged as a variety of sexual pleasure only in the last decade. The existence of wall paintings in the ruins of Pompeii that show figures engaged in fisting is rumored among the men who practice it, though I have never seen Pompeii or such illustrations. They would not surprise me; Rome probably exceeded even our own culture in its fascination with mixing pain and pleasure, violence and eroticism, sexual boredom and outrageous sexual variety. One of the moralists of Augustus' reign, the Golden Age, remarked with distaste on the practice of some wealthy matrons of keeping a resident flogger among the household.

Psychologists like Freud and Theodor Reik have been interested in sadomasochism because they regard it as so widely practiced, the most prevalent heterosexual perversity, and because the literature—beginning with the work of de Sade—is so ample, they have been able to discourse upon it in a context that is historical and cultural; long before psychology claimed to be a science, sadomasochism was a well-documented perversion. Recently, intellectuals like Georges Bataille, Gilles Deleuze, and Michel Foucault have seen in the subject meanings more central to the history of sexuality and the relationship of sexuality to culture than have been speculated on before. The ideas are indeed provocative, central to our notions of emotional well-being and sexual freedom and fulfillment: ideas of passivity and dominance, sexual boredom and sexual anxiety, the unpredictability of erotic excitement, the need for fantasy that dwells on the taboo, the need to liberate the self from guilt and anomie.

I am concerned with the subject because of its growing prominence in gay culture, emerging from its closetry in every major gay ghetto, and because it relates to the idea of sexual freedom that is the central issue of gay history. I am not really interested in moralistic judgments about the perverse, but I am interested in clarifying how aggressiveness signifies for gay men, how fantasies of dominion and helplessness, erotic visions of power, are mirrors and dreams of their sense of powerlessness in the larger world. In their desire for and fear of power, their relationship to passivity and to self-control, and their ambivalence about responsibility for their own lives, gay men enact many of the motifs of sadomasochism.

1

The subject is sensational and it is hard to write about with genuine detachment. Of all the topics I am exploring, it is the most confusing, the most difficult to make sense of. But it is also the one that contrasts most dramatically the fantasy of powerlessness and the fact of it in gay life.

Diana Trilling, reviewing J. R. Ackerly's *My Father and Myself* ("Our Uncomplaining Homosexuals" *We Must March My Darlings,* 1978), praised the book highly for its simplicity and lack of sensationalism in depicting what it is like to be homosexual. She added, "Presumably, if we are honest about our sexual selves, we cannot be false to any man or woman and we are on the way to saying something useful about the general life of feeling, perhaps even about the general life of mankind."

The dictionary is a lot clearer about perversion than psychology texts; it says, "an aberrant sexual practice habitually preferred to normal coitus." Unfortunately, it has nothing to say about normal coitus. By such a definition, perversion is hardly a static condition. Any variety of sexual play including most foreplay, if it did not lead to heterosexual male orgasm, might be perverse. The best synonyms Merriam-Webster supplies are "incorrect, improper, obstinate in opposing what is right, reasonable, or accepted." What is right is a matter for philosophers; what is reasonable or accepted is something most adults are fully qualified to judge. This obstinate opposition to reasonableness and conventionality is what intellectuals find so fascinating about the subject, particularly about the life and work of de Sade. This opposition as erotic rebellion outrages most people because it aspires to experience sexuality as taboo, to transgress violently what is interdicted.

In *Story of the Eye* by Georges Bataille, the narrator champions indecency as necessary to sharpen perception: "To others, the universe seems decent, because decent people have gelded eyes." Peter Brooks, reviewing the book *(The New York Times,* February 12, 1978), finds it a serious examination of eroticism as "an encounter with death and evil, to the realization of man's most liberating and frightening capacities." Simone de Beauvoir, in her essay *Must We Burn de Sade?* also sees his life, even more than his work, as an example of these capacities. Michel Foucault in *Madness and Civilization* and his more recent *History of Sexuality,* Volume I: An Introduction is also interested in these capacities.

At the moment, Foucault is probably the most influential writer on the history of sexuality, and some of his ideas are very provocative. In *Madness and Civilization,* he insists that sadism appeared precisely at the end of the eighteenth century with the man whose name created the word. In sadism, which infers masochism—except for Deleuze—Foucault finds a transformation in the imagination of Western civilization, one in which love and death enter "an insane dialogue . . . (on) the limitless presumption of appetite." It is almost as if the paradoxes of Christianity and the glorification of suffering were to be finally understood exclusively in sensual terms.

Freud is less flamboyant, but he also finds masochism and its lesser counterpart, sadism, rooted in the struggle between love and death, Eros and Thanatos, in a theater where the two most profound human instincts are embattled. Freud is very precise about masochism as simply passive sadism, normal aggression turned violently against the self. For a moment these two psychic forces cooperate in sexual obsession: the sadistic energy as part of the life force, the masochistic passivity the emblem of non-being, of death. Freud's view, which I shall return to shortly, would disagree in an important respect with Foucault's: if this erotic conflict is instinctual, it was not born with the life of de Sade.

Foucault is interested in sexual repression and sexual freedom which he finds modern society meaninglessly preoccupied with. In *The History of Sexuality,* he tries to account for the repressiveness by two changes in the culture relating to ideas of procreation and sin. First, religious authority eroded and the sense of the power of sin weakened; second, the attitudes toward procreation in Western society have changed. Both have led to replacing the idea of the soul with the idea of the body. In the Renaissance and the seventeenth century, the soul dwelt as a guest in the house of the body, and often it was a strange dwelling. In modern times, the body simply has become the soul.

Carnal behavior and emotional health become linked in a new way, with a new importance that leads to new authorities—the psychiatric, the medical, the legal—on sexual issues. Finally, Foucault adds, the modern need to "know," to have sexual knowledge, makes us even more dependent on authority than before to interpret the meaning of our sexuality: "Understanding about us what we do not understand ourselves they gain the right to show us how to behave." Psychoanalysis replaces religious confession, sexuality becomes subject to classification and arrangement, quantitative and material data are taken for truth. Foucault sees this as the antithesis of freedom. Scientific knowledge tells us nothing about sensuality, what has been called the aestheticism of the erotic: knowing how to make love does not replace knowing how to love. Foucault, opposed to Freud, aims to discredit our belief in a fixed human nature, particularly regarding the nature of sexual desire.

Freudians presume a fixed nature for sexuality which determines the nature of mankind. They are more interested in masochism than in sadism since it is even more removed from normality, which acknowledges that human nature is to some degree sadistic. It begins with the child's perception of sexual intercourse as sadistic, a primal scene in which the woman is mistreated or humiliated; sexual writhing is understood as the response to assault ("Of the Sexual Theories of Children," 1908). In 1920, Freud formulated his concept of the death instinct in *Beyond the Pleasure Principle*; the wish to revert to an earlier state of being, ultimately non-being, is thwarted by Eros, the sexual instinct that needs to procreate. These two opposing forces in the mind have equal "validity and status," and their constant struggle paraphrases the human condition. What might have been a touch of the misanthropic in Freud's earlier work blooms into a full pessimism that becomes the final tragic vision of humanity in *Civilization and Its Discontents*.

Freud sought to "classify" masochism; his three types were erotic, moral (by which he meant social), and feminine. In "The Economic Problem of Masochism," he offered the idea of the feminine as basically masochistic, since women have been enjoined by society, and "by their constitutions," to repress rage and aggression and replace them with the wish for romantic bliss, for merging and union in ecstatic love. To be dominated, even beaten, is interpreted as being loved, and the essential purpose of such feminine love is to submerge one's whole personality in another's. The argument about the feminine that arises here is currently raging in every aspect of discussion about women's nature, role, and aspiration. While all feminists agree that society has indeed conditioned women to accept passivity as normal to femininity and to invest in dependence on others as the means of personal fulfillment, none agree that such conditioning has biological or constitutional support. I am interested in the formulation of passivity and masochism and, by contrast, aggression and an early perception of sexuality as sadistic that then becomes incorporated into the traditional or normal *gestalt* of masculinity.

Indeed, society has arranged matters between men and women so that what is traditional, passive-feminine, dominant-masculine, becomes the murky ideal of the normal and the natural. This then becomes the model for what psychologists as early as Krafft-Ebing (who coined the term "masochism" about 1900) see as the predominant perversion of heterosexual men: the need to be "feminine" or masochistic. Out of their guilt and failure to be masculine is created the desire to mix pain and pleasure.

Psychologists and some of the polemicists agree that sadomasochism is more than "a special variety of sexual play," which is the description its apologists prefer; it is an aspect of personality rather than an isolated erotic technique. Perhaps the question is one of degree, but it is not disputable that sexual taste is expressive of personality, that those erotic skills we master tell much of character. S-M devices may be used in conventional sexuality to sustain sexual play, to postpone the final pleasure of orgasm, to experiment with the taboo as the most exciting kind of foreplay. But a taste of the perverse is not an appetite for banquets. For the masochist the postponement of pleasure by pain creates another kind of pleasure that is only his.

In his pessimism about humanity, Freud knew he was entering "the darkest and most inaccessible sphere of psychic life" in exploring sexuality, much of which was left speculative; he was less hesitant in his conviction that "man is a wolf to man . . . a savage beast to whom consideration of his own kind is something alien." Man's nature constantly threatens civilization with disintegration; to survive, all its institutions must lend their energies in the service of limiting man's aggressiveness. These efforts Freud called the claim of culture, the reality principle. Monogamous heterosexual love, restrictions upon the sexual life, perhaps most demanding of all, the ideal of Christian love, to love one's neighbor as oneself, are all part of culture's effort to contain aggression, though Freud added about brotherly love that "nothing else runs so strongly counter to the original nature of man."

On such premises, the life of de Sade is seen as heroic rebellion against the constraints of a civilization too corrupt to justify its own authority, and as de Beauvoir said, "He made of his sexuality an ethic." De Sade's sexuality was inseparable from his misanthropy; compared to the demands of culture, sexuality in any form was positive. All experience, life itself, became libidinous, an extention of the sexual; what de Sade sought to find were the limitations, if any, to sexuality; certainly, the distinction between pleasure and pain, the licit and the taboo, heterosexual and homosexual, invited experimentation in order to violate such categorization and make it meaningless. By championing the outrageousness of abnormality, de Sade gave more clarity to what was called normality.

His early sexual adventures concerned flagellation. Those comparatively innocent spankings with prostitutes made him vulnerable to blackmail and finally to imprisonment on charges trumped up by his vindictive mother-in-law. But imprisonment triggered that passion for rebellion that would later make his name synonymous with "monstrous."

By 1792, de Sade was experimenting with homosexuality; he would whip and be whipped, bugger and be buggered (by his valet, Latour), sometimes simultaneously. These episodes in flagellation and buggery were the basis of what came to be called sadism. He and his valet were charged with sodomy, and *in absentia* they were sentenced to be executed, de Sade by decapitation and Latour by strangling. Since they had fled from the jurisdiction of the court, they were burned in effigy in Aix. While his ventures into whipping had made de Sade subject to blackmail, not until he voyaged into sodomy did he risk his life.

De Sade's explorations seem to be in the service of self-mastery rather than of surrender, mastery of the human capacity for violence and cruelty in the knowledge of them. Sensation and pleasure were primal laws, more legitimate because their authority was in biology, not the pieties of his society. But de Sade also insisted upon the futility of separating mastery and submission, power and helplessness, and that one could not be experienced or understood without knowledge of the other: in the end, the nature of pleasure could only be learnt in pain.

Simone de Beauvoir warned that "to sympathize with de Sade too readily is to betray him." Like romanticizing the satanic which misreads it, to see in de Sade a victim of anything but his own sensibility and his passionate willfulness is to sentimentalize his great achievement—to pioneer questions about sexual freedom that had not been heard, perhaps not thought of before. De Sade willed perversity to serve him; he was not to be its servant, a far cry from the perverse condition that is the "commonest," perhaps a commonplace, of male heterosexuality.

2

Erotic masochism is a closet drama, not a sexual epic. Everyone—its detractors, analysts, and defenders—agree that the penchant begins in childhood; what is acquired in maturity is a need to ritualize earlier experience that is either unresolved or conflicted or perhaps simply a given about sexual pleasure. Sexologists like Freud insist that every important physical process can contribute to sexual excitement, that the body is erogenous in ways and parts that are limited only to what the imagination can conceive. They also agree that provided pain and discomfort are not excessive, sexual excitement and function continue unimpaired. Theodor Reik in *Masochism and Modern Man,* still one of the most informative single works on the subject, makes a telling distinction between pain and discomfort. Pain can be perceived only by the tactile sense of touch, the sensitivity of skin and membranes. Discomfort concerns the tolerance for pain, which varies highly within and among individuals.

Reik is not sure that sadomasochism has instinctual connection, but he respects the theory. Whether it is instinct or partial instinct, a defense mechanism or a formation of the conscience, its complexities are not easily reduced. Reik is sure that the idea that the masochist reverses all the pleasure values and delights in pain is an illusion. The masochist pursues pleasure like anyone else, but he is detoured by pain because he cannot approach pleasure directly. What causes the detour is sexual anxiety capable of extraordinary intimidation. The masochist is in flight from a terrifying, torturous anxiety that all sexual excitement raises for him, and the pains he courts are lesser ones and manageable: he defends himself in punishment; first he atones, then he sins, as Reik puts it.

Pleasure is the reward after the labor of humiliation, the necessary price. It sounds somewhat like mere puritanical conscience: make yourself uncomfortable, then remove the discomfort and see how good it feels. Reik sees the plot as more complex than that small deception we all practice to enhance pleasure, saving the best for last, creating obstacles for the gratification of overcoming them, letting things get messier to restore and enjoy order. The masochist is guilty by his own sexual admission: desire condemns him. But he is also defiant, unsure this verdict is just. By voluntarily submitting to humiliation and suffering, he triumphs over his guilt and anxiety, which he has substantiated in the person of his tormentor, who is both the symbol of authority that forbids him pleasure and the actual instrument for the pleasure he seeks. By anticipating punishment in self-chastisement, he controls it and makes it ineffectual, a variety of play. Authority which he feels is denying him sexual gratification now becomes an ally, and the arm that whips him is disarmed by his consent. Punishment is now transformed into an enticement by which he seduces his aggressor. All that has inhibited him in culture fails, since the acquiescence is a pretense, a fantasy, while the spirit is stubbornly defiant. To make punishment the condition of pleasure makes authority a sham, a meaningless inhibition. The masochist is sustained in his discomfort and pain by both the foretaste and the foreknowledge that the conquest of authority is finally his.

Reik defines the masochist as one with a strongly sadistic disposition inhibited by his anxiety, in conflict with an urge for pleasure that is resolved by creating a manageable humiliation or shame. Sexual desire writhes in a mime of passivity that signals to the sadist what needs to be done. This performance is choreographed with precision. Writhing itself is active, full of momentous movement, the opposite of stillness and acquiescence. Even lust is so powerful it can hardly be called "passive."

This drama demands its own momentum and suspense, a studied development of tension vascillating between fear and excitement. It is sophisticated and civilized in the sense that it is entirely *contra natura,* postponing the natural impulse to discharge or climax and, in fact, making that a by-product of the action whose central concern is the conversion of anxiety into pleasure. Since part of the pleasure for the masochist has come from anticipating pain and preparing himself for it, the focus has partly shifted from action to expectation: "anxiety-ridden pleasure is transformed into pleasurable anxiety." Reik adds that this suspense is a forepleasure which is a "kind of sample orgasm," anticipating climax in small doses. The natural tension of sexuality is subverted because either orgasm or something associated with it is terrifying. The discomforts of pain or humiliation divert the masochist from the threat of climax. Punishment is "less essential than the fear of it," which increases if it appears to be unpredictable. The passive has become the active, the future fears are the present ones, the anxieties created in fantasies are resolved in the ritual actions of scripted performance.

This is delicate psychic manipulation; such fantasy depends more on ritual than any other erotic deviation does. In a bland defense, *S-M: The Last Taboo* by Gerald and Caroline Greene, authors who are practitioners define the ritualization of these fantasies of helplessness and power. Accidental pain is regarded neither as erotic nor as pleasurable. The session begins with the masochist having allegedly done something; some unspecified guilt therefore merits punishment, which is always threatened verbally and suspensefully withheld. Havelock Ellis is cited to argue: "The sadist is merely servicing the masocist. The sadist must develop extraordinary perceptiveness to know when to continue, despite cries and protests, and when to cease." Ellis, like the Greenes, insists on a context of trusting intimacy where pain is only a token of love; a contest of civilized reenactments of combat courtships still observable in lower species. But unlike animal mating, this script transcends biology, uniting the imagination and senses artfully. Ellis defines the proper conditions for such an achievement: the masochist (Ellis uses the pronoun "she") must be absolutely sure of the man's love and have perfect confidence in his judgment; the pain must always be calculated and inflicted with kindness, never in anger; it must be "a tidy pain, not excessive enough to interfere with arousal, and finally she must be sure of her own influence over the man."

This is the healthy model of loving male dominance and female submissiveness only slightly sabotaged by the masochist's passive aggression.

Though the Greenes imply their own relationship is in this classic mold, they allow for the piquancy of role reversal. The dominatrix is a venerable part, rarer than her "natural" male counterpart and thus more in demand. However, the Greenes are leery of the professional, no matter how skillful she is. Commercialism is debasing for the usual reason: it is loveless. It is better than nothing, and they cite the useful work of Monique von Cleef, who ran a "torture house" first in Staten Island and later in Newark. Von Cleef said, "They come to me to find what is missing in their lives. I think it's probably love. They feel on some level that to be beaten and humiliated is to be loved."

Ideally, sadomasochism is only handled properly by "those who exist in perfect confidence and love"; the Greenes are a bit self-congratulatory about the refinement of their emotional rapport but allow that in the quest for expressive sexual freedom, a polymorphous perversity is allowable; a fraternity of sexual plurality, "protean and transsexual," is possible—two women or two men or a man and woman reversing roles.

The Greenes and recent apologists follow similar lines of reasoning in a serious effort to help sadomasochism out of the closet into sexual respectability. It is really all about love; it is deeply sensitive, imaginative, and communicative; and, one notices, it is coupled. To the chagrin of gay liberationists, one of the justifications offered for the acceptance of sadomasochism is the measure of public response to homosexuality. There are interesting analogies: in homosexual culture, casual cruising demands that men regard themselves as sex objects. Some men devote themselves to such objectification, which corresponds to the basis for humiliation in sadomasochism where being held as a sexual object is meant to be deprecating and insulting, the foundation for humiliation. Gay liberation claims the right of sexual self-determination, the right to be free to explore even the fringes of the self, demanding that liberal society acknowledge the justice of its claims, and, as that support is given increasingly, other sexualities demand equal permissiveness.

It is also why conservative America focuses its anger on homosexuals, why its sexual anxieties are inflamed into murderous hatreds: we will not only destroy the family and seduce the children but also pioneer the corruption of all modesties, all restraints, and, most threatening, all privacies. We are speaking of the unspeakable; to do so is already to give it some quarter. To demand that society tolerate the display of sexual variety is to condone it.

The ritualized theatricality of S-M, with its toys and costumes, its careful scenario manipulating suspense, also needs to express what Reik called its "demonstrative" factor, its need for display, exhibition, publicity, exactly like the demands for visibility and confrontation that gay liberationists insist upon.

Like the claims homosexuals once made about elitist sensibilities, sadomasochists insist on the superiority of their imaginations, more vivid and excitable than ordinary people's; de Beauvoir says, "The world of the masochist is a magical one, and that is why he is almost always a fetishist," supporting the idea of both the theatrical and the rarified. Like all deviance, it is ambivalent, linking biology and imagination, claiming an elitism in higher responsiveness that would prefer the bedroom to the barricade, but it also needs to proclaim itself, command an audience, demand justice.

Part of the publicity stems from its roots in rebelliousness, making a claim for legitimacy in a society where technology and violence increasingly question all civilized proprieties, and where both are amazing and unpredictable. An unknown assailant whose motive will never be comprehensible and whose violence is truly random shoves a lovely young flutist in front of a subway train which severs her hand; hours later, technology repairs the damage in miraculous microsurgery. We have yet to understand fully the intimate connection between those two events. Less mysterious is the vulgarization of hedonism, the consumerism that makes prurience profitable and therefore respectable. But sadomasochism inverts ideas of authority and aggression, defying the punitive father, paternalism, and patriarchal culture. Compared to commercial ordinary society which encourages everyone to treat his or her body as an object, in sadomasochism, the individual is claimed at least to be an object "of fascination."

It does not demand genital sex; it may even diffuse the frustrations that technocratic society has created whose commonest outlet is the unmotivated violence on every urban street. In its claims for imagination and intimacy, it seems, as the Greenes note, above the judgment of a whore civilization that turns every experience into a commercially exploitative commodity.

If sadomasochism is the commonest perversion among heterosexual men, impotence is the commonest complaint among normal ones. Not only is violence mindlessly eroticized and commercialized, but it is then coupled with male sexual performance. The Greenes suggest that men who are confused and frightened by the demands of women—even ones who do not call themselves liberated—for male performance, who have been told by publications as mild as *Family Circle* that sexual performance is a rite and a right, may find anxieties so anguishing that impotence is their respite, but a little male sadism might restore such blemished confidence; if not, there is always the feasibility of a Sadean woman.

Thus, the logic of the times calls bondage "fettering," and tight black leather evokes delectable *frissons* along with the Gestapo. Urinating on one another is "water imagery, a delicious shame" (though scatology is pathological), and a tidy pain, like spanking, conveying the mere naughtiness of the small helpless dependent child, will give "people comfortable lives and violence will go away." The transformed parent in this fantasy joins the sexual play rather than forbids it. Trust and intimacy are ritualized as discipline, and what seems ungovernable passion is ordered and governed autocratically.

Gay defenders of sadomasochism are less utopian and more aware that they are as feared or detested by homosexual as heterosexual opponents. They emphasize that in submission symbolic pain is as valid as physical torment. Ian Young, a proponent who has written more than once on the subject ("Inside Sado-masochism" in *The New Gay Liberation Book,* edited by Len Richmond and Gary Noguera, 1979), talks about keeping his slave off-balance, "anxious but curious, a bit apprehensive, yet eager." He emphasizes the trust and intimacy between the couple, the sensitivity and awareness of the master, who does not even have to be turned on, for if he is a really good "S" he can function without desire, unlike the "M" who both sets up the ritual and must be excited. He illustrates how a good master calms the initial panic of his slave when he first handcuffs him into helplessness. He grants that for some, S-M has become a lifestyle rather than a variety of sexuality, but he does not tell us what that signifies. For him, it is the last taboo: "That's part of its attraction."

He quotes from a pamphlet by Robert Payne, "The Care and Training of the Male Slave":

> Remember, to truly dominate, you must have as your key knowledge of things that turn him on. As your dominance increases, you will find yourself doing the thinking and planning for the two of you. . . . Psychologically, you will have found humiliation, rough talk, mild but constant punishment and not-to-be-ignored instructions useful. But the desire to serve you, care for you, wait on you and identify himself as part of you, is an intangible that depends on your charisma.

Omit the third sentence and the gender of the pronouns and this might be a Victorian guide to the new groom, completely premised on what Freud called feminine masochism, an imitation—or perhaps the real thing these days—of romantic blissful surrender to male pride, the dreamy "charisma."

Young thinks the rules need not be so textual; there is room for creative or spontaneous play, as long as the psychodrama yields its goal: "An altered state of consciousness, a heightened awareness." The gratification not only harmlessly satisfies the need to master aggression and submission, but it is a profound romantic communication where observing the effect on the other party is tender and mezmerizing. The issue of submission is dismissed as "not different than being fucked in the ass," the "incidental harms" not worse than the harms of sexual repression.

Lyn Rosen, a lesbian proponent in a forum on the subject *(Lavender Culture,* edited by Karla Jay and Allen Young), sees it as a sexual act, "not an act of violence." She underscores that it is a consensual relationship different for lesbians and for gay men, who tend much more to separate sex and emotional involvement: "Men see it as a kink, an escape from boredom." Lesbians, even sexually liberated sadomasochistic ones, are more loving than gay men, closer to the heterosexual model of the Greenes. Pat Califa in recent issues of *The Advocate* (#283) has written about lesbian sadomasochism, and her experience and observation contradict Rosen's premise pretty thoroughly. Califa is perhaps the only gay woman in print who asserts that sadomasochism is a stronger bond than either gender or sexual persuasion. She declares she is a lesbian feminist whose sexual tastes are strongly S-M and, furthermore, that there is no conflict among her lesbianism, feminism, and sadomasochism.

Both Rosen and Young dismiss the dangers: the psychopathic sadist who assaults, rapes, maims, kills is partly driven to desperation because he is deprived of access to those who would consent. With sufficient publicity and permissiveness, much of this driven furtiveness would dissipate. But in minimizing psychopathic violence as the result of ignorance, they quietly assume despite all the insistence that the sadist is merely the character in the masochist's fantasy, that there are some fantasies of consent to just such fury.

3

In homosexual life, the sexual demands of women are apparently irrelevant while the anxieties about performance are the condition of promiscuity. One may never become inured to it, and it may worsen, but among those men for whom casual sex is what it says, performance anxiety is well controlled, managed by whatever defenses the individual creates. Why then is impotence increasingly obvious among gay men, proportionately as high among them as among their straight counterparts (this is conjecture with the force of faith)? Possibly, the answer is boredom.

The prodigious appetite of the perverse has also been attributed to homosexuals, and it can be easily verified in the large gay urban centers and playgrounds. But largeness of appetite does not automatically require variety. Presumably, an ample and intense sexual life is available to the monogamous. Unfortunately, what has not been verified is this ideal couple—Sadean or not—loving, intimate, trusting, monogamous, and hot.

The prodigiousness of sex really depends deeply on change, and promiscuity is the easiest kind of change for gay men. They find themselves with the choice of indifference and impotence or of variety and innovation. But the force of this boredom is not the dullness of their partners or the sameness of the scene; it is rooted in a narcissism that is powerfully present in homosexual life, the most primitive sense of self that precedes pride and precludes interest in anything else. The myth of Narcissus is about beauty and self-absorption, but it is not about vanity. When Narcissus discovers his own reflection in the pool, he falls in love with it, subjectively experiencing it as another person. Unwittingly he falls sexually, or more precisely homosexually, in love. In the myth, he is also chaste until he discovers himself; he has spurned everyone, both male and female pursuers, though his treatment of women in the story of the nymph Echo is particularly unpleasant. Narcissus' first sexual discovery is also self-discovery. Sexual passion and sense of self become identified as the same thing. Objectively, he loves his own reflection; subjectively, he loves another. In his obsession, he becomes simultaneously asocial and antisocial, self-absorbed and self-defeating. Freud claims that everyone begins life in a state of primary narcissism, meaning that we discover that we can be in love with the self in just the same way we can love another, the object outside ourselves, like the parent. Our boredom arises from our inability to respond to others or things with genuine interest. When the boredom becomes constitutional, it is because only the self is interesting, and sometimes even that does not entice. A common compensation for narcissistic boredom is aggression, whose violence at least is not dull.

In "The Most Prevalent Form of Degradation in Erotic Life" *(Contributions to the Psychology of Love,* 1912), Freud tells how tenderness and familiarity inhibit sensuality, how this is the condition of civilized sexuality for most people. In a healthy love, "two currents of feeling have to unite . . . the tender, affectionate feelings and the sensual feelings." When there is some psychic disorder, these strains of feeling separate, are dissociated from each other. In severe cases, they become exclusive: "The erotic life of such people remains dissociated, divided between two channels, the same two that are personified in art as heavenly and earthly (or animal) love. Where such men love they have no desire and where they desire they cannot love." The perverse is one attempt to resolve that separation, to break the sexual taboo surrounding the tender figure. What used to be the neurotic exceptional condition of fifty years ago has now become one of the commonplaces of urban adult life; the sexual expectations that are presumed now in marriage have created an intolerable burden on the institution. No coupled relationship of any sort, from heterosexual marriage to homosexual master-slave, seems to have solved the problem of sustaining sexual excitement and nurturing that tender trust the textbooks speak of so glowingly. That is Narcissus' precocious intuition: only that exciting stranger who is beyond his grasp is truly interesting.

Perversity and promiscuity hold in common an intolerance for habitual boredom and a propensity for aggression and hostility. Among the perverse, the hostility is ritualized for the sadist and internalized for the masochist. Among the promiscuous, that hostility is in the game of sexual enticement and rebuff, the omnipresent teasing and shame. In homosexual life, there are few humiliations equal to the sexual rebuff in a scene where one has presented himself voluntarily as a sexual object. That scene, enacted in every gay bar and nearly every bath—places created to expedite sexual liaison and devoted to libertinism—that scene is the experience of nearly all gay men and many women, and it is an experience they return to again and again. It is not surprising if someone is so beautiful or so sexual that he or she is immune to rebuff and finds such places congenial, but the majority of men who frequent bars complain: despite the pitch-black fuck room in the basement where anyone can score, up front the same tedious appraisals go on.

Shame is not limited to sexual rejection: one can experience it in any competitive defeat, when one is ridiculed or even socially slighted; a special kind of shame is felt when one's privacy is invaded, which illustrates the irrationality and difficulty of such response. People talk about how they feel after having discovered their apartments burglarized, as if "someone shit in the living room." Unlike guilt, which can be lived with and made gratifying, shame triggers rage. When a gay man enters such a situation forearmed with awareness, his rage often turns against himself in self-disgust. It is a miniature of the same process by which sadistic aggression is internalized and transformed into masochism.

Freud called it moral masochism, an unconscious tendency to seek pain or failure and enjoy it, a need to punish oneself, translated into the idea of being beaten by God or destiny or society. In short, the loser. To a degree, this experience is common to every civilized man, present in his response to his helplessness, powerlessness, or sense of guilt. Eric Fromm popularized the idea in books like *Escape from Freedom;* these strivings help us evade the unbearable feeling of isolation and powerlessness. Unlike the erotic masochist who wants pleasure even at the cost of pain and who is obstinate in his pursuit, the moral masochist finds pleasure in his punishment, or in the self-pity that accompanies it.

If we accept the idea that perversion is an expression of character in general, what has traditionally been called the perverse is now becoming only the ordinary *in extremis,* eroticized in those people who by nature or conditioning express the deepest sense of self in sexuality.

Put in a context larger than the bedroom, it cannot be regarded merely as exotic foreplay, especially since sadomasochists increasingly demand both publicity and, if not approval, acknowledgement. Psychologists tend to see the masochist as either an intensely suffering victim, ultimately of his culture, or the opposite: blackmailing, coercive, or paranoid, someone who uses suffering to excuse himself from the responsibilities of his own life by manipulating others into taking care of him. The theories on character range from the placating and completely acquiescent, passively enslaved, to one that sees the individual as demanding, contentious, armed for a power struggle that he understands better than his antagonist, whom he has handicapped as his cruel but loving master. The sadist in turn is viewed as weak, with a crippled sense of self, intent on self-aggrandizement, exploiting others psychically to disembowel them. In both roles, the deception and illusion about dominance are central: the sadist's strength devolves on his feeling of mastery over someone else which depends on the volition of his subject.

What is then enacted is highly political in content. The sadistic figure of authority represents not only the father with the strap but patriarchy, Freud's civilization itself, which the masochist temporarily believes he controls. The real antagonist which is culture is represented by a player whose momentary credence is his script and costume. The mixture of renouncing autonomy but enjoying it by proxy is the common condition of political life and the life of orthodox religious communities. The cults of the seventies, most notoriously the Jim Jones cult, would seem to verify completely Freud's idea of moral masochism.

Reik believes that the "more violent and brutal the ambition of the individual . . . deprived of the right of self-determination, the more pliant and resignedly will he surrender to the will of the autocrat or the leader who replaces him. The sadist becomes the executor of the suppressed yet not vanished brutality of the masochist." Therapists testify that, in treatment, when the patient begins to master his masochistic tendencies, what inevitably begin to emerge are sadistic fantasies. In such a reading, sadomasochism betrays its social history as subversion; instead, it is deeply conservative if not reactionary, surrendering to fantasies about power while suffering, psychically writhing, under the demands of omnipotent culture. The disillusionments of childhood are permanent legacies for withdrawal and closetry. The bedroom becomes the playroom, and the outside world remains fearful, disagreeable, and unchangeable.

In a critical rather than clinical study, *Masochism: An Interpretation of Coldness and Cruelty,* Gilles Deleuze argues that sadomasochism is a syndrome where true sadism must be distinguished from a pretended one. He begins with an idea borrowed from Georges Bataille on de Sade's work: "It is a language which repudiates a relationship between speaker and audience." Deleuze then denies the idea of consent: the sadist is sometimes *coincidentally* involved with the masochist, but the real pleasure for the former is in inflicting pain on "those who do *not* consent nor are persuaded." What is cruel and disgusting to others is the source of pleasure for the cold-blooded and libertine sadist. He is a "speculator" on death in a gothic world. He has no shame, remorse, or repressed desire for punishment. His world is cold; anti-emotional, for feelings compete with sensation, dissipating sexual energy. This hedonistic sadism must inflict pain, unlike Freud's perversion which is purely aggressive and only aims at domination. Deleuze contrasts the masochist's infantile world, the realm of the fairy tale: if the sadist controls by possession, the masochist does so by contract, which acts as law and creates order.

Deleuze's disputes with Freud are really minor; he subscribes entirely to the Oedipal construction of both sadism and masochism, and his discussion is quite orthodox. In masochism, "the father is totally expelled": in sadism, "paternalism and patriarchy predominate." Sadism negates the mother, the maternal, and the feminine to exalt the father beyond all law, into something akin to what De Sade meant when he talked of "intelligent evil." Deleuze quotes Nietzsche: "If pain and suffering have any meaning, it must be that they are enjoyable to someone." That someone is God the Father as he is embodied in patriarchy. Deleuze concludes by itemizing in that meticulous French fashion the true differences between sadism and its false counterpart masochism: besides inflating the father who is abolished in the masochist's world, sadism gives fetishism and fantasy an entirely different significance. The masochist is imaginative, aesthetic, idealizing his experience; the sadist is hostile to all that—his experience is speculative. The list is much longer, but it adds up to a theory of eroticism based on the idea of transformation. Like all theory about sadomasochism, Deleuze's involves ideas of pain as pleasure, dominance and passivity that are transformations of ideas about gender, about the meaning of masculinity and femininity. In homosexual sadomasochism, what is psychically imitated are heterosexual conflicts about patriarchy.

4

The moral outrage against sadomasochism from heterosexual and homosexual critics is often less than useful; it creates a desire to defend the underdog against dogma. To say that it is an eroticization of violence and powerlessness is no longer illuminating or critical in modern America. To say that it is allied to death and motivated by guilt, or a pederastic displacement in which an adult uses a consenting masochist as a surrogate for a child, is an interesting notion, but unclear as moral criticism. As to guilt, after Vietnam, what does that term mean morally? If one cites Freud's argument about instinct, can one then use it against the subject one has conceded is powerfully based in biology? To say it is a surrogate for pederasty is hardly to make it worse but seems to support the idea that S-M is a safety valve for forbidden, destructive impulses.

But there are more serious criticisms: first, consent is not choice, and no defender of this faith has touched on the compulsive nature of this sexuality. Second, in celebrating submission and slavery, sadomasochism may betray entirely the idea of sexual liberation.

Most of this discussion has made little distinction between heterosexual and homosexual sadomasochism because it is a perversion where such differences are much less meaningful, when men and women who regard themselves as heterosexual will perform sexually with members of their own sex without later questioning their own identity. When stores like The Pleasure Chest first opened, their clientele was the gay leather crowd and a few tourists. Now the catalogue for the seven stores, "The Pleasure Chest Compendium of Amorous and Prurient Paraphernalia," is 192 pages long, fully illustrated, and ambisexual, as devoted to straight as to gay usage. Indeed, some of the more elaborate equipment indicates that someday technology may create autoerotic masochism. When I browsed through the Greenwich Village shop, there were two couples there: one appeared modishly straight Madison Avenue, and the other couple looked like your everyday liberated lesbians: sandaled, braless, sexily boyish, unself-conscious.

Sadomasochism truly seems to transcend the kind of categorization that has been so polarizing in sexual politics. It is also true that gay men are more extreme, more intrigued by danger and risk than their heterosexual and lesbian counterparts who tend to be coupled. And gay men are much more intense and insistent upon borrowing the trappings of Fascism for their rituals, finding the concentration camp and the Gestapo titillating setting and character for their variety of sexual play. And among gay men, the issue of potency and erection is more relevant than it is among others who claim the genital is not nearly as important as the anal.

Gay S-M is more intrigued with experimentations with urine and feces; scatology has its own organizations. For its brief moment, The

Toilet, an S-M bar near the docks, lived up to its name and, from some of the gossip, exceeded anyone's expectations. Whether piss and shit are really substitutes for semen, part of a fetish about virility and ingestation, or whether they are part of the search for that exciting humiliation is unclear, though nothing prevents them from being both.

It is a standard observation that sadomasochism is particularly prevalent in "clean" countries like Sweden, Denmark, England, Switzerland, Germany, and of course America, where hygiene is a virtue. If masochism is biologically rooted in destructive instinct, excrement is the closest thing to the principle of decay this side of death. Also, the anality of S-M is omnipresent. Psychologists relate its origins to toilet training. It is in that first difficult socialization of the child that punctuality, control, and cleanliness are united in an experience that demands the child bear discomfort temporarily in order to secure parental approval and love. Children think their feces are gifts to the parent, and babies, we are told, only wet those they love. The dabbling in the excremental is documented as early as de Sade; to my knowledge, it is the first recording in literature of heterosexual rimming (my familiarity with Latin erotica is limited). Analingus has long been a homosexual variety of foreplay, particularly when it precedes anal intercourse. That it is also forbidden, dangerous to health, and held as disgusting by most of society does nothing to diminish its popularity.

In rimming, homosexual eroticism shares with sadomasochism the excitement of humiliation, precisely the experience of shame. What counters the shame of the performer is his invasion of the privacy of the body of his partner, which differs from anal intercourse in that it is so overwhelmingly tactile and intimate, and which bears no resemblance to heterosexual intercourse, to normal coitus. The privacy of the bowels opened to access is also a drama of submission and dominion where the roles are not clearly active or passive, where the one pursuing the shame is active, using his partner; as in masochism, the active performer controls the shame; as in sadism, he also gives the pleasure.

That gay men are exuberant in their practice is now verified in the epidemic proportion of amebiasis in recent years. What used to be a speciality of tropical medicine ("Did you drink the water in Mexico?") has now become a venereal disease in these temperate climes. What was once the unlucky tourist's hazard is now the average risk of promiscuous gay life. That it is widespread conveys not only its practice, since conventional venereal disease also indicates that, but also the fact that its popularity is recent. Only in the last decades has it entered the vernacular; I would venture that the attraction is partly that it is still taboo, that more than fucking or sucking which has heterosexual counterparts, analingus is forbidden and therefore seductive. It is risky to health, but not nearly as serious as syphillis or the new resistant strains of gonorrhea which are so widespread that they are demanding national medical interest to research preventive vaccines. Of course that attention is largely the result of the epidemic among heterosexual adolescents.

To break the taboo is always to experience shame and triumph. What is taboo is set apart, too sacred or too profane. Among primitive people, it is charged with danger—supernatural power—or subject to supernatural reprisal. In homosexual culture, what is taboo is part of an entire life style that is set apart and regarded by society as already profane, dangerous, and subject to reprisal. To break the taboo among primitive and civilized peoples alike is to enter the perverse. If one is homosexual and has heard all his life that he is already perverse, the inhibitions are lowered, the threshold to the experimental much easier to cross.

In the last decade, a new threshold called fist-fucking or fisting has beckoned more and more gay men. The practice, like so much that is innovative and American, soon demanded an organization, and in the early seventies news of the F.F.A. (Fist Fuckers of America) centered in Philadelphia leaked into gay culture. Martin Duberman in his journals records meeting a man calling himself "Berlin" in January 1972; Berlin first told him of the practice and the new organization. When asked what the experience felt like, Berlin replied, "It's like the feeling your funny bone gets when it's hit, only it travels all over your body."

The early members of F.F.A. were men with some experience in sadomasochism, fond of leather and butchness, but who were now in their late forties and fifties, isolated by their age in gay culture. With the advent of handkerchief signaling, communication between fisters became much easier, and both the information and the experimentation spread quickly through the gay scene. That piece of red cotton in left (top man) or right (bottom) pocket was first a signal and soon a trigger, a fraternal sign inviting boldness.

From the men I interviewed who have been into fisting for some years, I learned much which was startling, not least of all about my own attitudes toward sexual innovation. While I explored the sadomasochism scene, I checked my own impulse to judge or dismiss or disapprove by analogizing. Those impulses must be just what much of heterosexual America feels when confronted with garden-variety homosexuality. My fears of what I did not understand and was embarrassed by are probably very like the fears and disgust of homosexuality in conventional society.

5

I first met John and Pete in the summer of 1968 at Fire Island Pines. They had already been lovers for more than six years (they are now entering their eighteenth year together). They met in the army; John had had no significant gay experiences before, and Pete had had no gratifying ones. They became lovers in the service, and when I met them, they had developed an easy, familiar, monogamous relationship that seemed successful and attractive. They were both in their late twenties and beginning to explore their careers. John thought he might like to be a writer; Pete knew he would have something to do with the technical production of popular music. They had little money and not much direction, but they were optimistic and not overly ambitious. Pete was always cheerful and buoyant, cute and campy and extravagant about his enthusiasm for New York: for the opera and the theater, the bar life and the drugs.

The following summer, we were roommates in a house on the island that we rented for August. Their relationship had changed little even as I saw it more fully. John had given up the idea of writing and was working on Wall Street; Pete was part of a lighting and sound company. They were more ambitious for money, for clothes, and for every new record, more trippy about drugs, but easy companions, rarely quarrelsome or irritable, interested in good times. I also learned that their relationship was sexually fixed in ways it was not fixed socially, where the two men acted fairly spontaneously and unstereotypically. Sexually, John was always dominant because Pete insisted on being anally passive. Socially, they were flexible: John liked to cook and was quieter and more domestic than Pete, who made more money and was profligate with it. John managed the bills and the social calendar, but Pete made new friends more easily. Both were attractive, but nothing special at Fire Island Pines. Their appeal was boy-ishness; their style was gregarious and hedonistic. Pete never read any-thing, not even the newspaper, but could not bear a room without music. He was a Californian, a native of Los Angeles, and seemed to have found in the East everything he wanted: a lover, the gay life, fast drugs and fast dancing, a profitable job, and endless amusement. John usually had his nose in a book; he came from working-class suburban Long Island; New York was nearly as new an experience for him.

In the last few years I saw them infrequently; we had drifted as people do so easily in the city. When I went to their parties, these were novelties of heavy drug taking, sexually charged dancing, camping, and booze, all diverting and exhausting. At their last party in Christmas week of 1978 I met a hunky Latin who danced me into a giddy state and invited me home. John had been watching us and came up to me as I began to look for my coat and forbade me to leave. Julio was definitely not for me: he was a sadistic fist-fucker who had already sent three men to the hospital, one of whom ended with a colostomy. When I asked why Julio was there, John said he had crashed the party. No one asked him any place anymore; he had even been thrown out of F.F.A., creating a precedent.

When I decided to write this chapter, I called John and Pete, who readily agreed to be interviewed; their enthusiasm and volubility filled three hours of tape. Pete did most of the talking; he has changed the most since they discovered F.F.A. He travels all over the country on his job, and in every city he has names of members; he rarely has to go to a gay bar. It is like a fraternal order; there is always a welcome arm for a buddy.

After ten monogamous years, both men had agreed that for them the sexual scene was with other people, but most of their experiences before F.F.A. were unsatisfying. Neither had much patience cruising the bars, and threesomes were less exciting than they had hoped. In 1976, Pete was fisted for the first time by someone he'd known for years and who spe-cialized as a top man. From then on, Pete has been an enthusiast; he is involved with his new sexual discovery exclusively and, outside of his work, entirely. In 1978, he joined F.F.A., the first organization he has ever been a member of. John was willing to oblige. After intimacy of such standing, he did not take long learning to be a good top man, but he was not satisfied. He demanded that if he were to fist Pete, Pete at least should make a serious effort to fuck him, for John had never been successfully fucked. It took some months of patience, and after fourteen years, Pete succeeded, his first time as a fucker. From John's first experience being fucked to being fisted took less than six months. Now both are fully involved, and John's capacities are nearly as large as his lover's.

Fisting has decreased the amount of sexual time they spend alone with each other, but the quality of their sexual life is better now than it has been since the early years. They are now very open with each other, less jealous and competitive than before, and they talk to each other more. Neither foresees any risk of falling in love with someone else despite the hundreds of men they go through annually. They feel even more coupled, unthreatened by romantic infidelity, satisfied and assured that the friendship they feel is enduring. Oh, there are occasional crushes, but those infatuations are reserved for the orgies they habituate.

They find most of their old friends a bit boring now—"G.A.A. types, those politicos are so dull," they tell me with cheerful malice. John's social habits have changed as much as Pete's: "I never cook now; I've forgotten how. Besides, we don't eat on weekends, what with all the douching and the drugs; it's best to keep your stomach a little empty. You don't want to eat heavily anyway because of all the drugs you're taking. On a full stomach you'd throw up. Maybe what I should do is write *The Fist-Fucker's Cook Book*—all omelettes and soup."

When they prepare for a sexual evening, say an orgy at The Loft starting promptly at twelve (the doors are locked for the night and everyone has checked his clothes by midnight), they begin hours before. Sometimes it starts the night before with their last solid meal. They then have no breakfast or dinner the day of the orgy. "Some people won't eat for two days, the whole weekend." Drugs depress their appetites, and the dieting keeps their weight down. Pete, who has an ulcer and colitis, has to eat some "light stuff."

Douching is the main topic of conversation among fisters. It takes two or three hours to ensure that the body is as empty as one can hope. Between sessions of douching, they begin their drugs. The douching is now expedited by an attachment to their shower, a six-inch cylinder with six holes, at the end of a long flexible steel pipe. They each douche two or three times as the body relaxes more and more on the downers they take and the food in their systems descends lower into the intestines. Before a fisting party or orgy, they check each other out. Sometimes, Pete gets so excited during the hygiene inspection that he has an orgasm.

Each prefers his own cocktail. John likes a tab of mescaline and five milligrams of Valium to begin the night with: they can keep him hard for hours. During the orgy he will take some M.D.A., a form of speed, of course grass and poppers, and, if he is particularly heedless, a toke of Angel Dust. Both take Mydol, sold over the counter to relieve menstrual pain, which they say prevents intestinal cramps. However, both can be fisted on nothing more than grass, and Pete has been done sober. The poppers are used mostly when they are tops, to keep them excited. "But it's M.D.A. that's the fister's drug—that's what gives duration."

The Loft is their favorite orgy place, but it is not as far out as The Catacombs in San Francisco where straight S-M couples sometimes appear, and the gay men watch while a woman fists her husband or lover. I am surprised both at the mixture of straight and gay, of F-F and S-M, and at John's interest in such a scene. He confesses he never was interested before, but since fisting he now loves straight pornography and even has some bisexual fantasies. I ask them whether they think the man being fisted by a woman is straight just because he says so. Pete replies, "Well, to take a fist is a pretty macho thing." John tells me of a Latin American who likes his wife to fist him, but when he travels to the States, he goes with gay men; he won't do anything else: "Straight guys who have no desire to be fucked by a dick can get into fists."

They explain that most of the men regard fisting as macho: their epic fucking and heroic endurance are not for frail types; one has to be strong, patient, and usually silent to sustain the right mood. Pete adds, "I don't like nelly people—it's a turn-off. We went through that period, beads and French poodles. Now we can be like everyone else."

They are very opinionated about the proprieties. In contrast to ordinary or "straight" gay sex which they call "vanilla," in fisting there is no rigid role playing. Every bottom man knows how to fist though some don't especially like to and some are not very good at it. The men they know and they themselves will not be fisted by anyone who has not already been on the bottom and knows what it's all about. There is foreplay, but it has little to do with kisses or whispered endearments. Instead, it is usual to begin to fist a man by rimming him first, "if you acquire a taste for Crisco," John adds, relaxing the sphincter with the tongue before exploring it with the fingers and the hand. Pete likes to have his nipples played with and tolerates a lot of discomfort which he finds exciting, but he draws a distinction between that and the actions of some of the masochists he has seen who have their nipples pierced with needles or clamped and weighted. There is also some theatricality, but it is partyish, not nearly as pretentious as the leather scene. Pete thinks it is groovy to see a guy in a cowboy hat, boots, and a jockstrap, or a black leather motorcycle cap and nothing else. "People who'd never look at you otherwise suddenly are interested if you're wearing a cowboy hat or a baseball cap." Despite this flair and a pleasure in exhibitionism which Pete once heedlessly expressed when he got fisted by all comers on the pool table at The Mine Shaft, sharing the limelight with a successful proctologist with the same fondness, they insist that theirs is the opposite of the S-M scene.

Fisting is anti-"scat"; the whole point of the douching is to be clean. "There are occasional mishaps. The tensest moment is with the first entry: are you clean or dirty?" Pete adds, "Enema queens, like scat queens, are really the scum of the earth." It is the opposite of bondage and discipline because it is action not fantasy that is central, and because the men are flexible in their roles.

"S-M is all in the head; it's artificial and kinky; they have to build their fantasy with so much mental preparation, it's sort of sick. Besides, sometimes I think they're not even into sex. Those motorcycle groups just parade around and get drunk. They don't have much sex—most of it's strut."

The distinctions they were emphasizing seem to be more telling than the similarities to sadomasochism. Fisting has moved sexuality into the center of their lives in an unprecedented way. They socialize almost exclusively with other men like themselves. Outside work and time they spend privately with each other, the rest of their energy is given to fisting. "Now life is sex and work. The sex and the social are merged completely. Our time is for sex and for ourselves alone." Even what is erotic has changed for them. Pete says, "In summer, when I'm on the streets, I get turned on by guys in their sandals, with their tits showing through their T-shirts, and their hands, their arms—you can see everything that matters but their dicks—but who cares, the hand's always hard and doesn't get tired." John adds, "I've taken vanilla home, but when they see the leather sling in the bedroom, they freak out and make for the door. Sex is much hotter now. I've gotten rid of cruising. If we're horny, we use the phone. We have a hundred numbers to call. None of that posing shit in the bars—it's far more liberating psychologically now."

While the rituals of hygiene sound overwhelming, there is also a delight in piggishness, in rolling in "a sea of grease." The pig is the emblem of F.F.A.; pig power is the motto. Miss Piggy is the Judy Garland of this scene. "We're pigs. A true pig is hot, a number who knows what he's doing." Each man has discovered a sexual appetite he had never suspected, and a new sensuality that is more gratifying than anything in his prior erotic life. If Pete has no other sexual outlet, he masturbates while sitting on one of the enormous dildoes they keep in the bathroom tub, but it is a rare day without a sexual session. The orgies are reserved for the weekends: large ones twice a month, otherwise a party of six men or so: "Six is a nice combo; everybody can make it with each other." In the last few years, they have been to a hundred orgies. At first, they were a bit nervous, as if they were at a cocktail party, unsure of how to behave. Now they know the rules and no longer feel insecure. Pete says they are very "cocky." In a single night, he will have long sessions with each of ten or eleven men, most of whom he already knows; he prefers to have at least one or two new men in a long evening. John is nearly as prodigious. His maximum was nine men; usually he averages fewer. These sessions are of some duration, as long as an hour with a man, and it is always coupled, even amid fifty other couples. One does not join a pair or interfere or try to excite the top man by fellating him or fucking him. That might be too dangerous to the man being fisted.

The fister must maintain a balance, controlling his excitement with alertness and skill. He must begin gently; no one rams it in. After his partner is relaxed he can be rough, but he must always be sensitive. "Fisting requires incredible control, but if you're into it, you get very good at it. I'm lucky, I have small hands; I've gotten into people further than anyone else can. People trust me because I'm patient, though John is even more patient than I. When you've got your arm up somebody's ass and they've got this blissful look, it's an entirely different thing than what happens when you fuck. It's kind of a temporary concentration of affection and lust that's a supreme sexual moment, intensely emotional as well as a sensual feeling." John agrees and adds that fisting may start as a head trip, but it gets less and less so. It does not stand for anything else; it's not "psychological"; there is no competition. "Very few bottoms control; they're really passive—that ass is yours, baby, do what you want." Pete interrupts: "Everything in my body has gone to my ass; I'm just a big asshole. They can do anything they want with me. It's *real* passivity."

Pete has become a skillful and popular top man, a marked change from his exclusive preference for being fucked. He still does not like to fuck. He explains, "I've got a six-inch dick; it's cute but nothing much. I never liked to fuck because I'd get shit out so easily. But with fist-fuckers it's different; their ass is so loose." The size of the penis is no longer important; many good tops are small. When I asked them whether they think there is some relationship between penis size and developing skill as a top man, they didn't think so, though Pete agreed that had been his case. In fact, phallicism is generally peripheral and sometimes irrelevant. Many top men perform without erection, and only a few have orgasm. They sustain excitement with poppers. John is one of the exceptions. He gets hard when he's topping, and he sometimes comes while he's fisting. He has even jerked himself off inside someone, an unusual feat even in his crowd. But neither erection nor orgasm are required in performance, and orgasm is often entirely absent in an evening.

John and Pete say it is difficult to generalize about coming. They agree there is less impotence in this scene because people are less nervous, and because performance is based on manual skill. Pete says beginners should not even try for erection since the pressure in tumescence tightens all the muscles and makes getting fisted more difficult. There is also an investment in postponement, which is one of the reasons Pete does not like to be genitally fondled when he is dominant; it provokes orgasm too quickly which then tires him.

Orgasm is commoner for the bottom man who either can masturbate himself or let his partner do it. Both men prefer to be positioned on their backs, best of all in a sling designed for the purpose with leather cuffs that buckle around the ankles to support the legs. That is ideally comfortable for long sessions. They like to watch the men fisting them, and if there is a mirror above the sling, they also like to watch themselves. Pete says he recently came four times, though the last time was dry coming. When I ask him how he manages, he tells me that he doesn't ejaculate entirely. There is too much pressure inside him to release all his semen. The orgasms are partial, allowing him to continue without ending excitement. When an orgasm has been heavy and he wants to rest, it is different from straight gay sex where one partner's ejaculation sometimes ends the session. Pete can go right from bottom to top; often after he's been fisted and come, he wants to fist his partner or someone else. The drugs and the images of the other men all around him are very sustaining.

But both men insist that orgasm is relatively unimportant, like penis size and even erection. Some of the men never come at all at the scene. It is the fisting that is central, and while the drama is all with the man on the bottom, he depends utterly on the skill of the one on top. The techniques vary. Some men just want the motion at the sphincter; some want depth; some want what the mood of the moment dictates. Pete says you try a little of this, a little of that, miming with his hand some of the snaky motions he uses. Usually, the prostate is so stimulated that the sexual tension never ends, building to an aching sensation that wants release at the same time that the heavy motion of the arm produces too much pressure for spontaneous ejaculation.

Pete is very advanced now on the bottom as well as skillful on top. He likes to be punched fucked and have his second "sphincter" handled. "It's like a double fuck. As the ass opens and you relax more and more, you can get your arm up to the second sphincter, the point where the large colon ends, and curve your hand into the opening. Then both sphincters and the colon are getting it." But best for him is to be punched. After the hand has explored him, massaged him till he is completely relaxed, he wants his partner literally to use his fist, to punch him like a pneumatic drill. The sensations deep inside his body which he cannot articulate are the most blissful he has ever known.

When I ask him about his fantasies, he says he doesn't have any when he's punched. "Maybe it's because I don't read," he laughs, "but I don't like talk, rough or any kind; I just sort of drift off, see colors, sometimes a fucking scene, sometimes a beefcake image." John always fantasizes when he is on the bottom, but not when he is on top; then, watching the man he is fisting is interesting enough. Lots of the men are into horses; that's the fist-fucker's dream: up behind the barn door with a stallion. They have heard of a man in northern California who claims to have tried it.

I try to generalize: the arm is then an enormous penis. They both deny it. "Fisters prefer fists to cocks; it's the hand and the arm I cruise these days when I see a red hanky sticking out the back pocket of a trick on the street, or when I go to The Ramrod, where I've already balled with thirty or forty of the men in the place. Lots of older numbers who are not lookers, a bit paunchy maybe, are fun to fuck with because they're good tops—I don't mean ugly, but who gives a shit about pretty? I mean by the end of the evening we all have little pot bellies from the fisting. Everything inside gets pushed around a little. It all settles down later."

It's not that fucking is entirely absent, but it is regarded as a kind of foreplay, or perhaps a postorgasmic stimulation between fisting sessions. To my surprise, John says being fucked after being fisted is terrific because everything is so sensitive that even a small penis can create enormous sensation. I ask what happens to the sphincter and the colon after such sessions: is there any constriction, any of the grip that most gay men find desirable and necessary in anal sex? Both of them laugh at me: a tight ass is as admired in the fisting scene as a limp penis in any other. There is of course some contraction when the arm is removed, but the colon feels like "jello"; John says fucking that is wonderful, but it's an acquired taste.

John and Pete have minimized the dangers of psychopaths or sadists like Julio. They do not perform now with men who are completely strange to them, or spontaneously at a place or a time when they are not prepared. They claim they are much more careful about their bodies now than they've been before, alert to danger signals, confident of what they can withstand physically, more knowledgeable about how much drugs they can tolerate. Like most of the men who are serious about fisting, not only do they douche routinely, but they manicure their nails meticulously since even a slight scratch will put someone out of commission. Like other pro- miscuous gay men, they accept with resignation venereal disease as a haz- ard, particularly amebiasis, which they come down with at least annually. Since they douche so frequently, they are never diarrhetic, nor are the other men; thus, they are asymptomatic, and some men are simply carriers. John jokes, "I'm glad when I get it; I need the break."

When the visit is nearly over, I ask them what's next. They say it's the high plateau of their sexual lives; there's nothing after it, and there's no going down. They are happy and fulfilled. They have explored their sensuality and their bodies as never before; sexuality has assumed an importance and given them a pleasure they had never before expected. They cannot imagine the adventure will lose its thrill. Pete adds, "I can do anything now: top, bottom, I'm good at both ends. I'm cocky now because I'm good at so many things. Of course, I don't suck cock; I never liked that."

6

Pete and John were always reckless about drugs and hedonistic about sexual pleasure. Their frankness is disarming; nothing they have said invites the patronization I have had to deal with exploring the literature of sadomasochism. First of all, I do not understand the psychology of this scene, nor am I sure that there is much to understand in the sense of "interpret." The fancy scenario of sadomasochism with its inversions and anxieties, its fragile ironies and denials, the escapism into a closet psychodrama about power and control, seem absent among fisters. Nor is there the need for pain. Instead, there is the incessant action in a setting free of some of the worst experiences that have beset gay life: sexual guilt and erotic humiliation, rigid role playing, the adoration of beauty and youth, the anxiety about performance, the coldness and hauteur of cruising, the worship of the penis.

There is also a profound surrender to passivity that is never clearly present in S-M, and an exploration of physicality and the body I have never heard of before, testimony about sensation and sensuality, intensities of pleasure I know nothing about.

When I come to interview Ethan, my friend who began to explore fist-fucking when it had hardly been named ten years ago, there is much I want to verify. We have known each other since graduate school, but our friendship has been sporadic. When he was younger, Ethan combined an unusual delicate beauty with a quiet persistant streak of self-destructiveness that was as arresting as his startling eyes. I had not seen him for some years since the break-up of a long affair with a lover I had come to dislike and since he had left academia for more engaging work. He was generous about talking to me; we had missed each other, and this was a chance to strengthen ties that were nearly gone.

When I arrived at his Village loft, I was stunned by his appearance. At forty-four, he is now one of the most beautiful of men; maturity has ripened what was delicate and somewhat evanescent. The boyishness is gone; an air of petulance has also passed away. What remains is serene and seductive, sweet and more than a little sad.

The loft is an entire floor, newly converted, deluxe, spacious of course, but somehow homey. David, his lover of four years, a younger man of thirty-six, handsome in a conventional way, greeted me politely and then absented himself somewhere in the apartment.

Ethan and I chatted about old times, ex-lovers, old and new jobs, his new affluence, his new relationship. He is, plainly, "married." When his lover leaves for his monthly weekend out of town to see his children, Ethan uses the occasion to go to the Beacon Baths and be fisted; it is his exclusive infidelity, and it is never discussed between the men. What happens outside the relationship that might be hurtful to know about is left to silence. When they are together they are tightly coupled, with a small social life in the city and a narrower one in the country where they have a house they visit most weekends during the year.

The first thing Ethan verifies is that fisting is not orgasmic, not even phallic. He never comes at the baths and is rarely erect. There is no foreplay, no kissing or embracing for him. He also prefers to be positioned on his back so he can see his partner, but partly, it is to be protective: he can push a man off with his legs if he has to. That has rarely happened because Ethan says he is good at psyching out a prospect; his intuitions have been reliable. Not only is the man's appearance and demeanor evidence, but Ethan judges how much he can trust him by the touch, by the degrees of gentleness and firmness that signal the *gestalt* he needs.

Ethan has no interest in topping: "The top is boring; as the bottom, I'm the center." The heart of the experience is surrender, the passivity. He is also anally passive with his lover, but between them the lovemaking is varied, romantically full of passionate foreplay, and Ethan is as reactive in his own responsiveness as his lover. In the beginning of the relationship, David fisted him because Ethan wanted him to, but he soon sensed that David got little from it other than giving his lover pleasure. They have now dropped fisting from their sexual lives, and Ethan does not miss it. "I began to see it as an unfair demand," he explains, adding that his sexual life with his lover is completely satisfying.

Ethan claims that he is in control of the situation at the baths, that there is as much control by the passive party as there is in S-M, but he adds that obviously there is a great deal of self-deception, particularly since he always uses quaaludes when he is there, as well as grass and poppers: "But I *feel* I'm in control at any rate."

So far, that is the result of his luck. He has never been injured, has had no health problem more serious than a hemorrhoid, and has escaped amebiasis. Perhaps his luck has some relation to his foresight. He always has sex in a private room with one man at a time. He has no interest in group sex or exhibitionism. Like Pete's, his capacity is enormous, averaging six to eight men in an evening, long sessions using the entire night that end only when he is physically exhausted. "I'm anally erotic, which is not climactic—the night ends with exhaustion." At no time does he feel any phallic interest in himself or his partner. While Ethan has never been a joiner and would be embarrassed at F.F.A., the red hanky in a pocket is still a trigger of fraternal recognition, reminding him of the place of that sexual pleasure in his life, and he feels toward that man "what I feel when there's just one other Jew in a room of gentiles." But he does not act on that trigger; he does not cruise the man, acknowledge the signal, or wear one himself. All he is interested in is his monthly excursion to the baths, and "finishing it there." He says the problems connected with fisting are the same psychological ones he has elsewhere in his life about anxiety and authority. Before his present relationship, with its domestic tranquility, he was out every night looking; sex was much more obstrusive, anxiety ridden, and provocative. Then, he felt his appetite controlled him.

I'm skeptical about his notion of control during a session. Even if he could push a man off with his strong legs, he could easily be torn during ejection, and how can he rely on his judgment or intuition when he is so stoned?

"I can do without drugs, but I prefer to be stoned, to be out of myself.

My fantasy is to take as much as possible; my pleasure is in depth, in feeling someone deep inside me, the deeper the better. Drugs help me open up. I don't like to speed or trip because when it's over, I want to come down when I want to—I want to get home and go right to sleep. It's all over then."

Ethan laughs at Pete's notion that fisting is macho; he dismisses it as thoughtless if not silly. For him, this has little to do with ideas of gender. He never imagines the arm is a penis, no more than his anus is a vagina. It is another variety of sexuality, and at this time in his life, not especially significant. He concedes he has been lucky avoiding injury and pain, contrasting that with his early experiences getting fucked, which were painful for some years "till I acquired the taste."

With fisting, he began experimentally; he didn't know what he was doing or what was going to happen. He had not heard of fist-fucking before it happened to him; it was all inductive. He liked being played with and slowly discovered what was possible. His first full experience was at the baths. He now thinks it'll end sometime; it is already boring to wait between men for the next prospect; waiting takes half the time, and it is full of ennui. There are no fantasies he has not used up to occupy the time or sustain excitement. The pleasures are in action; the anticipation is nothing. Ethan suspects that he has already peaked, perhaps some years ago. If fisting made trouble in his relationship with David, he would give it up. His life with his lover is the romantic center that sustains him in work and in the world.

Perhaps the only legacy from fisting that he now finds a necessary pleasure is the douching. As a procedure, he only discovered it relatively late, some four or five years ago. Since then he has douched as a preparation with his lover, and even when he is alone. It is the highest autoerotic excitement he knows, almost masturbatory, a deeply sensual experience. If he is stoned and uses a popper while he douches, fantasizing about being fisted, the experience is as intense as any with men.

7

Ethan and Pete and John are finding a sensuality that was unimagined before it was discovered and that seems now the furthest outreach of pleasure in homosexuality. Unlike sadomasochists, they are avid for the plea-sure, "bliss" as distinct from fervent sexual excitement that can override pain. Like everyone's sexual life, theirs is colored by character: the conflicts of personality and the moods of temperament are present, as troublesome or supportive here as elsewhere in their lives.

There is a common ground with sadomasochism, but I suspect that on it are similarities to all sexual variety, all erotic play among those who are so experienced and so engaged in sexuality that change of some or even any sort is welcome, perhaps necessary. Once when I was in my twenties, I ended up somewhat drunk in bed with a stranger. He was very skillful, and I was soon lost in my excitement and myself, foggily congratulating myself on my luck, when suddenly he slapped me hard across the face, twice, fast. When I looked at him speechless in outrage and panic, he was smiling, a knowing sweet smile. The rest of the lovemaking was shadowed with fear and anticipation; I was off-balance, and while I cannot say the experience was more pleasurable than others, it was memorable. My own temperament is too cowardly, too intolerant of pain, too conflicted about control and surrender to dabble. My body is too much a stranger to me; its executors are my physicians upon whom I hostilely rely; they know it better than I do when it ails. But in its normal state, it is taken for granted, forgotten in a way that my appearance never is. I will abuse my health casually in ways that I am never as careless about with appearances.

Erotic sadomasochism seems much concerned with surfaces, skin-deep, and that skin is sometimes in glacé kid or butch leather. Fisting appears what it is: a daring flirtation with mortality, ignoring risk for promises of sensual intensity where the self is blissfully lost, surrendered into other hands. Fisting, with its intimacies that regard kissing and fon-dling and embracing as uninteresting, naive, is really fuelled by a more intense romanticism than conventional sexuality. If the mouth and the hand and the arms are used in new ways, they still refer to the earlier more innocent usage. What these men who fist delight in is that surrender, that momentary trust that fixes the body on another, that joins two people in a new image of coupling that has its only analogy in impalement: pain and death are indeed symbols of these lovers.

I leave it to the doctors and the moralists to sum up the degree of hazard and the long-term risks. Are those fisters who end up with colostomies proportionately higher in number than ordinary patients with such surgery from years of ulcerating their bodies with frustration and repression? When I first heard of fisting, I assumed that psychologically and physically it would be a point of no return, ending other kinds of sexuality, especially anal fucking. How could one go back after this voyage? But Ethan can go back and forth at will, and he is already a little bored with the journey. When he truly tires, he will head for safe harbor, not scuttle the ship.

Masochism is defined by negatives, consistent with Freud's negative concept of pleasure as the cessation of excitement, the sudden discharge in orgasm of pent-up tension. For many men, this has been what they seek: the pleasure that is the end of pleasure, the orgasm that is the finale after which there can be rest, and normal safe life may resume. Sensuality is entirely in the service of this end product. Orgasm becomes crucially important, often the sole criterion of sexual success, and erection, potency, and phallicism are strict concerns; performance can be as much a labor as a delight.

One of the questions about masochism relates to the impact upon men of ambivalent and prismatic images of women. The focus has usually been on the symbolic father who is always the figure of dominance no matter what gender the aggressive partner is. That sounded reasonable enough to Krafft-Ebing and Wilhelm Stekel; Freud and Reik thought they had sufficient answer when they classified masochism as feminine. But the question now is about the importance of passivity and feeling powerless, and how we respond to them in our lives.

The book by J. R. Ackerly that Diana Trilling found so simple and so moving is also the story of a life of unrelenting loneliness and unhappiness. Ackerly's idea of homosexuality was indeed simple: there are men who want women and men who want men. In Edwardian England, upper-class culture allowed and even encouraged such a choice for adolescent boys, even assumed that it was a free choice, that one could change sexual direction at will. Maturity would encourage heterosexuality and conventional life. That was how Ackerly saw his own father's life, one where it was possible to move from youthful homosexuality (and a hint of male prostitution) to adult heterosexuality, though Ackerly's father was bigamous.

But Ackerly had no such self-determination. His own sexual life was criminal by a number of standards. The laws of 1885 which sent Oscar Wilde to prison hung over every law-abiding homosexual, and Ackerly's own tastes were quite limited: for "young, clean, healthy boys as nearly heterosexual as possible." Searching for his ideal friend, for whom he expected to pay ready cash, cost more than money; as Trilling says, "life for Ackerly was in fact hell."

His sexuality was limited to mutual masturbation and hugging. He felt no desire for oral or anal experience. He attempted fellatio once with the young sailor whom he loved, but that provoked the youth's disgust and his prompt disappearance from Ackerly's life. He confesses he somewhat sympathized with that disgust. The rest of his sexual history was confined to male prostitutes, until premature ejaculation and finally complete impotence made even those encounters futile.

He found peace when he fell in love with his dog, an Alsatian he named Tulip and about whom he wrote a remarkable book in 1956. If Ackerly was stoic and uncomplaining, so admirable in the disposition of a writer and so pleasant for his readers, those virtues had little to do with giving him pleasure or lessening his misery. He had intelligence, education, taste, and talent, and his life was hell. For some men, those gifts might balance the deprivations or inadequacies of their sexuality, but that was not Ackerly's case. The longing for affection and for sexual excitement did not abate until he found his strange deep tie to his pet, and then perhaps there was enough to make him resigned to sexual failure. His story illuminates many things about English culture and its odd tolerances about sexuality, the arrangements people make for their emotional well-being, the childhood with a bisexual and bigamous father, but it is also the story of sexual imprisonment, of powerlessness before one's own desires, and of desires so self- defeating that a guilt-ridden solitude seemed an inevitable relief.

The impoverishment and arrestment that Ackerly describes was common to men of his class and his time, though his is an extreme example. More and more, we are learning through biography how little freedom there has been in male homosexuality, even when it was consentual and when it was called a choice. In 1976, Howard Sturgis' *Belchamber* was reissued by AMS Press. Written originally in 1904, it is a closeted novel of manners about sexual inhibition. Sturgis, a cousin of George Santayana, was famous for his effeminacy and for his witty deflations of pomposity.

Wit was the only weapon for the anger of a man described as gentle, intuitive, vulnerable, and nervous, who hated violence and delighted in the arts, who cultivated feminine friendship, and whose work advocated a tolerance for human diversity of any kind. But he could not help praising and insulting in the same breath; the charm and the rage were so intermixed they were an entity. The anger is not difficult to understand: it is his outrage that in the entire erotic world, he had nothing that mattered. He was not even pleasing to other homosexuals as effeminate as he.

Gay men have learned to behave differently, to divorce appearance and proclivity, to appear powerful and controlled even amid the most ardent romantic pursuit. What they have not learned is to tolerate diversity despite their own experience with ostracism, to respond to character rather than charisma, to regard personality as more valuable than person. Liberationists call this the internalization of oppression, and it is surely that. But no one is exonerated for his self-destructiveness, his moral masochism, not when he has access to privilege and opportunity to explore the self and its sexuality with more freedom than ever before.

In Paul Goodman's essay, "The Politics of Being Queer" *(Nature Heals: The Psychological Essays of Paul Goodman,* edited by Taylor Stoehr), Goodman says, "What we need is not defiant pride and self-consciousness, but social space to live and breathe." To live and breathe is no minor demand in a culture where life is cheap and what we breathe nearly poisoned. He likes the political potential of the gay world because it is so profoundly democratizing, but he wonders whether that is really not an appalling superficiality. What is democratic and crosses lines of ethnicity, class, and race in the gay world is beauty; what is distributed equally among gay men is their powerlessness before their sexual obsessiveness and their helplessness to protect themselves from scorn and harm. Goodman adds, "For both bad and good, homosexual life retains some of the alarm and excitement of childish sexuality." Well, it is easy to see the good: the liberation from moral hypocrisy, the delight in variety, the courage or daring or madness to risk new experience in the search for pleasure which everyone is told is the modern architect of happiness. What is bad is the failure to make of the good something lasting, so that, unlike Ackerly or Sturgis, we can claim, despite all, that it has been a good life; freely chosen or not, it has sufficed.

For those who have accepted their homosexuality, there is consent; perhaps choice is irrelevant now. But consent means awareness and responsibility. The growing need to deny the burden of helplessness is not consent. Sadomasochism is many things; among them is a flight from the anxiety of pleasure, an anxiety more powerful than hatred or rage.

I do not want to moralize about matters of hygiene and health in a nation that subsidizes the tobacco industry and turns its countryside carcinogenic. Perhaps the real standard of well-being is nothing more reliable than an intimate connection with one's own body. But fisters acknowledge in the thrill of passivity more than a preferred sexual posture. They tell of dispositions that are unresolved about aggression and acquiescence. To be thrilled by delicious punches deep in one's body is to find a bliss in sexual violence that no ordinary relationship can sustain. At least the passivity and the blows are real, and the pleasure not fantastic.

Ultimately, Freud's claims of culture must be confronted. If those claims are unjust, then it is reasonable and good to demand justice. To play with powerlessness is to deny it, and worse, to immune oneself from sympathy for those who are truly helpless prisoners, whether in the penal institutions our nation keeps building or in the solitary confinement of old age.

CHAPTER EIGHT

Prisoners:

The Three R's: Reading, Rape, and Riot

1

At Roberto's sentencing, he wept: "I told that judge, 'I don't know if any of the victim's relatives are here, but I want them to know how truly sorry I am,' and I broke down and cried—it was really, I really felt bad about what I did, and I knew I didn't mean to do it, but it was something that happened, and I could never bring him back—hey, if they had given me a chance to stay in the community, to do something positive with my life, I would have made a tremendous asset to the community, I would have worked with the old, the retarded, I would have helped. In that moment, I knew I was really sorry." Roberto's sorrow and his fervent need to make restitution were not relevant. The district attorney had already reduced the charge from first-degree murder to first-degree manslaughter. Since society did not insist on literal revenge, on taking Roberto's life for the one he had taken, it could at least waste his life in prison.

When he was twenty-four, Roberto killed a man, a gay man, a client. Hustling the New York bars, habitually drunk, he was always at the edge of rage. Though he had been a prostitute in Chicago for several years before he came to New York, he describes himself before the crime as still "square." The night of the killing, he was already high when a client propositioned him for a threesome. Roberto didn't like the looks of the friend and turned down the offer; however, he agreed to go home with him alone. At the apartment, Roberto got drunker, and "the sex didn't work out—I came first or something—and then the john tried to throw me out, but I was supposed to stay the night. Anyway, we started to quarrel and suddenly it got violent: the guy smashed me in the face and broke my nose. I pulled out my knife just to scare him off, but that got him really angry. He said, 'Now I'm going to get you' and yelled out for his buddy next door."

Roberto panicked; his bluff was called, and he stabbed the man. When he ran out the door, covered in his own blood, he collided with the buddy who was just entering. In a cab on the way to St. Vincent's Hospital, he threw the knife away. After his broken nose was X-rayed and set—a piece of evidence that helped reduce the charge to manslaughter—Roberto went home to wait. When the police arrived, tracing him through the hospital, he was still waiting. He was told he was being booked on a charge of assault; not until he was at the station did he learn that the charge was homicide. Roberto screamed and got hysterical when he realized he'd killed the man. There and then, he was interrogated and asked to confess, which he did. At the indictment, the charge was first-degree murder. Some months later when he finally got a lawyer, he agreed to cop the plea, for it was not until the indictment that he learned that he had gone berzerk at the time of the killing and stabbed the man twenty-six times. He recalled having done it only once. Roberto believes he must have been temporarily insane. "I'll always believe that."

Toward the end of the interview when I asked him whether that anger would have erupted so explosively in another kind of life, he was unsure: "Hard to say—I didn't even know I had the anger. But hustling is so self-destructive, you have to put up with such a lot of shit. Well, maybe if I'd been gainfully employed, I wouldn't have drunk so much."

Gainfully employed? Is Roberto being ironic? But looking closely at him, one is no longer sure what he is. A quick glance and one thinks he is another hunky Hispanic in his late twenties, sexy and vibrant like so many of New York's Latins. It is late June, and he wears a tight plain T-shirt, cheap khakis, and black basketball sneakers. The body is strong and sexual, but nothing extraordinary on Columbus Avenue in Manhattan's West Seventies. It is his face that eludes one's preconceptions until he tells you he is Mexican, not Puerto Rican. Then what seemed vaguely familiar is identified: he is Indian, the same face one sees on the sculptured heads from pre-Columbian America. The high cheekbones and slanted eyes, the long coarse black hair, the heavy lips and wide sensual mouth are more Mongol than Spanish.

We are brunching at Ruskay's, sitting outside at a cramped table, eating and taping. I'm worried that the tape will be useless since the street is so noisy, but Roberto has said, not quite casually, that he hates being cooped up. Besides, if the tape is inaudible, I'll abandon the piece which I've been working on for two months, which I am sick of, which confuses me and frightens me more than a little. Neither interviewing ex-offenders, nor visiting prisons, nor talking to those involved in prison reform, nor even my own political and human sympathies have washed away the shadowy anxieties that travel with me in this research.

Roberto suddenly calls out to a passing acquaintance, a young black man in a baseball outfit heading toward Central Park. After introductions, Roberto flirts with his friend very boldly, teases him for not joining us, and, when he leaves, returns to his food greedily, explaining that he is into blacks and has been after this particular young man for some time.

Oddly, Roberto neither speaks nor understands Spanish, much to his chagrin. He was the youngest of eight children when his mother abandoned the family; without emotion, he describes her as an alcoholic prostitute. His father tried to keep the family together, but in St. Paul, Minnesota, that was impossible for a Mexican migrant worker. Like his brothers and sisters, Roberto was raised in a Catholic orphanage until he was twelve, when he began to live in a series of foster homes. It was when he left the orphanage that he recognized that he had homosexual feelings. They disturbed him deeply since he wanted to become a priest. Guilt kept his sexual encounters confined to forays in parks and tea rooms with older men, and not until he was twenty did he discover there was another gay life.

Roberto describes himself in his adolescence as a good boy, a hard worker and eager student, religious if not devout, but alone, isolated even when all seven brothers and sisters were in the same institution. For some reason he was not close to anyone. Though his father tried to see the children on weekends, Roberto has few memories of him. He died while Roberto was in prison, and no one from his family ever visited him during his sentence.

He served nearly five of his one-to-seven-year term at Auburn Prison. He would have been paroled earlier had he managed to find a sponsor and had he not been accused by officials of inciting discontentment among black prisoners by "lecturing to them in Spanish." Though he explained that he knew no Spanish, having grown up in Minnesota, he convinced no one. When his parole was almost a certainty, that skepticism returned to lengthen his stay. He had decided to become a Trappist monk, and through his former church contacts he had arranged to be paroled to a Wisconsin monastery. Then the parole officer told the brothers "something" that made them reject him. Roberto had to stay in prison until he could make new arrangements some seven months later. When I asked what that "something" was, he was puzzled; he had been open about his homosexuality; indeed, given the circumstances of his crime there was no point trying to conceal it.

Like others, Roberto was openly gay in prison, but unlike most whites, he chose his lovers among black prisoners, defiantly crossing the color line and cutting himself off from other Hispanic prisoners (he was already isolated from the rest of the white minority). I suggested that it may have been this, more than his gayness, that infuriated prison officials and provoked the charges against him.

Roberto was welcomed by blacks since he was an attractive macho man, a "cute guy," and he was educated, articulate as well as literate. I'm uncomfortably curious about sexual matters and finally ask more bluntly than necessary what he and his lovers did: where did they go? What were their roles? Roberto explains that he is always active, that though he is gay, he always does the fucking. He laughs, "I had a lot of trouble explaining that to them in prison: that I was gay but active. Anyway, in four years there, I only got down maybe twenty times. I didn't want to be a fuckin' whore like those queens who'd take care of business for a pack of cigarettes. I guess I have a high sense of moral values. I couldn't live with myself." When Roberto starts describing his contempt for queens who he thinks are "very pathetic, they're a segment of the population I don't identify with, that stereotype of swishy up-the-ass," I turn the subject away.

Roberto spent a significant amount of his prison time working out, and the legacy of those years is his strong youthful body and his boyishness even in his mid-thirties. "I had to be in shape because they knew I was gay, and if you didn't show you were strong, you'd be ripped off—raped." Fear of rape was always with him. From the moment he began his sentence until he was paroled, that never lessened. Neither did the racial tensions or sexual frustrations, nor did the constant boredom. His job was filing, and he made some extra money typing legal briefs for other prisoners, an easy job but a waste of time. He wanted to go to college, and there was a local work-release training program held at a nearby junior college, but the violent nature of his crime disqualified him. Ironically, Roberto was one of the very few men sufficiently educated to qualify for college entrance.

Like all the ex-offenders I spoke to, Roberto agrees that prison was totally unredeeming, worse than useless, that the damage done there was beyond repair. Speaking of those years, his voice is anguished and he becomes quieter and finally depressed. "The stigma is always with me—an ex-offender. There was no rehabilitation. Listen, I reject the society that sent me to prison and then decided that it was time for me to go back into it. The only thing they do, they take away your manhood, they dehuman-ize you—that's the classic wrong. They take away your self-respect, your pride."

And I'm thinking: but you were a hustler and a killer; you killed one of your own, and you cannot even find sympathy for them when their style isn't like your own sinister virility. What were you proud of?

And of course the answer is: surviving. A Mexican in America would be proud simply because he had survived, because he had come through two of the most depriving institutions in modern society, the orphanage and the prison, and emerged with his sanity and intelligence. I understand, but I can never understand.

Roberto tries to convey how sick the prisons are. He doesn't use the word in its psychological sense; he uses it morally. He has little use for psychology. He says he is not introspective. He rejected therapy in and after prison claiming he couldn't get into it, but he rather approves the suggestion one psychologist made that the killing may have been cathartic for him, exorcising the legacy of hatreds from the years in the orphanage and on the streets.

"I don't know why—why I did it or anything—it's still a mystery. Life is. When you try to understand it, it gets less clear." But the murder, the prison, all of it is still with him, in dreams, in memories. Now both the nightmare and the stigma have to be used, have to be made into something.

When he was paroled, he had good luck. He was sent to Harlem Halfway House, where he was given room and board and access to work, and eventually to occupational training. He left reluctantly since he felt safe at the House, but the shortage of space was severe. Now Roberto would like to head his own halfway house, preferably for gay prisoners, to channel the reminders of his past into the restitution he was denied in the courts. Roberto's vision of his halfway house is a place men would not have to leave; it would be a stable community where mutual help and solidarity would give parolees fresh from prison a home. He is convinced that only prisoners can really help each other; society's concern is unreliable.

"Look at Attica. It didn't last. Straight society forgot. It doesn't care; it's not interested. Like Dostoievsky said, prisons, they're the mirror of the society, indifferent, demoralized."

I thank him for his time and his frankness. He cheers up when I click off the tape recorder, and he is free to pursue his pleasures on this stunning June day. And I wonder who he is, this man I've spent nearly three hours with and probably will never see again, this gay Mexican-American macho man with middle-class skills and a Catholic education, who hustled and killed, this man who cites Dostoevsky: "The degree of civilization in a society can be judged by entering its prisons." If that is true, then we all live in *The House of the Dead*.

2

The issues that brought Roberto and me together are ideological, political. Our homosexuality is the basis for talk about prison and reform, but even there, few of our experiences are mutual. I envy him his sexual vigor, his appetite, his ability to survive; perhaps he envies me my nights free of dreams of violence and claustrophobia.

I admire Roberto's boldness in Auburn, his crossing the color line and recklessly defying this taboo, probably the most infuriating one to break. As long as prisons vibrate with racial tension, truly the mirror of the society that needs them—both the prisons and the tension—then prison authorities will tolerate or even encourage the men to sexualize that tension. The aura of violence, especially as rape, will keep the men suspicious and wary of each other; raw strength is then sustained as the only real penal power. In such an atmosphere, the prisoners cooperate with their jailers to make might the only right and thus perpetuate their own brutality. This is why prison officials fear men crossing the color lines and why they are vengeful toward those who do: such attempts may be the beginning of a solidarity that leads politically either to Attica or to liberation, to the nihilistic bitter rage of riot or to change in the prison system, change that only a few reformers, some ex-offenders, and the prisoners have a stake in. Roberto's homosexuality could be accommodated in Auburn; his freedom from racial contempt could not.

In Roberto's history there is much of contemporary life. His oppression in an ethnic minority, his exploitation as a young homosexual, his yearning for order, particularly the comforts of the Catholic church, which was turned into guilt and self-hatred, his murderous anger, and finally his haunted nights and lifelong shame at the humiliations of the past make up a model chronicle of modern times. Yet he survived. Why then am I so dogged by a sense of futility that deepens over the months even as I talk to men and women optimistically and humanely trying to alleviate the problems of prisoners?

I began eagerly enough. A friend referred me to Lambda Legal Defense and Education Fund. Lambda is representing the National Gay Task Force, *Gay Community News, Off Our Backs,* the Inside-Outside Collective, and Calvin Keach, currently a prisoner, as joint plaintiffs in a suit against Norman Carlson, Director of the Federal Bureau of Prisons. The issue is prisoners' access to printed gay materials which are now prohibited. Early in 1977, Calvin Keach, an inmate then in Leavenworth (now transferred to a federal institution somewhere in Texas) was denied literature written by or about homosexuals. He asked Lambda to sue to secure his rights because such censorship violates the First, Fourth, Fifth, and Ninth Amendments. The suit is the basis of a class action, since Carlson's policy directives stated that all literature identifiable as homosexual is to be banned. Carlson maintains that prisoners' receiving such material poses a threat to the "security, discipline, and order" of the institutions since it would identify those who receive it as homosexual and therefore subject them to sexual assault.

I found the case provocative and was eager to work on it. Literature as an invitation to rape! Gay prisoners fighting for their right to read, for their literature as a means of sustaining their dignity, perhaps even as a source for their psychological liberation. It was perfect for me, a political activist, a teacher of literature. With contempt, I read the federal directives. Though it was assumed that gay men would be raped and that assault is inevitable in prisons, the term "homosexual rape" was used repeatedly to characterize the sexual violence committed by men who will fight to kill if their heterosexuality is impugned but who assault other men, usually straight, who are younger and weaker than their assailants.

In the spring of 1977, some attempt to correct this attitude was begun. Among others, the National Gay Task Force, Lambda, and the Fortune Society (a rehabilitation agency run by ex-prisoners), met with Carlson through the efforts of then presidential assistant Midge Costanza. Everyone agreed that their common goal was to eliminate prison violence. Toward that end, Carlson has now issued a policy statement to all prison staffs to replace "homosexual rape" and "homosexual assault" with "rape" or "sexual assault." This is an important first step. Next would be to allow gay teachers, ministers, and representatives of the different organizations into the prisons to counsel and instruct inmates. So far, no discussion about this has taken place. Traditionally, prison officials cope with sexual assault by segregating gay prisoners either in inferior overcrowded prison housing or worse in solitary confinement. This approach is also under attack in the courts, both in the States and in Canada.

Now, some six months after that initial meeting with Lambda, after reading hundreds of pages on prison problems, after helpful talks with David Rothenberg of the Fortune Society, Tom O'Connor of the Prison Reform Task Force, and Adam McQuillan of the Correctional Association, after consulting with officials in the State Department of Corrections and with librarians and teachers running programs in institutions, after visiting Riker's Island, I am filled with a sense of futility. Tear the prisons down. Burn them.

3

Rape is the subject that unfailingly elicits everyone's interest. Sex in prison, "normal" men having sex with other men: this proves fascinating to those who run the system, those who are in it, and those who are trying to reform it. The brutal, useless, vindictive wastefulness of prisons is just taken for granted. The possibility of keeping nonviolent offenders in the community where they could make restitution is ignored. Neither society nor the judicial system is interested in restitution. Neither are the victims of crime, particularly. Most people prefer vengeance to mercy; most approve of prisons as punitive institutions. I do not think prisons are solely reflective of social callousness; any public institution will do for that. But people's approval of imprisonment does reflect their impotence, their fear about their powerlessness to protect themselves against violence. The ordinary citizen approves: all those black and Hispanic men locked up and wasted and, even more gratifying, terrified themselves of something worse than their victims' muggings: anal rape. Grim justice indeed.

The image of prison rape is a central myth of gay oppression. This is the essential fag: the asshole to be taken. And the darkest side of the issue is the erotic fascination with the subject among gay men.

But what are homosexual men to make of an attitude toward anal intercourse which so many practice with fervid pleasure, here regarded as the worst of punishments? Aside from reinforcing again the idea that what we love heterosexuals detest as unimaginably debasing, what is involved in such mythography? True, most homosexuals would not be turned on by the sadism of rape, the desire to hurt the object of one's lust. Women may love to be fucked, but they hate rape; however, the heterosexual act in itself is not regarded as disgusting, nor is it necessarily physically painful. What is violation is coercion, to be taken without consent, and often victims testify that even more scarifying and traumatic are other sexual acts. Those same acts, fellatio and anal intercourse, that are ordinary among gay men, are instruments of debasement among prisoners.

Prison rape has been written about extensively; documented by psychologists, sociologists, and penologists; examined by gay writers in fiction, poetry, and drama. All agree on its horror; all report its devastating effect on naive and invariably straight young men: almost a fate worse than death. In a dreary but well-meaning book, *Terror in the Prisons: Homosexual Rape and Why Society Condones It,* by Carl Weiss and David Friar, the answer given is that society is callous and puritanical: it does not wish to acknowledge that the problem exists. But that puritanism is not explored, nor is the homophobia it is deeply connected to. Instead, the book dwells vividly on the rapes, devoting more than half the space to case histories; another third is spent on the narratives of the rapists. The material could easily be converted into homosexual pornography.

No issue connected with gay prisoners is untouched by the question of rape: not what they read, nor where they sleep, nor their chances for work or training. Yet overwhelmingly, the victims and rapists are men who think of themselves as straight, which is why the crime horrifies liberals and reformers. In the play which gave rise to the Fortune Society, John Herbert's *Fortune and Men's Eyes,* there are two rape victims, one gay and one straight. But the gay one is pathetic, if not contemptible, in his helplessness. The most graphic scene in the film version of the play, and the most pornographic, is the gang rape of the gay man. The straight prisoner is treated quite differently; the assault on him is depicted as painful; his facial expressions are emphasized. There is nothing but his pain and his rapist's sadism. With the rape of the effeminate homosexual, the camera focuses on the rapists disrobing, on their lust. Clearly, the straight man has to be beaten into submission, while the fag is there for the taking. Why should he resist? What manhood is there left for him to lose? Later, when the straight victim turns the tables and rapes his tormentor, audiences cheer, presumably largely gay audiences. What are they cheering about? Has the straight man come out? Has he turned gay? Of course not: anal penetration is seen entirely as an issue of submission and power: that is its only source of pleasure. It is a matter of masculine domination. That it might be erotically powerful or sexually pleasurable is not hinted at: the idea is bizarre. The rapist "has" to do it: he is compelled by deprivation. The victim, whether straight or gay, is tainted, his manhood lost.

Is it surprising that when "experts" explore the subject, somehow their findings always manage to aid prison authorities in the oppression of gay prisoners? Director Carlson uses as his major argument for the supression of gay literature the supposition that the material will "mark" the recipient, singling him out for even more aggravated assault. His evidence is a monograph by penologist Peter Boffum, "Homosexuality in Prisons" (U.S. Government Printing Office, 1972). Boffum's findings are based on the observation that gay men are harassed and sexually molested in prison, as any gay prisoner will confirm.

But the report is inaccurate because it is euphemistic. It does not mean that gay men will be subject to rape if they're identified as gay: witness Roberto who is just one of many gays who were never assaulted in prison. It means effeminate or feminine or youthful or slight gay men, it means nonmacho or nonviolent gay men will be easier marks. How serious an argument is this? Are gay men who are convicted of violent crime most of whom are Hispanic or black, likely to fit this description of the victim?

Much more pertinent research which the federal director does not mention has been done recently. In *Urban Life* (January 1977), Leo Carrol wrote an article called "Humanitarian Reform and Biracial Sexual Assault in a Maximum Security Prison." His conclusion is not surprising but it is chilling. Most rapists are black men; most victims are white. The motivation is less sexual frustration than it is racial hatred. One man sums it up: "It's getting even, I guess. You whites been cutting our balls off ever since we been in this country. Punking whites is just one way of getting even." The assumption is that hundreds of years of racial oppression can be avenged by treating straight white men as homosexuals. One injustice will balance the other.

The Bureau of Prisons is fully aware of these racial tensions. Why then does it ignore the real issue? Partly it is expressing the wishes of the dominant society that supports it. Whites in urban America are frightened of black aggressiveness. The assertion is now seen everywhere, but most of all among young black and Hispanic men. Charles Silberman's *Criminal Violence, Criminal Justice* discusses the effect on blacks of their discovery of white fear: "It would be hard to overestimate what an extraordinarily liberating force this discovery is." Silberman talks of the high proportion of blacks among those who commit violent crimes as a sign of the growing awareness of black power. The young black man, the "bad nigger" so much in evidence in pop culture and in street life, is probably the most hated and feared stereotype in white America. And the prisons are the one place a frightened society can safely appease its anxiety about black men by punishing them for its own helplessness.

That same society, so profoundly racist, is deeply homophobic. If tolerating rape will pacify men at the edge of violence, it is safer and cheaper than hiring more guards and risking *their* lives. If only black studs just raped fags, respectable people could slam the lid on that can of worms. But there are straight victims. Black men are using the most humiliating of weapons: they are turning white men into women. White women. By fucking them. It is the nightmare of lynch-law America come true. What can be done?

Well, the government has a ready answer: build more prisons. At a time when every respectable penologist has acknowledged the utter failure of the prison system to rehabilitate, the Federal Bureau of Prisons is embarking on a building campaign. The most prestigious study of the problem is Michel Foucault's *Discipline and Punish: The Birth of the Prison*. Foucault has been exploring the relationship of sexuality and power for the last decade: it is *the* subject. He thinks the day of the prison may actually be over, since prison is both too inept and too corrupt for the efficiencies of capitalism. As long as there are still inhibitions about converting them into concentration camps or extermination centers, they are increasingly expensive and useless. Well, perhaps in France. After all, how many unemployed blacks or Hispanics are there in France? In America, we are building.

The 1980 Winter Olympics site at Lake Placid is now being converted into a federal prison for five hundred youths, some three hundred miles from the nearest urban center. Even though the newer prisons are more humane, architecturally sophisticated, and attuned to the populations they serve, there is no doubt of the absolute zero return in terms of rehabilitation. At the present cost of nearly $30,000 per cell this is staggering. Sweden, the Western nation with the most progressive prisons, has abandoned all hope of rehabilitation through prison. The United States, with the largest prison population (over three hundred thousand), continues to build.

Well, what are we to do with criminals? The sensible answer is to separate those who are hard-core violent from the rest of the population.

Most experts put that figure at no more than 10 percent of the present prison population. Another 20 percent may be guilty of violent crimes of a singular nature; that is, they are not likely to repeat their offenses. Undoubtedly, the other 70 percent of those in prison could be released to the community where the cost of maintaining and retaining them would be a fraction of what it costs to keep them in prison. No one in the power establishment supports the expanding prison program. Newspapers like *The New York Times,* hardly radical, have repeatedly advocated an end to such futility.

It doesn't stop. Short of utopian intervention, the building program will continue. The prison population, obeying some demonic law of supply and demand, will expand, and the situation will worsen. Susan Sheehan's *A Prisoner and A Prison* pessimistically documents the failure of Green Haven (!), the newest of New York State's five maximum-security prisons, to change anything. A $35,000 turret lathe lies unused; inmates claim that vocational training is a dupe, for no one will employ them outside. But surely to know how to use a lathe *might* be useful, *might* alleviate the endless boredom of prison days. The answer to the neglected machine, to the failed educational programs is that in maximum-security prisons, men are too bereft of hope to care.

Why then are they still being built? I think the reason is not indifference but something more sinister: middle-class America feels less anxious as the prison walls go up. Yet their anxiety is truly existential. The new prisons will not deter nor reduce crime. The cells will fill up as soon as they are finished.

Most people say something like, "Listen, I have just so much sympathy, and the violent mugger whose life is wasted in jail is at the end of the line. Go peddle your bleeding heart somewhere else." But what happens in prisons does not leave the rest of us sublimely untouched, and I do not have to examine my political ideology to insist on changing it. Without change, the likelihood of someone's mugging me or killing me in a "senseless" crime increases appallingly.

If self-interest alone were not enough, then being a teacher and a writer and a gay man would commit me to reform. In fact, it is in my capacity as an English teacher, a teacher of both literature and remedial English, that some hope lies for effecting reform. There are no ready

statistics, but I would confidently say that there is a high correlation between illiteracy, the lack of what Roberto called gainful employment, and
violent crime. One step toward ensuring my safety is to make men ineligi-
ble for violence by giving them some stake in respectability.

So far, only a small minority of men have been rescued through
education, but since the odds they have had to work against are so sheer,
the results are impressive. Tom O'Connor, an ex-offender, is now head of
the Prison Reform Task Force. Tom was one of the few men who were
literate before entering prison. In his isolation, he turned to reading, discovered in himself a voracious appetite, and essentially educated himself.
One of the major jobs of the Task Force is teaching inmates and ex-
offenders how to read and write. The same goal occupies the Fortune
Society. Every reform organization emphasizes the necessity of literacy,
now crucial in an economy that no longer needs the unskilled labor that
historically dominated its work force. Last spring in the *Soho News,* a
sympathetic column describing Fortune's one-to-one tutoring program was
succinctly entitled, "If He Can't Read, He May Kill You."

Literacy is the beginning. If a man who is literate is less likely to kill a
stranger, a man who can read literature is less likely to kill anyone. In fact,
he may even begin to write literature if he can read it. I am not suggesting
that being a criminal in prison automatically makes one a victim, nor does
either status help one become a writer. While prisons rarely produce Jean
Genets, the recent works of Chester Himes, Eddie Morris, Malcom Braly,
Charles McGregor, and Ron LeFlore are testimony to the liberating and
redeeming power to tell of one's experience, to exorcise the past by writing
it out. (The fullest and most up-to-date bibliography on prison writing is in
H. Bruce Franklin's *The Victim as Criminal and Artist: Literature from the
American Prison.*) To testify, to bear witness is often all that is left for those
who are victims, the last resort for damages beyond any reparations, certainly beyond the capacity of human justice to balance the scales.

4

I arranged to visit Riker's Island to see the educational facilities—the
library and the classrooms—to meet the teachers, and to study the course

outlines. The library has a complete set of law books as federal law now demands. All the information, all the legal codes and laws that a prisoner might need in order to reopen his case or prepare his defense are here. There were three men reading in the library when I was there. I opened the books; the bindings crackled; the pages were sometimes uncut. But it is better that the books are here, if largely unread, than not. If three men can find in these books some relief from the hopelessness of prison, the books are not a luxury. Likewise, if receiving gay literature marks a man, he nevertheless must be given the right to determine that risk for himself. That is what prisons have taken away from men: the adult prerogative of determining for oneself.

I went to Riker's Island because I wanted "local color"; how could I write about prisons without seeing the inside of one? And the answer is that I couldn't, that it would be meaningless to try. That sunny afternoon in June at Riker's was enough to make me want to tear up my notes, erase my tapes, and forget everything I'd seen and heard. Even in a moderate municipal prison like Riker's the truth is central and blatant. It is a place where white men lock up black men.

Here, the power relationships confirm for both the prisoner and his jailers the state of racial equity in America. True, there are now enough black guards to replace the traditional Irish one (who's now their supervisor) so that the tension is less stark, but for black men, being jailed by black guards may be even more enraging than being jailed by white ones. I didn't ask.

I talked with the prison psychologist, with the director of educational services, with the librarian from the New York Public Library's Office of Special Services which distributes books among inmates on permanent "loan." I marveled at their endurance or patience or cheerfulness. Somehow they did not seem to see where they were or who was there.

Despite all the articles—and every program or office mentioned in these pages has been written about in newspapers or journals more than once—little changes. Every day the same incompetence and stupidity is documented. Recently, a professor of education from Queens College wrote a letter of protest. A former student was now in prison and wished to complete a course he had left unfinished, so he asked his professor to send him the books he needed. The works in question were by Eldridge

Cleaver and Malcolm X and George Jackson. They were returned to the professor by the mail clerk, who was also the institution's censor: they were "unsuitable," they had no "redeeming social value," and therefore no prisoner is allowed to read them.

Of course the point in works like these is their efforts to redeem society, to give value to pain and injustice and brutality. The logic of the prison is to invert everything, to reject books because they are redeeming, to let mail clerks tell professors what has social value. Why are there such efforts to keep black and gay literature out? What difference could it make to those who run the prisons what prisoners *read?*

Such books illustrate that one must protest one's misery by demanding to be treated as more than an illiterate felon. Through literacy, there is access to the literature of oppression, to the hundreds of voices that have illuminated their rage without succumbing to despair, that have humanized their pain by giving it political meaning: to be helpless in America is to always be in prison. Those in jail for their crimes of violence and for their antisocialism discover through reading that they are no longer merely criminals; they have become political prisoners. They may still be too powerless to make a revolution, but they can find a liberation from the humiliation of their imprisonment, from the loss of dignity and self-determination that Roberto talked of. And from such liberations come the changes that will tear down the prison walls, that will make prison obsolete.

CHAPTER NINE

Those Dying Generations:
Harry and His Friends

That is no country for old men. The young
In one another's arms, birds in the trees
—Those dying generations—at their song,
The salmon falls, the mackerel-crowded seas,
Fish, flesh, or fowl, commend all summer long
Whatever is begotten, born, and dies.
Caught in that sensual music all neglect
Monuments of unageing intellect.

—William Butler Yeats, "Sailing to Byzantium"

Poets see things earlier than ordinary men; poets like Yeats see them more
clearly and tell us more movingly what we may expect from the present.
In 1928 when he published his tragic lyric about the expendability of old
men, Western society had not grown as phobic and callous toward old age
as it is now. One cliché claims that old age is more difficult in youth-mad
America than elsewhere. True, America is the advance guard of all those
forces which seem to provoke and promote social decline, but the condition
of the aged is as bad in Europe and in socialist societies as it is here—if the
old men and women happen to be gay.

When one is old and gay, one acquires a universal burden of social indifference or contempt to add to a lifelong oppression as a homosexual man or lesbian. With the men I interviewed, one question was central: has being gay made aging more difficult? Hearteningly, the answer seems to be, "No, not especially," even given the notorious exaggerated investment in youthfullness in gay life. In some cases, it has made it easier. For men in their late sixties and seventies, living gay in this century and surviving those miseries has alleviated the traumas of aging. The long closeted life has often hardened them; some are even more fortunate than their heterosexual counterparts for whom widowhood and loneliness and loss of social place are terminal griefs. The men I interviewed, despite the diversity of their lives, are more than literal survivors.

I began to explore the subject accidentally. I intended to write about the instability of romantic sexuality when I lost my lover of three years to a new man. Depressed and bitter, I wanted to document this particular sad story among others. When I found that the bars and baths and organizations I had once been active in were dead ends as far as meeting someone "serious" went, I decided to join a small C.R. group and answered an ad in *Gay Community News* directed to men forty or older. Although, as one friend later put it, "You should have known that any fag admitting to forty is really sixty," I was not prepared for the group I entered: Ted is sixty-seven, Bert is sixty-nine, Michael seventy-two, Harry seventy-five, Rudi seventy-nine, and Alex eighty-two. A half-dozen other men were in their fifties, but I was the baby.

When the discussion leader calmly announced that the topic of the session was attitudes toward dying, I felt a double wave of anxiety. I had been having totally irrational fears and fantasies about dying (promising myself every day to stop smoking). But the idea of discussing death with men who might keel over from natural causes during the hour was more than I'd bargained for.

As one might expect, only the younger men in the group seemed burdened by fears because the issue for them was not dying, but its corollary: not living. Those in their old age who had "lived" regarded the subject as somehow irrelevant. They were going to die; none really denied that or seemed to find the idea horrifying, although all were concerned with the manner of their deaths and hoped they would not be cursed with senility or agony. But all of them, including one in remission from cancer, agreed that they lived exclusively in the present. Tomorrow is Monday or Tuesday; the fantasy future of younger people had finally disappeared.

As I listened, I was struck with the richness of their collective past. These men had been homosexual in the twenties and the Depression, in libertine New York of World War II; their pasts were a valuable document of gay history. Here was a subject of great immediacy. At the next meeting I asked the older men whether I could interview them. They seemed surprised and consented, with some reservation since I was a stranger. This is about how five of those men live now. Some day the fuller story of their lives should be told.

1

No one would believe that Harry is nearly seventy-six. Not only is his face almost unlined, but he moves with vigor and ease; he is tanned and firm, sweet and outgoing. An Englishman, he has an accent which does not define his class, though it is neither Cockney nor Oxbridge. When Harry agreed to an interview, he gave me a small card from his wallet identifying his career field as industrial electronics, which I later learned meant he was a highly skilled electrician. The card was a bit stained and yellow; the business address was inked out, and in one corner he had written his home address. Harry retired at sixty-four, a year earlier than necessary, because he feared losing his pension when his union voted to strike. When I suggested that this was a strike-breaking tactic, he looked pained and agreed that perhaps it was, but he chose to use his accumulated sick days to retire early.

Harry attributes his physical fitness to a "lucky" constitution, but he is also an avid hiker and walker, a nature lover, and a devotée of nude sunbathing. He spends as much time as he can in the country with old friends where he combines his taste for nature and exercise with what he calls "having a party." When I asked him whether that is a euphemism for fucking, he paused and admitted that he and his friends have always described casual sex as "having a party." Since I once edited an anthology of gay short stories, including Tennessee Williams' "Two on a Party," without paying particular attention to the title, I began to see how informative my research was going to be.

Harry's English background also appears in his small, trimmed gray moustache, in the Bermuda shorts he wears daily in the summer with forest-green knee socks, sensible wing-tip shoes that I haven't seen outside Brooks Brothers for twenty years, and freshly pressed button-down shirts. It only takes a moment to figure out that the shoes and shirts *are* twenty years old, still meticulously polished and darned.

Harry is different in other ways. For example, his mother was a lesbian. He is not sure when he learned this, but by his teens he was certain. Harry says his mother knew *he* was gay though the subject was not discussed. His father and mother separated before World War I. When Harry was seventeen, he had his first love affair in the Boy Scouts with a twenty-three-year-old Swiss living in England. When his lover left, Harry confided his grief to his Scoutmaster, who counseled discretion and then seduced him.

In 1922, Harry's mother sent him to the United States to live with his father, a jeweler who had emigrated here earlier. She wanted more freedom and thought he would now do better with his father. At first Harry lived in the East Fifties, then a working-class neighborhood, and in the 1930s on West 97th Street. His sexual adventures were sporadic, limited mostly to pickups in Central and Riverside Parks. Harry sometimes cruised the West Seventies, which he claims was the gayest neighborhood in the city, though not as bohemian as the Village. During the Depression, he discovered gay bars and baths.

Early in the interview he confessed that he is worried about sex: he is having too much and perhaps it isn't good for his health.

"What is 'too much' at seventy-five, Harry?"

"Well, since my lover died, I've been having some wild parties. I feel I'm oversexed. But perhaps it's good for my longevity?"

I hoped so too. Harry usually has sex twice a week, almost always with men he knows well. Dave, a librarian in New Haven, is a boyfriend of fifty-eight whom Harry visits twice a month for long weekends. He also pays a monthly visit to Norman, a long-standing friend whom he most enjoys sleeping with, now retired from active service in the Mattachine

Society and living in the country. His friend Rudi, who lives in Queens, is seventy-nine, and he visits him weekly for dinner and partying. Then there is the young thirty-eight-year-old hospital worker, whom Harry describes as "hard of hearing, and he slurs when he speaks. He's very self-conscious, but he feels comfortable with me. He's very affectionate." He drops by regularly at Harry's North Bronx apartment on his way home. Finally, there is an occasional adventure which develops from an early evening at Carr's Bar or an afternoon at the baths.

Harry did not blurt out his erotic schedule. He does not brag about his virility though he knows he is unusual. As I solicited answers, I wondered how coarse I could get. Harry appeared forthright and he talked easily, but he was also decorous, unflirtatious, and genuinely friendly. His sex life seemed extravagant for a man of seventy-five; maybe he and his friends simply cuddled a lot. As we talked it was apparent that he enjoyed speaking frankly, even if he was unused to doing so with a stranger. Our terms had to be clarified. Harry didn't say "fuck"; he said "brown" or "up the back." When he said he had sex, he took for granted that we meant oral sex and that being affectionate implied oral reciprocation. Though my vocabulary was blunter, Harry didn't shy when I said fuck or suck or rim; he just responded in his own idiom.

Later, I understood that while Harry had no sexual prudery, the subject was just not as fascinating to him as it is to me. It was not sleeping with Dave but going to the Trolley Museum that he relished from his recent weekend in New Haven. It was not the party with Norman that was memorable, but sunbathing nude in Norman's isolated backyard with only an occasional cow meandering by. Harry's need for civilized, affectionate sexuality makes sexual encounters without friendliness and emotional responsiveness less exciting. Even when he spoke of the young man of thirty-eight who drops by occasionally, whom he described as somewhat clumsy and inexperienced, he denied that the man was selfish or unemotional.

"Yes, it's true, I usually blow him, or sometimes he browns me, though I don't particularly care for that, but he's not a quickie. He likes to stay in bed a long time. Once, he stayed overnight."

Though Harry is no stranger to the baths, having discovered them forty-five years ago, he finds men nearer his own age more satisfying, even if their activities are less exotic. What they do—mutual masturbation, oral sex, or dry fucking—is not so important. When I asked whether there are things he does not do or disapproves of, he said, surprisingly, that he never enjoyed 69'ing. "It's too distracting." Concerning the apparent excesses and novel tastes of the younger generation, Harry confessed that he could not understand the blatant interest in scatology or sadism. However, he admitted, giggling, to "perhaps a slight fetish you might call sadistic—I love to have my thighs bit. Norman bites me and it turns me on. I guess I love men's thighs. I go to soccer games to watch the players with their muscular thighs. A few years ago when I was seventy-three, my lover had just died and I went to Everards. I came three times! It never happened before, but this young fellow knew just what to do. My legs were very red the next day."

Harry uses no drugs, and he won't sleep with anyone who uses poppers. He sometimes feels self-conscious about his age at the baths since it's obvious people want younger men, but it doesn't bother him terribly. He also thinks himself more fastidious than younger men. He has never had any form of V.D., never contracted a sexually related disease nor experienced impotence. For a moment, the expression on my face must have been peculiar, for he hastened to add, "Well, it takes me longer to come now . . . sometimes."

Harry's lover Bob died of diabetic complications in 1973 when he was sixty-one. Talking of his lover, Harry lost his customary cheer but otherwise showed little of what that loss means. Harry and Bob were together twenty-seven years. During World War II, both men were employed in essential industry and thus were draft exempt. Bob was the dispatcher for a fleet of trucks. They had known each other nearly a year before they became friends and waited almost as long before they became lovers. At first, they would meet at Riverside Drive near the George Washington Bridge to make love. When they could afford it, they'd rent a room in one of the small hotels in the West Thirties since they both lived at home with parents. Though they made their emotional commitment gradually, it was solid enough to exclude jealousy and accommodate a mutual if mild promiscuity. Both would go together to the raunchy steamroom in the basement of the Penn Post Hotel. Occasionally, Harry would spend the night with Norman or another man, and though Bob did not like this very much, he did not regard it as serious.

It was Bob who first interested Harry in gay issues, in Mattachine, and in a community of gay friends. Bob wrote as an avocation; his special interest was vaudeville, which they went to regularly. Harry, in turn, introduced Bob to the ballet, which he'd always liked. He tells of seeing Martha Graham in the 1932 American premiere of Stravinsky's *Le Sacre du Printemps* for which "I squandered all my money."

Bob's other interest was drag. He wrote about American vaudeville for British trade journals, and about drag for some early homosexual newspapers. Drag, in fact, was one of Bob's delights, though photographs show him to have been wiry and craggy-faced, and by the late 1950s to have grown a beard. The pictures of Bob in drag, with blond teased hair, sequin shift, long white gloves, gold purse, etc., grinning broadly, indicate the drag was mostly a lark. Harry said that no matter how carefully he himself tried, in drag he always looked like Mrs. Roosevelt, so he gave it up.

When the men traveled to Europe, Bob got in touch with the newspaper correspondent Oscar Weibel, founder of *Der Kreis* or the Circle, a homophile organization in Zurich that dated from the Thirties. Through him and Bob's interest in drag, they became friends of Quentin Crisp. Bob was planning to write a book about drag that he had been researching for years when he became diabetic, and Harry still has the notes carefully stored in his apartment.

Harry assured me that while there were squabbles and ups and downs, it was a very smooth relationship and essentially monogamous. Only when Bob's health began to fail and when some emotional stress forced a kind of permanent withdrawal from an active social life did he become possessive or jealous. In the early years, Bob worked nights and Harry days, so they saw each other only on weekends, and in the hectic last year of the war, they even worked then. When they would meet, their favorite places were Beckman's Bar on Third Avenue and 34th Street or The Pepper Pot on West 4th, where I gather a McDonald's now stands.

In the seventh year of their relationship, they decided to live together. Bob's parents had died, his father of cancer and his mother by suicide, and he asked Harry to live with him. They then "officially" became a couple, sharing household duties, entertaining, and meeting other couples, both homosexual and lesbian. Bob's fondness for drag and his hobby of writing about it brought occasional glitter to their Washington Heights home.

After a piece on Francis Renault, Bob and the famous impersonator became friends. Renault would turn up at their gatherings with celebrities like Nita Naldi in tow.

They became close friends with another gay couple, Peter and Eddie, especially Eddie, a Puerto Rican. Eddie introduced them to gay life in New Jersey and to bars which catered to working-class couples like themselves. In the 1960s, Bob became mysteriously withdrawn and despondent. "He was always touchy, but now he began to lose his friends." Easily offended by them, he became more reclusive and decided to stop working. "He suddenly became a housewife." Their sexual life diminished and became more role defined, Bob insisting that Harry always be dominant. Gradually, they stopped seeing Eddie and lost contact with their other friends. They gave up working for the Mattachine library and stopped helping with the mail and the newsletter.

Bob became insomniac, and so they stopped sleeping in the same bed. In the middle of the night, Harry would discover Bob eating bread and butter thickly spread with sugar. Increasingly, Bob turned to masturbation "to help him sleep, he said." Then he collapsed and was rushed to Fordham Hospital where he was diagnosed as diabetic. After being under observation in a public ward for a month, he begged Harry to take him home. Once he was released and housebound, Harry discovered Bob was alcoholic. He would drink till he became sick and rage if he could not drink. Two months later, Bob collapsed again and died in the emergency room. I suggested that Bob's reclusiveness might mean that he had been drinking far longer than Harry suspected, and though the idea seemed plausible, Harry regards Bob's behavior in his last months as an ugly mystery.

Bob died intestate. His only surviving relative, a sister who had cut off all communications when he and Harry began living together, took all Bob's assets, some $10,000, "though she paid the funeral expenses," Harry added generously. However, there was a complication. Harry had bonds in Bob's safe deposit box which he was able to claim only after much red tape cluttered his life and his mourning for the lover of twenty-seven years. Since Harry had named Bob *his* beneficiary, he thought it strange that Bob never made out a will, but inasmuch as he was ten years the elder, it had seemed an academic as well as a tactless issue.

After Bob's death, Harry tried to find Eddie, but his only lead was a straight brother who refused him any information. Mattachine was finished. It was at the West Side Discussion Group the following year that Harry met Dave and, through West Side, heard of the C.R. group where I met him. Dave has invited Harry to live with him in New Haven, but Harry is ambivalent. He likes the freedom his pension and Social Security give him to travel, usually to Europe every year. He likes his habitual walks all over the city or sunning at Orchard Beach when he can't get to the country. He likes meeting friends at Carr's, where the clientele is friendly and older than at the usual Village bar. He does not cruise: "If I go to a gay bar, I'm not so concerned with meeting someone. I just like to be with gay people and talk." His complaint about the C.R. group is that it is too unsocial. He needs sociability; his consciousness is already raised. Like most men his age, he admires the openness of younger men and women but fears we are heading for a "backlash; things are going too fast, too quick." He means, of course, for straight people.

I asked him finally whether he had serious regrets about the past, about never marrying or having children as some gay men in his generation had done. "I guess I once did seriously consider it, but no—I never have regrets about the past. And I don't look back. I'm not nostalgic."

2

Rudi, one of Harry's steadies, is seventy-nine. He came out when he was sixty-four. Married over thirty years, he became a widower with a grown son when he was sixty-three. The following year at the racetrack, one of his favorite haunts, he struck up an acquaintance with a Cuban refugee, John, a man his own age. For the next fourteen years they were lovers, until John died in 1976. John was not only Rudi's first gay lover, but also his first gay experience. Rudi did not think of himself as homosexual nor did he experience closeted yearnings before he met John.

Rudi was obviously a beauty; photographs of him over the years document his sustained handsomeness. He is still good-looking, a small man with an innocent smile and a well-shaped youthful body. His health is remarkably intact. In pictures from the 1920s and 1930s, he looks very dapper, sporting boutonnieres in his well-cut lapels. He showed me a pair of white kid gloves, folded in a fine yellowing silk handkerchief, that he wore on his wedding day. He is fond of looking fashionable. A recent snapshop of him at Acapulco in a bikini shows he has little to be self-conscious about and not much to hide. It isn't clear what Rudi looks like ethnically, though somehow he does not look American. In fact, he was born to "real illiterate peasants" he says with some contempt, one of four-teen children, somewhere near Zemplin in Czechoslovakia. When he was nine, with eleven surviving siblings living in near-serfdom, he left home with his parents' indifferent blessing. He was hired as a servant by a mid-dle-class couple who took charge of his welfare and schooling, virtually adopting him.

At fifteen, he went to work as a clerk for the railroads where his adoptive father held an important position. When World War I broke out, sixteen-year-old Rudi volunteered to serve the Hapsburg Empire. He be-came a hero accidentally when he and another cavalryman captured a hundred Russian deserters lost in the Carpathian Mountains. Though they were outnumbered fifty to one, their offer of bread induced the starving, freezing, practically unarmed Russians to surrender.

Shortly after the war, in Budapest, he struck up an acquaintance with a captain in the Imperial Horse Guards, "such a beautiful man," he sighed. Rudi said he was not aware of any sexual attraction on the part of either; he was just struck by the beauty of the man who, it seemed, had intentions. He took Rudi into his home and soon arranged an engagement with his unmarried daughter.

Rudi went to work in America for a few years to save a nest egg, and through Hungarian emigrés, he became a waiter in one of the posh beach-front hotels in Atlantic City. Two years later, on the night of his departure for Europe, he was mugged, robbed of everything including his passport, and left unconscious in the streets of New York while the ship sailed. In the hospital, the police found an interpreter (after fifty years, Rudi still speaks English with a thick accent) and located his boss. When he returned to work, the staff and guests had raised $1,000 for him. Ironically, an anonymous letter he wouldn't have received had he sailed earlier informed him that his bride-to-be had just given birth to an illegitimate child. Rudi returned to Europe to hire a detective and confront his handsome Hussar father-in-law, all of which he tells with a mixture of scorn and mild incredulity. Soon after, he met the woman he married and emigrated permanently.

Rudi described his marriage as uneventful. He praised his wife as a good woman. Rudi's son, a bachelor in his early forties who teaches in New Jersey, keeps a room in his father's house but owns a house somewhere in the Hamptons. Naturally, I asked whether his son is gay and whether he knows that Rudi is. Emphatic and politely outraged denials followed both questions.

Rudi's son and John seemed to have tolerated each other, but there was little affection between them. When John came to live with Rudi, he ostensibly rented a studio apartment in the basement of Rudi's small two-family house. They did not decide to live together immediately; Rudi was cautious, if not suspicious. From their initial meeting, John was aggressively ardent. At first, Rudi refused to give him his last name or telephone number, thinking him a racetrack sort. When they met again a few days later, John invited Rudi to visit him at his rooming house on West 14th Street. Rudi described his seduction laconically. John, who was experienced, was active, Rudi passive. The sex was exclusively oral.

Rudi is a pragmatic and compassionate man. Working forty years as a waiter (he retired as head waiter from a prominent midtown hotel), has made him careful about money. After two years of meeting at John's shabby expensive room, the move was made. Rudi said he also needed that length of time to accommodate himself to being gay. By the time of the move, the adjustment had been made. When I asked Rudi to describe the experience of learning to be homosexual after sixty-four heterosexual years, he brushed aside the question; he was awkward at first, but always responsive to John's tenderness. As he grew more adept, he found he could reciprocate fully. John slept in his own studio, but the rest of their routine they followed together. Both liked to bet on horses or play cards and dominos at a Spanish club in Manhattan that John belonged to. Their gambling was petty; Rudi's prudence and John's small income, if nothing else, kept it a reasonable pastime.

John was born in Spain; when his parents emigrated to Cuba, he became a grocer. In New York, he found work as a pants cutter in the garment district. He met an interior decorator from New Jersey, a younger man, who became very smitten with him. After a gift of an expensive diamond ring (which Rudi now wears), John considered himself engaged, quit his job, and kept house near Monmouth while his lover ran a successful antique and decorating business. Two years later when the lover died suddenly of a heart attack at the age of forty-five, intestate, John returned penniless to the garment industry until he retired with Social Security and some small savings.

As Rudi neared seventy, he found the winters too trying and decided to spend the harshest months in Acapulco. John, who was unable to swing such a vacation financially, agreed to stay in New York to take care of Rudi's house. Although consistently jealous and possessive, he succumbed to Rudi's plea: "John, if you love me, you want me to live longer, to stretch my life, so I must get away from the winter." For nearly ten years now, Rudi has taken a small apartment where he is free to bring boys at night and enjoy the Mexican sun all day.

In the winter of 1975–1976, John fell ill and went to relatives in Miami to recuperate. He was a poor letter writer, but as the months drew on, the silence from Florida grew foreboding. Rudi cut short his vacation; at Kennedy Airport his son met him, and Rudi demanded to know what was happening to John. His son avoided answering until Rudi made a small scene. He then learned that John was dead, had in fact died six weeks earlier. Rudi said his son had kept silent fearing that the news would shock his father, endangering his health. All Rudi's unopened letters had been forwarded to New York at his son's request to sustain the conspiracy. I suggested that this behavior indicated that his son was aware of the nature of the relationship, but with impatience, Rudi again denied it. John died of cirrhosis of the liver. He had always been a heavy drinker, and in Rudi's absence he'd returned to his boozing buddies at the club. When Rudi spoke of John, he showed much feeling. The grief was still fresh, and he was not sure he would return to Mexico this winter. There are complications, including his fear of leaving his house empty.

Just last spring, it seemed he found a solution. At the Church of the Beloved Disciple on 14th Street, he met Bill. They hit it off, and Bill moved in with Rudi almost immediately though he shared Rudi's bedroom rather than the old studio. At fifty-nine, Bill was just coming out. Aside from one furtive experience in a porno movie house, Rudi was his first gay relationship.

Bill is still married, though his wife threw him out in the fall of 1976 after thirty-five years of marriage. She simply said it was over for her: their two daughters and son are on their own, and she wished to be free. Bill claimed he was totally unprepared for her decision, for he thought he had a good marriage. His wife's behavior is inexplicable. Even more puzzling was Bill's response: for one dollar, he signed away to her his house and all his assets and had what he described as a slight nervous breakdown. He re-signed his position as music teacher in a local New Jersey high school where he had worked for many years (but not long enough for him to retire).

Bill is a medium-sized man, well built and cordial, eager to talk about his many problems, but he is also what most people would call homely. He looks his fifty-nine years, and his face and eyes are ravaged with sadness. When I said that he was overgenerous to his wife and that he might have suggested she leave instead of him, he said that he wanted to leave the way open for a reconciliation. Rudi looked at me skeptically. When we were alone, he told me he thought he could love Bill, if only he could forget the past and face where he is. I could not discover why Bill went to the Ramrod immediately upon arriving in New York, since he insisted that he was straight until the break-up.

At this point Rudi and I, who had been sitting on his porch, went inside the house where a third man was quietly watching the evening news. He was Ernie, who worked under Rudi for thirty years. He was recovering from a severe heart attack and looked it. He now lived in John's old studio apartment, and Rudi nursed him, cooked his meals, shopped for him, and generally shared his life with his old friend. Ernie wanted me to see his room and his collection of pin-ups of Hispanic wrestlers and his pornography.

Ernie is also seventy-nine. He was born in New Zealand, but his mother left for Australia when her husband deserted her. Like Harry, Ernie has a British accent, a typical Australian drawl to which he added his own campy intonations. I wanted to interview Ernie at length, but his illness, which has left him infirm, pallid, and slow to speak and move, has also jumbled his memory. He listened carefully and answered slowly but was preoccupied. He preferred to show me his collection of pictures and chatter, and I decided to postpone the interview.

I revisited Rudi and Ernie and Bill a week later. At the first visit, Rudi would not let me use my tape recorder and showed alarm every time I took notes, but now I was invited to dinner along with Harry, allowed to use my tape, and kissed paternally when I entered. Rudi took time from his cooking for me, and Ernie was contentedly watching an old movie with Harry, but Bill was absent. He had packed up and returned to New Jersey. Rudi was sad but not overwhelmed when he told me that Bill had decided that the gay life was too difficult, and living with his married daughter promised the best chance of resuming his own marriage. He has taken temporary work and promised to keep in touch. Rudi shook his head pessimistically and asked whether I thought Bill was truthful. He confided that Bill was impotent. "He would get hard in a minute, but he would never come! I even asked Harry, who's so good, you know, to . . . see if he could help Bill, but, well, it didn't work out. He said to me, 'Rudi, I'm still young, I have to try.' " I agreed that Bill is relatively young and that I did not think we got the whole picture.

Rudi was cooking goulash, which Ernie told me is one of his specialities. While I sipped a rum and Coke, bringing back memories of Cherry Grove in 1950, Rudi calmly chatted about his daily routine. He likes to bet if there's a race. For the four months that Bill was there, they could drive to Riis Park if the weather was good. Rudi had arranged to leave Bill in the apartment when he went to Acapulco, but now his winter plans are uncertain. He was also worried about Ernie. Just yesterday, Ernie foolishly went to Manhattan to visit an old trick whom Rudi dislikes. Ernie has always favored proletarian Hispanics and black men who mistreat him. Rudi has patiently listened to stories of Ernie's affairs, of stolen money, beatings, scenes, and neglect and is impatient with his friend's lack of self-esteem.

"John never liked Ernie. He was anti-gay. He would say, 'How can you walk down the street with him? He's such a fairy, aren't you ashamed to be seen with him?' " John never could tolerate effeminacy, and while Ernie is not flamboyant, he is soft-spoken, mild, a bit limp, and campy. The contrast between John's Hispanic machismo and Ernie's willowiness amused Rudi, who would always defend Ernie against John's antipathy, which he thought peculiar. While he had known that Ernie was gay for thirty years, he had not known that Ernie was effeminate until he was told.

Rudi sighed again over Bill's departure; he was hurt but by no means distraught. He thinks of John more than of Bill. We talked of the contemporary world, which Rudi regards as a great mistake. "We need another flood—wipe out everything and start again." Rudi finds conventional religious beliefs ridiculous. "If there's a heaven, it's up there on the moon." Suppose there is; what will he do if both John and his wife are waiting for him when he dies? "Introduce them, of course. I'll explain to her that she left me first, so I had to console myself." John apparently has the stronger, more recent claim.

Impatient to attend his goulash, Rudi said he would send Ernie to me but warned me that Ernie has had a bad week: his black friend was unfriendly, he has been feeling sick, and worst of all, his brother arrived from California at Rudi's behest and the reconciliation flopped. Ernie has not seen or had much contact with his brother for twenty-two years since their mother died. Rudi felt that Ernie's poor health called for the family reunion, and he phoned the brother, who is eighty-four. I asked Ernie about the meeting.

"Oh, he was so nasty. All he said was 'Why do you have pictures of those men all over your walls? It's disgusting.'" Ernie and his brother, neither of whom have ever married, never discuss their private lives.

I asked him when he came out, and he laughed as his memory was jogged. "It was awful, really, then. I was waiting table in Australia, and I had just moved to this boarding house. The lady gave me a room for the night; it was very crowded in the city, and rooms were scarce. This was 1915, and Australia wasn't so built up then. Well, in the middle of the night, this man comes into my room and says, 'What are you doing here? This is my room.' I told him the landlady put me here and it was my room, but he was drunk and big, and I didn't want to argue; I was only seventeen. 'All right, we'll straighten it out in the morning; shove over.' Well, when he got into bed, he suddenly said to me, 'I'm gonna fuck you.' I didn't know men even did that."

"Well, what happened?"

"Oh, he fucked me. I didn't like it at first," he smiled. Harry announced that dinner is on the table. It was 5:30, and I'm glad I skipped lunch. The kitchen table was carefully set. Rudi had cut long stems of rose of Sharon from his backyard and arrayed them all over the tablecloth.

When he poured Cherry Kijava for us all, Ernie winked at me, remarking that it was indeed a special occasion. The goulash was good, but Rudi took very little. He explained that for some years now he has been a vegetarian, and I noted his plate contained only stew vegetables. Dinner proceded amiably and quietly. I was a little sloshed on rum and Coke and worried about how cherry liqueur mixed with paprika. But as I watched Harry eating heartily, Ernie secure in his friend's beneficence, and Rudi serenely mothering us all, I was reminded of the calm of my own childhood meals. It seemed there are kitchen tables to gather round again.

3

Bert, who is sixty-nine, and Michael, seventy-two, have lived together for the last few years. They describe their relationship as a friendship. They began living together, after each lived alone for years, for all the obvious pragmatic reasons and because they found they could live with each other. Bert did most of the talking. He seemed frail compared to Michael, who is well over six feet and sports a Falstaffian belly. When Michael converses, his voice booms; the overall impression is one of gusto. Bert is a more meticulous man, and the image he suggests of being a retired school teacher is entirely accurate. He uses a cane, for he has worn a prosthesis since he lost his leg in an accident when he was twenty-two. But the Laurel and Hardy contrast is superficial. Bert dominated all the proceedings; Michael preferred to listen, commenting only when directly spoken to.

Bert is and always has been a pederast. He is unapologetic about it and, in fact, eager to explore the subject. His pederasty coupled with his career as a prep school and college teacher mark his story as the most politically volatile in these Save Our Children days. Bert feels that he has been as oppressed within the gay community as he has by straights.

"They're both so entirely ignorant of what pederasty means." When I asked him to clarify that, he became very articulate, with a nervous edge in his voice. "First of all, this constant talk about sex in relationships is overdone. I can love someone without having sex with him. It's more important to have a loving relationship whether there's sex or not."

Though he describes himself frankly as "low-sexed," he has been active as a homosexual since his early twenties and aware of his feelings much earlier. He was also married for fifteen years and has two grown daughters, both, he added, happily married.

Bert is the best educated of the men, the most active in his retirement, and the most restless. He taught English and drama for forty years before retiring, mainly at elitist private schools, which were the natural choice after graduating from Harvard and getting his M.A. from Cornell. Like many academics, he has been somewhat of a gypsy, teaching in different places for a few years each. Besides the prep schools where he began and ended his career, he has taught at Colby, the University of Michigan at Flint, and a community college in Westchester. His last job was as librarian and sole member of the English department of a boys' boarding school in Smithtown that was in its first year. He remarked that college teaching was always easier but less gratifying than prep school work. Because he responded more to younger boys, he especially enjoyed the opportunity to end his long career teaching adolescents again. The last experience was also special because he came out to the men who hired him. While he did not proselytize, he kept his collection of gay books visible whenever boys would visit him. Being out at work for the first time was a good experience, and he implied that he wished it had been possible sooner.

Being out at work was partly the result of some activism in the Mattachine Society, which he joined when he and his wife divorced. In the sixties he was the corresponding secretary, and with the demise of the organization, he began working with the Gay Academic Union, particularly with their speaker's bureau. Bert has spoken seven times to a class on Human Sexuality at C. W. Post College, though that was arranged by Mattachine rather than the G.A.U. He likes to serve on panels about homosexuality at high schools and colleges, though he claims his interest is more a social than a political service. Bert organized the C.R. group where I met the men, but he now finds it unsatisfactory, too unintellectual for his needs, and he no longer attends meetings even when they are held in his own home. He wants to organize a group of "college men" whose interests would be less exclusively social. He spends a great deal of time answering ads in *Gay Community News,* for pen pals in prison, and in *Holiday Bulletin,* a magazine devoted to relationships between older men and boys. He claims he has made good friends through the ads, perhaps a half-dozen, and "not all of them are youngsters; some are middle-aged men in their forties."

Writing is a pleasure for Bert. He has been writing poetry for many years, and before I left he gave me a small volume of his verse as well as an article on pederasty he had written for a journal devoted to the subject. He described his poems as metaphysical or mystical. On the covers of the eight-page booklet are idealized drawings of prepubescent boys. Bert complained about the history of the article. He had submitted it to Mattachine's newsletter a year before it ceased publication, but the article never appeared nor was it ever returned. He is sure it was suppressed or destroyed.

He is not naive about the political volatility of pederasty. While on a gay panel at a college lecture, he answered "Yes" when a member of the audience asked publicly whether he slept with his students. Later, a woman acquaintance representing Lesbian Feminist Liberation "hit the ceiling," berating him for his tactlessness in times when just such admissions were so welcome to reactionary forces. The distinction between "political" and "social" that Bert made is now clearer. He is not interested in what is politically wise; he is very concerned that people understand what he and men like him have been and still are.

"I've never had any moral doubts about myself. I don't think I've ever done anyone any harm. I see nothing wrong with any act when there has been love and consent." He illustrated by telling me of his current relation-ship with a newsboy. After becoming friends, Bert and the boy had sex. Some months later, on Christmas Eve, the boy showed up with a modest gift and asked whether he could spend the evening. Bert tried to send him home, pointing out that this was a family holiday, but the boy refused. "You see, he wanted *me;* it wasn't just a matter of sex."

Except during his marriage, Bert has had relations with young boys his entire sexual life. He actually came out when he was twenty-six, just before World War II. He was aware of his homosexual feelings in his teens, but he "smothered them" though he says he was deeply infatuated a number of times. Bert is clear that the impulse to teach and his attraction to young boys were parts of the same *gestalt.* Teaching has always had an erotic quality for him, and he has always preferred to teach in an all-male world. When Bert talks of his mixture of pedagogy and eroticism, and when he talks of his metaphysical poetry, he invokes Plato's *Symposium*. He regards himself as the descendent of the Greek teacher-lovers, a Romantic whose love of beauty has specified itself as pederasty. His preference for oral intercourse is part of his philosophy. "If a man's semen is the divine part, the life-giving part, then when I swallow it, it becomes part of me . . . it's wholesome. I'm not sure what happens to it if it goes up my ass."

Though he has had anal experiences, they are less satisfying in either role, active or passive. He smiled as he told me that in this respect he departs from Greek custom. With young men, his sexual relationships invariably develop out of social ones, like that with the newsboy, whom he befriended months before he took him to bed. He talked of another Michael whom he met when the boy was seventeen, a heavy drinker and already delinquent and unemployed. Now, four years later, they are "dear friends," and while Michael only drops by once a month for sporadic sex, they speak to each other a few times a week. Bert, who introduced Michael to his present lover, a man in his thirties, advises his protégé about his romantic problems.

The major relationship in Bert's life occurred when he was thirty-two, with a student nearly twenty years younger. When the boy was sixteen and Bert thirty-six, they became lovers. Bert emphasizes the mentor-student, nurturing character of the relationship. He does not feel that the boy was really gay. "He just fell in love with me." When they began to sleep together, they slowly advanced from masturbation to Bert's blowing the boy, to the boy's fucking him, and, after two years, to mutual oral sex. Altogether, they were involved eight years. They broke up when the boy went to California. Though Bert had the option of resigning his job and following, he thought that unwise.

Not long after, the boy married. Bert was then over forty, and soon after, he himself married. His wife was teaching at Mt. Holyoke and continued her career as a teacher and librarian. Bert has never considered himself bisexual. Heterosexual marriage was an important experience, but it was not satisfying sexually. By the time Bert was forty-five, he and his wife agreed to "go their own ways" when their two daughters were old enough. Divorced now for more than fifteen years, Bert has little contact with his wife, who retired to Vermont on a sizable inheritance. Bert himself lives frugally on Social Security and a small pension. He assumes his daughters know of his homosexuality, but it has never been discussed. However, when he writes them, he tells tham of his activities in the G.A.U., as he told them of his work for Mattachine. He confesses that he never wished for a more open dialogue with them. He hopes they will always regard him as Father and that categories or labels will not impose themselves. He feels he has been a good parent; he was virtually monogamous during his marriage, though he fell in love with a man when he was forty-five. He says his one regret is that he did not pursue that feeling, for he might have found the durable relationship of his life. But his commitment to his paternity and his responsibilities as a husband precluded that.

After the divorce, Bert was depressed and unable to deal with his freedom constructively. He began to drink heavily and spend most of his private time pursuing one-night stands. While his tastes had not altered, he now took up with men in their twenties. He thinks he may have become an alcoholic, for he is still unable to control drinking and usually abstains. This period, which lasted until he returned to prep school teaching and retired, is described with the most remorse. Though he was then sexually more active than at any other period of his life, he was also lonelier. Once he was beaten up. He picked up a young man, and when he took him home, three of the man's friends followed, forcing their way into the apartment. They made no attempt to rob him; it was "beat up a queer" time. He pleaded with them, and after an ugly roughing-up they left. During the incident and after, no neighbor made inquiries. Of course, Bert did not call the police.

The only other incident that Bert reports with equal distaste happened when he was teaching in a prep school and his affection for a sick boy was misunderstood. One of his students fell ill, and Bert visited him in his room. In a reassuring gesture, he squeezed the boy's shoulder before he left. The next day he was called to the headmaster's office for his version. The boy complained to his mother that Bert had made sexual advances. Bert says that the headmaster may have suspected that the mother was a crank, for after he explained what happened, he heard no more about it, at least from the headmaster. He did suddenly find that other housemasters were reluctant to let him visit boys in their houses.

When Bert first retired five years ago, he came eagerly to New York to pursue the theater and the arts. But he found he was lonely for the relationships with boys that had dominated his life. Through Mattachine, he began to offer his apartment to runaways and boys who arrived in New York without much resources. This worked well enough for a time until one boy robbed Bert and fled. The boy was arrested when he landed in Los Angeles; he had forged Bert's name to a check to buy his airplane ticket.

Though Bert has said he is low-sexed, the inactivity of his present sexual life is not satisfying. He is not driven, but he is not content. He sees the problems of his old age as qualitatively no different from those of his past. "Old age is a suffering time. I feel things as strongly now as I ever did."

Michael disagreed. Old age for him means the end of his sexuality, and he is relieved. For him, being old and discarded isn't as bad as being young and unhappy. "One feels the pain less." For Michael, being discarded was enforced retirement at sixty-five from a job he loved, a writer on interior decoration for *The New York Times*. Retirement has forced Michael to come out, to join Dignity and attend West Side and C.R. groups, though he would have preferred to remain absorbed in his occupation. For seven years he has been searching for ways to fill his time meaningfully. Michael was closeted his entire professional life, but he says everyone must have known; after all, he was an interior decorator. He is in some ways the most old-fashioned of the men. He would not, if he were young, be an activist. He claims not to like lesbians or the company of women. Bert interrupted to tell me that two of Michael's closest friends are women.

There is a contradictoriness about Michael that is difficult to explain. He characterizes himself as "extremely shy, very reserved . . . I hate giving interviews. If Bert hadn't broken the ice, I don't think I could say anything now." But he acknowledges that his lifelong shyness and his shame at being gay, his fear of public exposure, are tied together. He has never been enraged by his shame; he has tried to live a "normal"-looking life. He has passed as heterosexual in his social life, and he does not regret it. It was a way of protecting his privacy, and he regards himself as a very private person.

Despite these attitudes, he said, "I love being a homosexual. I love men. I love being in gay groups, at Mattachine or West Side or at the C.R. group. I have never regretted being gay; I can't imagine being anything else." When pressed, he said that he enjoys the company of gay men because "we all share the same weakness."

Michael said, "I'm very low-sexed, and I always have been. I have simple sexual tastes, mostly masturbation and some oral sex, but physical sex has never been very important to me, and I don't think it was to my lovers." Michael has been in love three times. He became aware that he was homosexual in his early twenties, but he does not discuss his early experiences which apparently were abortive.

In 1936, at thirty-one, he fell in love for the first time. Louie was half-Italian and half-Irish, "and you can imagine how beautiful a combination that was." They were together four years until Louie married. They did not live together, and Louie worried a great deal about being "queer." When Michael went into the Army in 1942, he met Lenny, who had been a dancer, and they became lovers. With peacetime, Lenny went to Julliard, so they did not live together. At school, Michael snorted, "he met this homely oboe player; she was really very plain. I guess Lenny preferred to be normal," for he soon married.

I was not sure whether the third love Michael referred to is Bert, but I suspect it is; somehow I did not ask. Michael would have liked a gay "marriage," but he knows these relationships cannot last, and he has never had much hope for one. "They always become roommates. It's then a matter of convenience, pleasant but unexciting." After Lenny, Michael had no relationships and little sex for twenty years. Though he went to the baths sometimes, it was mostly "to be there; just to see the beautiful men was often enough." He jokingly refers to himself as a voyeur, for he has a fondness for pornography and gay burlesque, but Bert contradicts him: "When I have a boy over, Michael takes a walk."

The organization Michael is most active in is Dignity. He is still a practicing Catholic, and I asked how he felt during the war when his relationship with Lenny put him in mortal sin as he risked his life every day. Did he feel angry at his special bind, caught between his feelings and his faith? He admitted that spiritual risks were greater when he was in his more enduring relationships. He thinks of himself as a sinner, but he is optimistic about forgiveness. He patiently explained that for Catholics, forgiveness is easily available if one is contrite, and Michael has lived in a state of constant contrition.

4

At sixty-seven, Ted is in remission from lymphatic cancer. He takes chemotherapy regularly and suspects that he may have to do so permanently, though the dosage is steadily decreasing. He is well informed about the disease, having been a practical nurse specializing in cancer care for fourteen years. Because he found his work with terminal patients depressing, when he was thirty-four he took civil service exams and became a payroll auditor, a dull job he held for the next thirty-one years. He would have liked to be a costume designer, and his present plans include designing and making some of his own clothes. He sews well, and on a recent trip to England he bought woolens and cottons that were a bargain. He is going to design a suit and make his own shirts. He would like to learn fine tailoring but has not found a teacher.

Ted was a little late for the interview, which was held in my apartment. He underestimated the traveling time, and the appointment was fixed so that he would not have to miss his favorite soap opera, to which he confessed he is addicted. When Ted retired four years ago, he thought he could immediately pursue something creative, but the adjustment period took longer than he thought, and then cancer preempted all other concerns.

To say he is casual talking about cancer is accurate, but inadequate. He is not resigned or bitter, nor is he overly optimistic. He feels he is lucky; the disease has been arrested, and he has not been immobilized by it. His routine accommodates the condition but is not changed by it. The drug he takes, cytoxin, is readily available in Europe, so he can travel whenever he wishes.

He is worried about his weight. "I'm so fat now from the treatment. The therapy seems to have increased my appetite, and I eat all the time." Otherwise, he says he feels fine, and indeed he looks healthy enough, agile and alert despite his cumbersome weight. Ted's style is laconic, and I was unsure whether he felt more than he showed. His demeanor is calm and thoughtful. When I asked questions, he took a few seconds to think about his answers, which often are witty and astute.

Ted is financially comfortable. With the civil service pension, Social Security, and bank interest on savings, he is free of money worries. His apartment costs $230 a month including utilities (he likes to be precise about costs) in a large complex where half the tenants are senior citizens.

"That's such an awful term, 'senior citizens.' No one I know likes it. Some of the people call themselves 'oldies'; I think that's much better, don't you?" Ted is very clear about his tastes and his dislikes. He likes to read and listen to music, watch old movies on television, and see new ones at the East Side houses where he is entitled to a half-priced ticket for matinees. He is an avid movie fan. When he retired, he went on a binge, going nearly every day for a year to the Museum of Modern Art's Hollywood retrospective. "But it was living in the past, going every day. I was sort of living for the movies. I lost all track of time. The days just disappeared."

Ted complained a bit about the West Side Discussion Group: he usually finds the talks tedious, and he doesn't go to the dances since he doesn't dance. But it's a night out. Sometimes he and Harry will meet in the afternoon for a matinee and then have an early dinner before ending the day at West Side. He has met no new friends there, though he does see some of the men from the C.R. group. Ted learned about West Side from a resident social worker, a lesbian, whom he described as pushy, always wanting him to be militant, to march in parades, to tell people he is gay. Ted thinks that for him telling and marching are unimportant.

He said some of the younger men in the group who are obsessed about their loneliness and their bad luck with lovers are "injustice collectors." He is not sympathetic to those men his own age who find the search for sex humiliating, haunting the baths and the porno houses, always exposed to rejection. The search for sex always bothered Ted, and he simply stopped looking in his mid-fifties. He became celibate.

"I just dropped out. After all, I was treating men as if they were sex objects; there was very little emotional involvement. Besides, I got syphilis at the baths, and it took a year to get rid of." Ted was an *habitué* of the baths all his sexual life, and though he sometimes went to bars, they never worked for him. "I never picked up anyone or even met anyone. And I don't like to drink. The only time I was ever really involved with anyone, it didn't work out because he was an alcoholic." With a faint sadness Ted talked of his one affair—with a promiscuous black man—which lasted a year in 1949. He described a period in his life when he was especially attracted to black men. He said his sexual drive is low, calling himself undersexed, "but there was enough to keep getting me in trouble." Of all the men, he seems to have the barest sexual history. Though he says he never wanted to be straight, he accuses the gay world of being "too narrow, too closed." When I asked him what gayness means to him, since he is not interested in sex and finds gay sensibility very limited, he replied that it doesn't mean much to him at all.

He would have liked a serious relationship, which he clarified to mean a monogamous marriage, but he does not regret not having had one, and at his age he has no further expectations. He is emphatically not interested in casual sex. He told of two men, both widowers with long gay histories, who live together and favor threesomes, and while he thought the offer flattering, it was irrelevant.

Though Ted has never had a sustained sexual relationship, he has had a gay friendship for fifty-two years. When his mother died, his friend wanted them to live together in a newly opened project at Rockaway Beach. But Ted stayed on in his home until the building was demolished. In 1967, he took an apartment down the hall from his friend. But in 1975, the year after his retirement, he moved to Manhattan, since he was traveling into the city every day to see the movies at the museum. He has begun to find his friend trying. "He's become a pathological liar. I can never tell what happens to him anymore. He exaggerates so much."

When I asked Ted how he came out, he described the friendly neighborhood cop who seduced him when he was fifteen and then took him to the Village bars. Ever since, he preferred anal sex; in fact, he says he has never really enjoyed orality no matter which end he was on.

Ted was the only one of the men rejected for service during World War II for being homosexual. "I was a C.P.I.: it means Constitutional Psychopathic Inferiority." I told him that I don't think that particular designation is still in use. How did he feel about the term? Had he wanted to go in the Army? He looked at me wryly and indicated that the questions were pointless.

The past, its inadequacies and pains, are as distant to Ted as they are to the others. He sees little of his two sisters, although he recuperated from his cancer with the younger of them and her husband in West Palm Beach. "That's when I got hooked on the soap opera. There was nothing else to do." He has never discussed his homosexuality with his family, but he suspects his Florida sister may know since she sent him all the clippings on the Anita Bryant campaign. Ted was close to his mother, whom he lived with until her death in 1957. She was Catholic and "a really good person." His father was a Jewish alcoholic who passed as gentile in the Irish bars he liked to get drunk in. I commented that an intermarriage in 1910 was fairly rare and asked how he regards himself, since he bears his father's Jewish-sounding name. But Ted has no interest in conventional religion. His mother's Catholicism was alien to him, especially after he recognized himself as homosexual, and he feels his father's family, who changed their name in order to pass, were hypocritical.

His one sustained interest is Theosophy, which centers on the belief in reincarnation. "It's the only thing that seems to make any sense. Otherwise, life is meaningless. When I had cancer, I was worried about suicide, because if you kill yourself, you have to do it all over again." Ted has no intention of doing it again.

5

Recently, over after-dinner drinks, Carol, a lesbian feminist lawyer, asked me what I thought of an idea she had about retirement homes for gays. "It would be complicated, buying land in Florida or the Hamptons or Hawaii; it would have to be covered by a single individual's name, but it's the coming thing. Now is the time to start." Her motives are certainly as pragmatic as they are social, for if she is right, the first entrepreneurs who succeed in organizing attractive retirement communities for gays will get very rich. I agreed the idea is marvelous; no doubt others are thinking of it as well, but my gut feelings reminded me of other utopian enthusiasms I have flung myself into.

It is not unfeasible. There are gay men and women in law, medicine, politics, social work, clinical psychology, architecture—every profession needed to make a retirement community successful. The question is the clientele. If the same statistics about population distribution are true for gays, there must be well over a million old gay men and women scattered across the nation. Why does the idea strike me as a fantasy when the evidence clearly indicates that it is reasonable? After all, where *are* they? One sees a negligible number of older men and women in the Hamptons, and a few older men at Cherry Grove, but where do old gays go when they retire?

But would Harry and his friends retire together? Would I want to retire to a gay community? Carol insisted the facilities would have to be segregated, lesbian and homosexual, with perhaps some impersonal territory for both. I started to argue: surely by that time gay men and women will have a dialogue which will make such arrangements superfluous. But we looked at each other, and it is difficult to imagine that time. We were both suddenly pessimistic. I ventured that by the time we're retired, perhaps Anita will have taken care of it for us: segregated gay concentration camps.

Old age for gay men and women presents more complicated problems than we have begun to name. All the men I have interviewed need a community. Most complain of the inadequacy of the West Side Discussion Group to deal with their problems, but they never mention any alternatives. West Side, however irrelevant its programs, at least acknowledges that old men and women are alive and in need. Perhaps West Side tries to do too much, but I doubt it. It is what it is, and one should be glad it is there and able to continue in times when the life span of most gay organizations keeps shrinking. When there was practically nothing, Mattachine and Daughters of Bilitis tenaciously held on. Militancy made them superfluous, with its contempt for the old styles and ideas, the closeted timidities. Now there are enough organizations in America to fill a telephone book (a thin one), but it can hardly be called an embarrassment of riches. As I write this, I feel the subject slipping away. I notice I am beginning to focus on my dissatisfaction with the movement.

Is it that one simply cannot imagine what it is like to live so exclusively in the present, with fantasies and rage alike burnt out? Perhaps the prejudices toward age are more potent than one suspects, cutting one off from empathy and understanding. When I told a friend, a reasonably intelligent woman, what I was writing about, she grimaced.

"Why? It's disgusting."

"What is?"

"The whole thing. Dirty old men." She is a professor of humanities, no youngster herself, and generally concerned about social oppression. But for her, these issues are not real; they have no priority. Tacitly, it is understood that death will resolve the problems sooner than later. My colleague hastens to clarify that her response has nothing to do with the fact that the men are gay; she would feel the same way if they were straight.

Some of the difficulties are identical for people of whatever sexual persuasion. On August 8, 1977, *The New York Times* devoted two-thirds of the Op Ed page to "How Old is Old" by Anonymous, an enraged woman of sixty-six forced to retire last year. She catalogued her dismay and anger, the stupidity of wasting her professionalism when it is still invested with the authority of experience without the bias of ambition. She is physically fit and has been educated to use her leisure in the richest possible ways; she has the money to do so. But she is immobilized with depression, with the sense of being unfit, rejected, subhuman. When she taught and had five sets of papers to mark over the weekend, she still found time to tend her family, bake bread, do a host of things: her energy was limitless. Now, completely free, she is imprisoned in fatigue and lassitude.

For those deprived of work "to make room for younger people," there may be no adequate compensation unless they find other work. But those who would work longer if they could are a small minority, less than 10 percent of the elderly. Most welcome retirement. The quality of work in America is not so ideal that forty-five years on the job are insufficient.

More universal is the sense of being useless, whether one is active or not. In the July 16, 1977, issue of *Gay Community News,* the cover story read "Older Gays: Our Neglected Roots." Writers in gay journals now understand the need to become amateur historians of the past before it is irrevocably gone. Well and good. While I was interviewing Harry and Rudi and Ted, no doubt they were flattered to enter gay history. Perhaps they'll enjoy reading this, and that will be another fleeting moment of esteem. However, this is *not* written for old men and women, but for the forty-seven-year-old babies who don't want to be old and peripheral in twenty years and who frankly doubt they'll arrive at seventy-five virile and healthy.

When I asked the men what they would want *now* that they don't have, the question was too vague. Of course, they would like a gay center devoted primarily to social needs, a place to be comfortable in where sexual issues are secondary, but sexual opportunities still viable. They would like a place to go where they are the majority. But most would also like to leave such places at the end of the evening and return to their own lives. When I said earlier that I thought gays coped better with being old, I certainly had in mind Anonymous in the *Times,* who seems self-indulgent compared to those men and women who are old and never had a decent job in their lives. These gay men cope better because deprivation had been their daily fare: social contempt is such an old story. Like bad weather, you just live with it. Unlike their heterosexual contemporaries, few gays have expected relationships to last.

When I compare these men to my relatives the same age, I understand that Harry and his friends had choices no larger than my father's and mother's. Foremost was a job, sometimes any job, in a Depression that marred their entire adult lives and materialized all their values. Then there was political survival in the forties when the anxieties were even more nightmarish. But they have come to be who they are despite the bitterness and injustice and limitations they testify to. They are dignified, mostly serene, and remarkably free of self-pity. I think of my aunts and uncles lushly retired in Miami, still enmeshed in their lifelong hysterias, still trapped in their children's lives, and I am certain that the strength these men have is special. It is not like the fortitude of old black matriarchs whose lives were worse, harder and more bitter, filled with far greater injustices than lovers dying intestate. It is not like the strength of Jews I know who have survived the Holocaust only to relive it endlessly.

But these men and lesbians like them lived their lives as something else, as heterosexuals, and that duplicity created for them a sense of self and privacy that no interviewer and no loneliness can readily violate. Their experience is still true for the majority of gays. No matter how many come out, no one is born out. One lives two lives until they are no longer tolerable. For many, "intolerable" is a luxury they can't yet afford. For some of the men, duplicity was very expensive, but I think for all of them it was the foundation of a stoicism that sustains them. Without any help from straight society and with precious little from gay society today, they survive decently. If they ask little, it is because their experience tells them it is wisest to ask for no more than what one can expect.

That is a lesson I have not quite learned, but I am skeptical of the quality of strength I can expect at their age. Right now, their possibilities are better than I imagined. What we with our advantage of youth all need to learn is who and what the Harrys are, so that our possibilities and choices are even greater. The next decade promises to be difficult for gays; it is also the last decade for Harry and Rudi and the others. Perhaps no ammunition will supply us better than to know where we have collectively come from. That is one of the surer ways of determining for ourselves where we are going.

CHAPTER TEN

Beyond Gay or Gloomy:
The Ordinary Miseries of Everyday Life

Near the end of the fifth year of my last analysis, I said to my therapist, spontaneously and sadly, "I feel I'm alone in this room, that I'm always alone in it, that I'm doing this all by myself." It was the harshest thing I could say of psychoanalysis, of my relationship to my doctor, and of my own enormous resistance and defiance. Behind that comment was an ocean of anger; ahead of it was the beginning of the end of this analysis, of all the years of therapy, of all the muddled striving and acidic self-recrimination. There had been long stretches of my adult life when I managed to live without therapy and the near-poverty it reduced me to. That was now so long ago I could not remember what those years had felt like. I could remember what I did with my money before half my salary went to my doctor: the travels, the furniture and rugs, the record collection, the books—I had them; I remembered buying them, going places.

For some years, I had gone no place, bought nothing, and often wondered whether I was getting anywhere. Was I now caught in that trap where my own masochism simply used therapy punitively, where I made of my therapist the very agent of society and deprivation I sought relief from? There was evidence that I was trying to; the remaining question was whether I was trying anything else. It had been a year of surrenders. An affair that seemed off to a good start failed quickly and utterly, and it precipitated a long depression; to crawl out of that, I had given up some cherished illusions about my lovableness and lack of ambition. But I had come to know more clearly what I did not want from love or work, what wasn't for me, and what I wouldn't put up with any longer.

One such discovery was that therapy and gay politics were somehow parallel experiences of coming out that would not meet. In both, I had yet to find myself; the evasions of the self were as sly as ever. The need to validate my life, my sense that my feelings were at once unreal but all that really mattered, remained unanswered. The pieces of my past were slippery; a fragment connected here dislocated the fit elsewhere. The degree to which I could recognize myself in sexuality, in gay life, and in society was reflected in therapy, that long dangerous intermittant voyage begun when I was seventeen. And thirty years later that mirror, like tarnished brass, still only showed a familiar stranger.

The work of therapy was resisted with excruciating cleverness, and the clarity I struggled for floundered in a sea of words where the life of feeling stayed submerged. In gay life, the feelings were often drowned in sensation. My past seemed in the stone age; the present with its astonishing confusions did not yield even a tentative sense of the future. Where were my high hopes of psychoanalysis, of gay liberation?

1

When I returned to New York in 1962, I began to read Freud and to meet people in psychoanalysis who were very elitist about it. I already had a therapeutic morality: what is bad is really sick and that results from some failure of love. Ideas of badness and goodness were less tangible than ideas of sickness and health. Lionel Trilling's *Freud and the Crisis of Our Culture* and Norman O. Brown's *Life Against Death* sent me to Freud's *Civilization and Its Discontents,* which I embraced like a law student preparing his first brief.

Here was confirmation of my worst expectations. Individual neurosis was an *essential* consequence of culture, which was itself neurotic. The price of civilization, the pressures of its sublimations and repressions, were that society was neurotic in the same way as individuals, and just as inadequate in coping with it. If I had a quarrel with things as they were, it was a just one. And justice itself was paranoid: all the submissions the self made to culture were countered by oppositions. Trilling said the self maintained "a standing quarrel with its great benefactor . . . and made greater legitimate demands than any culture could hope to satisfy." Here was evidence. All that effort of self-creation which had set me in conflict with others who represented themselves as Culture, as normal heterosexual life, was legitimate. The feeling that one was wrong when he wasn't—that paranoia I had felt as a Jew, as a homosexual, and as a radical—was in fact a genuine opposition to society. However, I did not quite believe that culture would not satisfy my demands now that others had helped me believe them legitimate.

What did I want more than work and love and to pursue them with some real freedom? I had other demands as well: achievement, play, art, loyal and supportive friends: these were not modest, I knew, but they were the demands for a healthy life. Of course, I was describing the ideal life. I had identified health and virtue without realizing it.

Life in New York fulfilled my hopes and thoroughly disillusioned me. Indeed, it is not America, and it certainly was no longer home. But whatever quarrel I had with America, I could pick up with ease in its least typical city. Far more than the sheltered genteel academic town, New York was Freud's civilization with a vengeance: everything attractive and coercive, every dazzling promise made and every promise broken. One was constantly invited to settle for nothing but everything, and to demand it instantly.

My response was to become reclusive, to move into a smaller world more refined than any I'd conceived or needed in my twenties. I suspected it was all neurosis: my disillusionments were proper payment for my grandiose aspirations. I now wanted self-sufficiency. Love seemed possible for others in preliberation gay New York, but not for me. About work, I was less cynical: I had no ambitions for scholarly or critical fame, but I was avid for success in the classroom.

Marie told me later how peculiar my classes were, what a forbidding intimacy I'd made my style. I had worked very hard for a reputation; the one I got had as its highest praise that the classes were not dull. Marie described the experience of hearing me read the poetry of the Renaissance or excerpts from Shakespeare with such odd understated intensity of feeling that the class was alarmed into silence. As soon as I left the text, my voice became ironic; the witty mocking questions would begin. I never acted the material, but I had only to loan it my own unused emotional life and read Donne or Herbert or Marvell with care for *their* feelings to overwhelm the class. I never quite knew what I was doing or how; my preparations were reserved for the analyses that followed the readings. When the reading was over, my persona became all cleverness. It was perverse but novel.

I had no argument with perversity. I had read Freud and liked the idea that it was the negative of the neurotic, acting out what others could only manifest in neurosis, in pressure and conflict, alienation and ennui. Freud offered the perverse as a kind of therapy: the misery of compulsion and the inability to make choices are dissipated in active deviance.

With friends, I argued that my troubles, my boredom and anomie, were the culture's. As a former Marxist, what should I have expected from late capitalism? I was having a crises of meaninglessness rather than neurotic withdrawal. And even if I were neurotic, which I never really doubted, what was the point of health in such a society?

But the residue of my hunger for the old values, for romantic love and worldly success, was my persistent anger, a reservoir always ready to supply real rage, and an increasing feeling of loss, of life emptying itself out. My first years of my thirties were the ones most free of pain. The less unhappy I grew, the colder I became to everything and everyone outside the shrinking circle of my life.

Sonia and Frances, both in psychoanalysis, thought I should reconsider: what did I have to lose? Now I was resigned, but perhaps I could be accepting. The consequences later would be very different. Did I really want to risk bitterness?

Ten years ago, psychoanalysis was at the height of its prestige in New York. Like caviar or cocaine, it appeared a rich indulgence for a strange pleasure, a narcissistic devotion to oneself. I knew that being analyzed would not make me handsome or sexy, more ambitious or amenable. I was lazy and abrasive and a cynic at the circus. Even Freud wasn't going to change that. I suspected that what Sonia and perhaps Frances really hoped was that since I was so misfitted for the gay life, in psychoanalysis, with its epic optimism about restructuring personality, I would finally be fitted for heterosexual living. Part of me concurred: it looked like I was going to flop as a fag. Becoming a grandly nasty queen or becoming a recluse were poor options.

One month after I began treatment, Sonia died. The shock of her death and my sense that I was not entitled to publicly mourn her, that I should be stoic, made the analytic hour a dirge: it was the only place to bring my grief. As I wept before this stranger, it was too late to ask whether I should trust him.

My other immediate response to her loss was to spend the summer at Fire Island Pines as devoted to drugs and sensation as I could manage. In Sonia's death I named the alienation that had plagued us both as a profound sense of unentitlement. The summer was a defiance of what was now clear. I would see if it were so: I would take all the pleasure I wanted, risk whatever I chose. I would test out these notions that I had no proper choices; perhaps it was only my cowardice; I had always been a coward.

I had an affair, was bolder sexually than I had ever been before and more successful, more daring about relinquishing control in trippy nights on those beautiful beaches, and when it was over, it was as if it had never happened. I could not remember the summer once I returned to the city where my grief, like my life, waited to be resumed.

Apparently, I was not entirely willing to: within a month Marie and I became lovers, and within a few months we were living together in romantic monogamy.

Even my analyst could not help commenting on my remarkable progress, though it was merely termed "change." Instead of following that epiphany of unentitlement, I would claim normality, escape from scorn, secure love, have children, join life reconciled. I was more surprised than anyone. When I began analysis mere months before, I presented myself as a homosexual unhappy about how I dealt with my choices but skeptical about improving them. I hoped therapy would give me more dignity. I had no intention of giving up being homosexual, only of giving up what made me so unhappy. The consulting analyst I had chosen was to find a therapist who would work on those terms: someone enlightened, undogmatic, and unthreatened by homosexuality. The search took more than the usual time.

In an article on the future of psychoanalysis in *The New York Times* (August 14, 1979), Kenneth Keniston, a therapist but not an analyst, tried to define the most valuable qualities of psychoanalysis as its "almost limitless respect for the individual, faith that understanding is better than illusion, insistence that our psyches harbor darker secrets than we care to confess, a refusal to promise too much, and a sense of the complexity, tragedy and wonder of human life."

The psychoanalyst's job is not so mysterious. In a sensible book for the perplexed, *A Complete Guide to Therapy: From Psychoanalysis to Behavior Modification* (New York, Pantheon, 1976), the author Joel Kovel says, "The analyst's business is strictly defined: to labor patiently, nonjudgmentally, tirelessly insistent at the edge of awareness, to dissolve those countless ways the analysand resists the emergence of his psychic interior." What is crucial between patient and doctor for that good working relationship founded on such mysterious trust, the key to treatment, are the fantasies of the patient which he transfers to that relationship—not what the patient is in the world or does there, but what he does on the couch.

Freud's statements about the treatment of homosexuality were not consistent over the course of his career. He was dubious about changing sexual orientation, but he was also uncertain about too much to be decisive. However, he was quite certain and decisive about the proper role of the analyst, of his absolute need to be analyzed himself before he could understand the therapy, and about the need for openness and a freedom from moralistic judgments. The analyst must listen to what the patient wants and help him discover that; it is the therapy that least allows being told what to do or what to want. The goal of a successful analysis is to discover how much is already psychically determined so that one can also know how much is free. After that, the real choices are clear. Then the self-reflectiveness of years of treatment can be brought to bear on the ordinary unhappiness that awaits everyone. As Freud said, "Neurotic suffering is transformed into everyday misery."

That confrontation and definition of limitation and freedom occur in Freudian analysis in what is called the transference neurosis: the reliving of the neurotic past in the relationship to the therapist. The therapist becomes an object of love or fear or both, the embodiment of moral authority, from the paternal to the patriarchal, from the first lover to all culture itself. For such a transference to take place, for the disabling past to be reentered, a special rapport of trust must be surrendered to by the patient. Kovel aptly describes this as an enthrallment of a particularly painful nature: the patient is enthralled with "someone pledged *not* to gratify the wishes set free." Only then can the patient resolve them, those wishes and conflicts of the past.

What happened in my psychoanalysis was that it was sabotaged without either the analyst's or my realizing it. The heartier my relationship with Marie became, the more tacit was the approval of my analyst, who now had become a comforting complicitous heterosexual, welcoming me, a man whose approval I was disarmed from exploring since it seemed not a neurotic transference but a social reward. But what in fact also happened was that self-estrangement began to metastasize in my life, as if I were watching myself in a play and acting better than I expected due to the quiet direction of Freud and my analyst. What was I? Which label did I really need? Was that feeling straight or gay? In all those distinctions, very telling now for I had memory and present experience to guide me, the way they meshed in me and whether they really mattered did not resolve itself. Or not in time.

After three years, I ran out of money. I'd been forced to move from Brooklyn Heights when the brownstone I lived in was sold, and I used the occasion for Marie and me to make a new home that was ours instead of mine. Somehow, debts mounted. I was playing out another part of the drama, but it appeared to be improvisation. My analyst suggested we interrupt until my finances improved.

By the time they did, my relationship with Marie had deteriorated badly. I made sure to keep my former analyst up to date—he was not to rest assuming all was well—but I did not want to return to treatment. Vaguely, it seemed to me that I had done too much for him and not enough for me, and neither of us had noticed that sufficiently.

Those three years of treatment were also more seductive than any prior experience, more intense, chronicling vaster changes than in any comparable period in adulthood. It was not that psychoanalysis had failed; it had hardly begun. When Marie and I split, I determined to return to gay life, to find there the relationship I had worked for with her, without the impediment of heterosexuality.

What seemed a career as a case history I decided was over, at cross-purposes with my life. I had written in my journal, when I first began to consider analysis, a quotation from *Life Against Death:* ". . . the goal of psychoanalytical therapy is to free him from the burden which compels him to go on having (and being) a case history. And the method of psycho-analytical therapy is to deepen the historical consciousness of the individual ('fill up the memory gaps') till he awakens from his own history as from a nightmare." That was what I thought I was buying: freedom from the past for a future of "more Eros and less strife."

But each time I had ventured more deeply into homosexual life, it had been checked by therapy, and each departure from therapy sent me back to homosexuality more hungry than before for romantic experience. I had always felt that I had to protect my homosexuality from my therapists, and so my idea of the therapeutic had been sacrificial: somehow I would end up with less. Less unhappiness for less sexuality, less conflict for less struggle. I had carefully programmed my efforts with my crises, with the deaths of father and friend that were such hallmarks. Perhaps I had only wanted resignation. That I was entitled to.

2

If I had found in homosexuality what so many others have, Freud's deviance which is a resolution to neurosis, I would have found what was gay in the life. But I had not. That was why I preferred queer or even faggot: they at least suggested some of my defiance and anger. But at forty, I was determined to try. The summer of Stonewall, I had been stoned at the Pines. The early exuberant years of gay liberation saw me feathering my heterosexual closet.

Now, I joined an informal group of gay academics. By the third meeting, word of mouth had trebled the numbers attending, and we de-cided to organize, to name ourselves and our purpose. I was among the four volunteers who worked on that first statement of purpose for the Gay Academic Union, along with Martin Duberman, Bert Hansen, and Jona-than Katz. At the next meeting, I met Richard, the man who was to become my lover.

The G.A.U. started loftily, even with its serious problem involving the overwhelming proportion of men to women and the desire of many of the lesbians to remain separatist but affiliated. We did not resolve the problem; instead, we focused our energies on the first conference, to be held Thanksgiving weekend. This was my second coming out, my "real" emergence as a homosexual in the public world, now based on my sense that I was at last entitled to be gay.

It was as exciting and confusing a time as I could remember. Among the highlights of the first conference, held at John Jay College, was a bomb scare. But for those of us who had worked without any clear expectations of what would happen, the large enthusiastic audience was elating, and at the end of the closing speeches, we were exhilarated. Here at last was a community, that included men and women (and at least acknowledged the problems of sexism within the ranks), and a network of friendship among men that was not competitive or primarily sexual in purpose. Adult life could still partake of the enthusiasm I saw in young activists. The only comparable feeling I'd ever had was during the great Washington march to protest the war in Vietnam, but this was so much more personal.

"They" could take their notions of sickness and shove it. That thought, after years of treatment with five different therapists and assorted evaluators and consultants, made me high. If gay men and women supported each other, the isolation that made secrecy so miserable could end, and the sexual search that was so overloaded because it was meant to end the isolation and self-denigration would be defused. I could end the secrecy at last if I sensed that gay people meant my people, that I could ask of them and feel for them what I had felt for Jews all my life and for radicals in my youth. I could be gay as I was Jewish.

I reminded myself that I was being too idealistic, that God was dead and patriotism a farce when it wasn't a vice, but these were strange vigorous times. The history of the G.A.U., which foundered on sexist issues and a failure to find a common ground for gay men and lesbians, was the first blow. Eventually, the G.A.U. became a male organization in New York City, but it decentralized nationally, and its character varies with each campus. But the arguments about sexual politics and the obstinance of some of the men to make concessions made me fully aware for the first time of my own attitudes, and what emerged was my own sympathy with feminism.

And I had another comfort. I had fallen seriously in love with a man who was a peer, for the first time since I was twenty-one. That comfort was more than balanced in the early months of the relationship by my mother's dying. In the six months between the diagnosis of Hodgkin's disease and her death in Miami, I barely managed my life, commuting often to Florida, working fervidly for the G.A.U. conference, and finding solace in romance and the business of gay liberation.

By January my mother was dead and my sense of family broken. I was forty-one and I called myself an orphan. My sister had her family to comfort her and I was invited to join them, but I did not. I sat *shiva* alone and in my way. The grief was deep and reminiscent, but losing one's mother is always a terrible and somehow final experience, different for sons and for daughters, and different for gay sons and straight ones. Somewhere we have remained romantically loyal; the child within is bereft again, and he cannot find the compensations of conventional maturity in wife or family.

My comfort now was that I was in love and believed I had finally found the relationship that would get me off the streets. I was surprised, somewhat puzzled at myself. I could scarcely believe that I had so impetuously committed myself to a relationship whose terms were so vague, so unarticulated. It was not the usual matters of monogamy and jealousy and priority, which I did have distinct ideas about, but the fact that none of my ideas seemed to matter beside my romanticism. Everything that I had previously reserved for women, respect and admiration, tenderness and empathy, I gave Richard, and it was the beginning, so of course it was ardent. That passion could acknowledge love without either's diminishing the other was a new experience for me, and its extreme tardiness made it an overwhelming one. After so much denigrating puritanism, I discovered that hedonism was licit, that romance was neither legend nor delusion.

Part of what was so new was that I was grateful to be homosexual for the first time in my life: if I were not, I would not have known Richard. I was still chagrined by my own prudery when he would be casually demonstrative in a restaurant or on the street, but I enjoyed chastising myself: serves you right for making that closet so snug and comfy; get used to living in larger quarters.

Ironically, it was my lover and my new politics rather than my mother's death that led me to decide to return to psychoanalysis and "finish" what I had started. My sense that my relationship with my lover would last had all the authority of religious belief. Almost as strong was the idea that my commitment to gay liberation would reward me with a network of relationships that would replace the extended family I no longer felt tied to. For a decade, I had not allowed heterosexual therapists to explore my homosexuality for a number of reasons, most of all that I did not trust them with it. When I had finally allowed it, it was to understand its origins, to see how the beginnings mattered when I tried to live life as a heterosexual.

Now I no longer cared how it had begun, but I was very interested in how feeling bad about being homosexual had originated. I wanted to scrape off the last of the crap that clung to my sense of myself as gay. If I had been so willing to understand myself and confront the disorders of personality and the limitations of character in order to be straight for Marie, I certainly wanted the same benefits for Richard.

I resumed psychoanalysis with a new doctor. I made it clear at the initial interview that I was in love with a man for the first time as an adult, but that I was fearful of my own past, of how damaged the goods were, and that I wanted what could be repaired and salvaged in the service of love. It was too late to ask how wise was this investment I'd made; all I wanted now was to protect it. There was no going back to that guardedness before Marie and before Sonia's death. Richard had subsumed the loss of Marie as Marie had the loss of Sonia. Gay liberation had armed me against heterosexual scorn. What I wanted from analysis was further defense against the enemy without who was still within.

Richard was sympathetic and supportive; he helped defray the deprivations by paying for all the luxuries in my life, all the ballet tickets, the restaurant checks, the traveling. My money covered room, board, and shrink. But I already had what I wanted; what did money matter?

I found out when the relationship ended and I was nearly forty-four without a penny to my name, and I also found out what wanting to be analyzed for the sake of others meant: when they left, one was trapped. Richard was gone, but I had entered a maze I could not leave unless I found my way out at the end.

It had been folly to do this for others, for Richard, for Marie, for my fantasies of what this therapist or that had wanted for me. In fact, it had never mattered to any of them. What they wanted from me had little to do with what happened in psychoanalysis. My sense of deprivation and inadequacy had not served them badly at all: I was an easy lover, and I was easy to leave.

For the next year I raged and would do little more. I adamantly turned an expensive and important experience into an infantile one. My feelings about love were echoed by my disillusionment with gay liberation: where was that network of support, those uncompetitive relationships? I had been a fool for a change, and I wanted an end to the follies.

After a summer in California, I returned to New York and began an affair with a younger man whom I thought beautiful and was excited by the prospect of being loved again. I felt he was too young for me, and I had doubts about duration—the memory of Marie who had outgrown what she first loved was still vivid—but then I asked myself again what had I to lose but some self-pity? Six months later, that too was over, but for the first time I was not left, the passive victim of someone else's decision or experience. This relationship ran aground because neither could meet the demands of the other: it was an ordinary failure; we were not right for each other.

It ended abruptly, as Marie and Richard had, over in an evening, my bridges burned before my eyes. It was a bad time, recalling other losses, but I had not been as deeply involved, had been ambivalent and wary from the first, and I knew I would not be as hurt because I was not as vulnerable: I was older, wiser, and I scarcely had begun to love this man when it was over.

Nevertheless, the break-up precipitated a depression as bad as any I had known, in its way even rivaling my misery at the time of Sonia's death, which I had sworn was the nadir. It seemed so meaningless: what was it about? I could not discover the subject of my despair. I understood that this last departure resounded with all the others: Richard, mother, Marie, Sonia, father, that by now one loss had a chorus of diminishments. But that was not it.

What was unutterably depressing was that I had to do it for myself, only for myself. To continue in analysis, I would really have to want it for me, not for "self-knowledge" or stoic dignity or any of the other abstractions that were designed to make it fail, and certainly not to be "healthier," more deserving of someone's love. I was deserving enough; any healthier, and I might be out of the running altogether. I was less needy, so I was more certain of what I could offer and what I should ask for. Love would solve nothing but lovelessness, an enormous solution, but not one inch more than that.

I had to finish this analysis to get it off my back, to get me off my back. My neuroticism and my oppression as a homosexual and my corrosive expectations of love were not different things: all of them had been evasions of the self, the opposite of that substantial self-infatuation called narcissism by psychologists and egoism by moralists. I had never been infatuated with my self-absorption. The mirror on the wall never told me I was the fairest of them all; in fact, it had been darkly silent.

The heart of this darkness, the fantasy that I was alone in the analyst's office as I was before the mirror, was the silence. I had thought in words were knowledge and in political action one could give power to the words. But analysis is so deeply conservative before the idea of a "reality" which one must come to terms with. Only then, rid of the impairment of fantasies, can he assume ordinary life, the everyday miseries. And all that I was politically still objected to the unmoveable condition of normal misery, no matter how flagrantly ordinary it was.

My political life with its infatuations, its *isms*, now seems promiscuous like my erotic adventures, exciting and evanescent. I had wanted social change to answer personal chaos. The injustices that angered me sluiced off private rage. I could not find comfort in radicalism because I was pessimistic, but I regarded that pessimism as defensive and neurotic.

That enthrallment to someone who would not gratify the wishes freed in words was also the enthrallment to patriarchy and paternalism which could never satisfy the fantasies or give me freedom, though it gave me plenty of words. Psychoanalysis is ever the father as political protest is again the son. The irony of it: I had come to paternal authority to bless my rejection of it, to help me find the will to define myself without its terminology, and I found myself without a real language. Psychoanalysis wishes to free the patient to define himself and what he wants, yet it assumes that what he wants is to enter ordinary life. Such a life is acquiescent, and such submission is the mother of rage. The analyst is pledged not to yield; now I understand that culture will not yield as well. But its seductiveness is waning. I have little stake in patriarchy, so I need ask less of it, less permission and less concession.

For me, neither words alone nor social change are now enough. I envy those women who have found in feminism a view of the world and their own experience that is connected. For them, there is a way to see the personal and public as coherent. I am an earnest fellow traveler believing that the possibilities for every kind of change in feminism are enormous, more convinced that it connects theory, action, and individual experience than other political ideas, but it cannot be for me what it is for women. As much as I borrow and translate what I read and see and hear into comparable terms for a gay man, it is still analogy.

I think feminism's insistence that gender has determined so much of how we see ourselves and are seen by the world is correct. I find exciting every rejection it makes in history, every convention it overturns, but unless those ideas are felt, they are only rhetoric. What I want now is to end the rhetorical, to stop the rhetoric of psychoanalytic confession, which is as betraying there as it is in political experience. Without understanding, feeling is a rush to the barricades, and there is nothing—nothing except event after endless event which never becomes experience.

The words in my mouth, the words on the page, so many words, only matter as felt thought. Without that connection, the serious life of the mind that is the microcosm of culture is barren, and all the powerful important confusions of feeling descend into whines and whimpers.